HUMAN RIGHTS AND PUBLIC FINANCE

This edited collection addresses some of the most important challenges in contemporary human rights law and practice. Its central theme is the linkage between public finance, particularly budget decisions, and the realisation (or not) of economic and social rights. While much academic and political debate on economic and social rights implementation has focused on the role of the courts, this work places the spotlight squarely on those organs of government that have the primary responsibility and the greatest capacity for giving effect to such rights: namely, the elected branches of government. The major actors considered in this book are politicians, public servants and civil society, with their role in realising economic and social rights the work's key focus. The book thus makes a crucial contribution to remedying the current imbalance in attention paid by economic and social rights scholars to the legislature and executive vis-a-vis the judiciary.

Featuring pioneering work by leading experts in the field of human rights and public finance, this multidisciplinary collection will be of great interest to academics, practitioners, public servants and students working in the areas of law, human rights, economics, development and political science.

Human Rights and Public Finance

Budgets and the Promotion of Economic and Social Rights

Edited by

Aoife Nolan
Rory O'Connell
and
Colin Harvey

·HART·
PUBLISHING
OXFORD AND PORTLAND, OREGON
2013

Published in the United Kingdom by Hart Publishing Ltd
16C Worcester Place, Oxford, OX1 2JW
Telephone: +44 (0)1865 517530
Fax: +44 (0)1865 510710
E-mail: mail@hartpub.co.uk
Website: http://www.hartpub.co.uk

Published in North America (US and Canada) by
Hart Publishing
c/o International Specialized Book Services
920 NE 58th Avenue, Suite 300
Portland, OR 97213-3786
USA
Tel: +1 503 287 3093 or toll-free: (1) 800 944 6190
Fax: +1 503 280 8832
E-mail: orders@isbs.com
Website: http://www.isbs.com

British Library Cataloguing in Publication Data
Data Available

ISBN: 978-1-84113-011-8

Typeset by Compuscript Ltd, Shannon
Printed and bound in Great Britain by
TJ International Ltd, Padstow, Cornwall

ACKNOWLEDGEMENTS

The idea for this book emerged from a two-year research project on 'Budget Analysis and the Advancement of Economic and Social Rights in Northern Ireland'. Based at the School of Law at Queen's University Belfast, this project was undertaken by the editors, together with Mira Dutschke and Eoin Rooney. It was funded by Atlantic Philanthropies. The project benefited from an outstanding International Advisory Board: Ann Blyberg, Debbie Budlender, Diane Elson, Ignacio Saiz, Martín Sígal and Sally-Anne Way. We would also like to express our gratitude to our Local Working Group members, Fiona Crowley (Amnesty Ireland), Oonagh Kane (Practice and Participation of Rights Project), Rosalind McKenna (Amnesty Ireland) and Alex Tennant (Save the Children, Northern Ireland). Especial thanks are due to Marie Lynch for superb research assistance with this volume. Jennie Finlay and Chris Wallace provided very able administrate support. Finally, we would like to thank our families and friends.

CONTENTS

ABBREVIATIONS

ADB	African Development Bank
AME	Annually Managed Expenditure
ACESS	Alliance for Children's Entitlement to Social Security
AWID	Association for Women's Rights in Development
BAME	Black, Asian and Minority Ethnic
BfC	Budget for Children
CBU	Children's Budget Unit
CEDAW	United Nations Convention on the Elimination of Discrimination against Women
CEDECA-CEARÁ	Centre for the Defence of Children and Adolescents (Brazil)
CESR	Center for Economic and Social Rights
CHRP	Centre for Human Rights in Practice
CIH	Chartered Institute of Housing
COC	Center of Concern
COE	Council of Europe
ComESCR	Committee on Economic, Social and Cultural Rights
ComRC	Committee on the Rights of the Child
CPG	Children Participating in Governance
CPS	Crown Prosecution Service
CRC	United Nations Convention on the Rights of the Child
CSCQBE	Civil Society Coalition for Quality Basic Education
CSO	Civil Society Organisation
CWGL	Center for Women's Global Leadership
CWV	Coventry Women's Voices
DAC	Development Assistance Committee
DEL	Departmental Expenditure Limit
DFP	Department for Finance and Personnel
DSD	Department for Social Development
DWP	Department for Work and Pensions
ECA	Children and Adolescents Act, Brazil
EHRC	Equality and Human Rights Commission
EHRIA	Equality and Human Rights Impact Assessment
EQIA	Equality Impact Assessment
ESCR	Economic, social and cultural rights
ESR	Economic and social rights
EU	European Union
FAO	Food and Agriculture Organization of United Nations
FTT	Financial Transaction Tax
GDP	Gross Domestic Product
GESTHA	National Union of Tax Inspectors (Spain)

GRB	Gender Responsive Budgeting
HAG	Housing Association Grant
HeRWAI	Health Rights of Women Assessment Instrument
HRIA	Human Rights Impact Assessment
IAWGCP	Inter-Agency Working Group on Children's Participation
ICEFI	Instituto Centroamericano de Estudios Fiscales
ICESCR	International Covenant on Economic, Social and Cultural Rights
ICPS	Integrated Child Protection Scheme
IDASA	Institute for Democracy in South Africa
IGO	Inter-governmental organisation
IHRIP	International Human Rights Internship Program
IMF	International Monetary Fund
LHA	Local Housing Allowance
MAR	Maximum of Available Resources
MDG	Millennium Development Goal
MNCs	Multinational Corporations
NGO	Non-governmental Organisation
NHS	National Health Service
NIFHA	Northern Ireland Federation of Housing Associations
NIHE	Northern Ireland Housing Executive
NISRA	Northern Ireland Research and Statistics Agency
NPA	National Programme of Action for Children (South Africa)
ODA	Official Development Assistance
OECD	Organisation for Economic Co-operation and Development
OFMDFM	Office of the First Minister and Deputy First Minister
OHCHR	Office of the High Commissioner for Human Rights
OSAR	Observatorio en Salud Reproductiva
OSCE	Organization for Security and Co-operation in Europe
PEM	Public Expenditure Management
PfG	Programme for Government (Northern Ireland)
PPP	Public–private Partnership
PRS	Private Rented Sector
PSA	Public Service Agreement
SCCYP	Scottish Commissioner for Children and Young People
UN	United Nations
UNDP	United Nations Development Programme
LHA	Local Housing Allowance
UDHR	Universal Declaration of Human Rights
UNECE	United Nations Economic Council for Europe
UNHCR	United Nations High Commissioner for Human Rights
UNICEF	United Nations Children's Fund
UNIFEM	United Nations Agency for Women (now UNWOMEN)
UN INSTRAW	United Nations Entity for Gender Equality and the Empowerment of Women

UNSCAP	United Nations Economic and Social Commission for Asia and the Pacific
VAT	Value Added Tax
WHO	World Health Organization

AUTHOR BIOGRAPHIES

Radhika Balakrishnan is Executive Director of the Center for Women's Global Leadership, and Professor in Women's and Gender Studies at Rutgers University. Previously, she was Professor of Economics and International Studies at Marymount Manhattan College. She has worked at the Ford Foundation as a programme officer in the Asia Regional Program. She is on the board of the Center for Constitutional Rights and the International Association for Feminist Economics. She is the co-editor with Diane Elson of *Economic Policy and Human Rights: Holding Governments to Account* (London, Zed Books, 2011). She has also authored numerous articles that have appeared in books and journals.

Mira Dutschke has a Master's degree in Human Rights Law and 10 years of experience of working in South Africa, Northern Ireland and the United States. Her focus is on the research, advocacy and enforcement of social, economic and cultural rights. She is currently working as an independent research consultant; is a part-time lecturer at the University of Cape Town; and produces independent environmental and human rights documentaries. Her academic work has been published in journals such as the *South African Journal of Human Rights*, the *European Human Rights Law Review* and the *International Journal of Social Work*. Her media work is distributed through LinkTV, the South African *Mail and Guardian* and *Global Post*.

Diane Elson is Emeritus Professor of Sociology and a member of the Human Rights Centre at the University of Essex, UK. She has published widely on gender equality, human rights and economic policy, including articles in *World Development*, *Journal of International Development*, *Feminist Economics*, *Essex Human Rights Review*, *Journal of Human Development and Capabilities* and *International Review of Applied Economics*. She has contributed many book chapters and edited several books, including, with Radhika Balakrishnan, *Economic Policy and Human Rights: Holding Governments to Account* (London, Zed Press, 2011) and with S Fukuda-Parr and P Vizard, *Human Rights and the Capabilities Approach: An Interdisciplinary Dialogue* (London, Routledge, 2012). Email: drelson@essex.ac.uk.

James Harrison is Associate Professor in the School of Law at the University of Warwick and Co-Director of the Centre for Human Rights in Practice. Much of his work involves analysis of the human rights and environmental impact of economic regulations, public spending decisions and activities of corporations. He has undertaken extensive work on human rights and equality impact assessments, and has produced a range of studies, academic articles, reports and methodological guidance in this field.

Colin Harvey is Professor of Human Rights Law, School of Law, Queen's University Belfast. He was Head of the Law School at Queen's (2007–12) and Director of the Human Rights Centre (2005–08). He has held visiting professorships at the London School of Economics, the University of Michigan and Fordham University, and he served on the Northern Ireland Higher Education Council (2002–06) and the Northern Ireland Human Rights Commission (2005–11).

James Heintz is Research Professor at the Political Economy Research Institute of the University of Massachusetts, Amherst. He has collaborated with numerous UN agencies, including the United Nations Development Programme, the International Labour Organization, the UN Research Institute for Social Development, the UN Economic Commission for Africa and UN Women. He has published in the areas of employment and labour markets, macroeconomic alternatives, the distributive effects of monetary policy and development strategies in sub-Saharan African countries.

Marie Lynch completed her PhD at Queen's University on the issues surrounding judicial appointments in Northern Ireland and the other jurisdictions within the UK. As well as continuing research in this area, she has also been working in the area of human trafficking and has co-created a database 'Slavery in Domestic Legislation'. See: www.qub.ac.uk/slavery/.

Aoife Nolan is Professor of International Human Rights Law at the School of Law, Nottingham University. She has published extensively in the areas of human rights, particularly in relation to children's rights and economic and social rights, as well as on constitutional law. She has worked with and acted as an expert advisor to a wide range of international and national organisations and bodies working on human rights issues. Her monograph, *Children's Socio-economic Rights, Democracy and the Courts* was published by Hart Publishing in 2011 and her edited collection, *Economic and Social Rights after the Global Financial Crisis* will be published by Cambridge University Press in 2014.

Paul O'Connell is Reader in Law at SOAS, University of London. He has published widely on socio-economic rights and the relationship of globalisation to law and human rights. His work has appeared in the *Modern Law Review*, the *Human Rights Law Review* and a number of edited collections. His recent monograph, *Vindicating Socio-Economic Rights: International Standards and Comparative Experiences* (Oxford, Routledge 2012) looks at how the relationship between socio-economic rights enforcement and the separation of powers has been dealt with in a number of jurisdictions, and articulates a model adjudicative framework for the protection of such rights.

Rory O'Connell is Professor of Human Rights and Constitutional Law at the Transitional Justice Institute/Law School, University of Ulster. He has published articles in the *International Journal of Constitutional Law*, *European Human Rights Law Review*, *European Law Journal*, and elsewhere, as well as contributing chapters for many edited collections. Rory was a member of the Queen's University Budget Analysis Project team. Email: r.oconnell@ulster.ac.uk; follow on twitter: @rjjoconnell.

Sheila Quinn is an independent consultant, providing consultancy, technical support, research and training, primarily in the area of gender mainstreaming and gender responsive budgeting (GRB). She also works on LGBT rights. She has written a number of manuals on GRB, including the seminal text for the Council of Europe. Her clients include UN Women, OSCE, the EU Commission, the ILO, the Equality Commission for Northern Ireland, the Department of Justice, Equality and Law Reform in Ireland, the Ministry of Social Affairs, Estonia, the Office of the Ombudsman, Lithuania. She is based in County Wicklow, Ireland. Email: sheilagquinn@gmail.com

Eoin Rooney is the Economic Research Officer with the Centre for Economic Empowerment, NICVA. He is carrying out a part-time PhD on Local Economic Development at the University of Ulster where he lectures on the social economy. Eoin was a member of the Queen's University Budget Analysis Project. E-mail: rooneyeoin@hotmail.com.

Ignacio Saiz is Executive Director of the Center for Economic and Social Rights (CESR), an international non-governmental organisation that works for the recognition and enforcement of these rights worldwide. Prior to joining CESR, Ignacio was Director of Policy at the International Secretariat of Amnesty International in London. He has worked for many years on a range of human rights issues in Latin America for Amnesty International and other human rights organisations. Ignacio holds an LLM in international human rights law with distinction from the University of Essex. Email: isaiz@cesr.org.

Mary-Ann Stephenson has worked as a writer, researcher and campaigner on gender equality and women's human rights for over twenty years. Her most recent publications include, with James Harrison, 'Unravelling Equality: A Human rights and Equality Impact Assessment of the Public Spending Cuts on Women in Coventry' (University of Warwick, 2011); 'Getting off Lightly or Feeling the Pinch: A Human Rights and Equality Impact Assessment of the Spending Cuts on Older Women in Coventry' (2012); and 'The TUC Women and the Cuts Toolkit' (2011). She is the coordinator of Coventry Women's Voices and a former Commissioner on the Women's National Commission.

Enakshi Ganguly Thukral is a human rights activist, researcher and trainer. For almost three decades she has been working on wide-ranging socio-legal issues such as those concerning women and children and development induced displacement. Since co-founding HAQ: Centre for Child Rights, New Delhi, in 1998, she has been working in a focused manner on children's rights. She has authored and co-authored a number of books, articles, manuals and handbooks on a wide range of issues. She has been part of several government committees for drafting plans, laws and policies. She has also been invited as an expert internationally. She was awarded the Ashoka Fellowship in 2002 in recognition of HAQ's work on children.

Introduction

AOIFE NOLAN, RORY O'CONNELL AND COLIN HARVEY

This book addresses one of the most important challenges in contemporary human rights law and practice: the linkage between public finance, particularly budget decisions, and the realisation (or not) of economic and social rights.[1] Much academic work and debate on economic and social rights (ESR) implementation has focused on the role of the courts. However, this work places the spotlight squarely on those organs of government that have the primary responsibility, and the greatest capacity, for giving effect to such rights: namely, the elected branches of government and public administration.

This volume is particularly timely given the impact of the 2007–08 global financial and economic crises. Post-crises budget cutbacks and reallocations have resulted in the domestic realisation of ESR being slowed in many countries and, in some cases, reversed. To achieve expenditure consolidation in the face of severely (and sometimes not-so-severely) constrained resources, developed and developing countries have adopted adjustment policies that are wide-ranging and severe. They include the cutting or capping of the public sector wage bill, the phasing out or removal of subsidies on basic goods and services such as fuel, cuts to social protection programmes, the reform of old-age pensions, and regressive taxation measures such as increased consumption taxes on basic goods.[2] All such measures are issues of public finance. All of them affect ESR enjoyment, whether directly or indirectly.

I. Foundations

Every human right potentially has implications for budgetary allocations and public finance generally. However, this collection's focus on economic and ESR is of especial significance given the strong linkage between the

[1] The terms 'economic and social rights' and 'socio-economic rights' will be used interchangeably in this collection. The term 'human rights' is used to denote the full spectrum of human rights, including civil, political and cultural rights—not simply economic and social rights.

[2] See eg, I Ortiz, J Chai and M Cummins, *Austerity Measures Threaten Children and Poor Households: Recent Evidence in Public Expenditures from 128 Developing Countries* (New York, UNICEF, 2011).

realisation of ESR and resource mobilisation and allocation, as well as the fact that the evaluation of budget decisions plays a key role in the assessment of states' compliance with their international ESR obligations. As such, the chapters in the first part of the book focus on fundamental issues regarding the interrelationship between ESR and central aspects of public finance, including macroeconomic policy, domestic and international fiscal policy, and budgetary decisions and processes.

In chapter one, Elson, Balakrishnan and Heintz explore a central umbrella obligation imposed by international ESR law: namely, the requirement under Article 2(1) of the International Covenant on Economic, Social Cultural Rights (ICESCR) that States Parties deploy the maximum of their available resources towards the realisation of ESR.[3] The authors outline how the human rights community has recognised the importance of government revenues, as well as public expenditure, to the concept of maximum available resources. Highlighting the different approaches adopted by neoclassical and Keynesian/human development approaches to economic policy, Elson et al demonstrate how the human rights understanding of 'maximum available resources' could be enriched by consideration of the concepts of fiscal and monetary space. The authors then proceed to relate 'maximum available resources' to different components of public finance: public expenditure, taxation, official development assistance (ODA), budget deficits, borrowing and debt and monetary policy and financial regulation. In doing so, they consider how specific understandings of concepts like 'efficiency' and 'effectiveness' will impact on the extent to which public expenditure will advance the realisation of ESR. They also highlight the way in which different perspectives on the desirability of tax revenue mobilisation will colour tax policy and, hence, mobilisation of resources for the achievement of ESR. The authors make clear the problems that may arise with regard to the conceptualisation, direction and employment of ODA in terms of the implementation of human rights, citing issues of recipient state capacity, human rights-compliant development and loan conditionality. The complex interplay between borrowing, debt and resource mobilisation is also explored, as is the role of monetary policy conducted by central banks. The chapter's central message is that governments *do* have alternatives, singly and together, which must be considered before public finance decisions are taken.

Concern with the linkage between international ESR obligations and public finance is also a major concern of Nolan's chapter (chapter two). She addresses conceptual challenges with regard to ESR-based budget analysis work that result from the current condition of the framework as set out in the International

[3] Art 2(1) states that 'Each State Party to the present Covenant undertakes to take steps, individually and through international assistance and co-operation, especially economic and technical, to the maximum of its available resources, with a view to achieving progressively the full realisation of the rights recognized in the present Covenant by all appropriate means, including particularly the adoption of legislative measures'.

Covenant on Economic, Social Cultural Rights (ICESR) and interpreted by the Committee on Economic, Social and Cultural Rights (the Committee). In doing so, she focuses in particular on retrogressive measures and the role of private (or non-state) actors and privatisation processes vis-a-vis ESR realisation. The author argues that these are issues highly relevant to the contemporary economic and policy context that have yet to be addressed adequately by the Committee so as to provide guidance to ESR-based budget analysis practitioners (or, indeed, states and ESR advocates more broadly). Nolan criticises the Committee's historic failure to engage convincingly with the concept of retrogressive measures, arguing that this has limited the capacity of anti-poverty and human rights campaigners to argue authoritatively that specific budgetary responses to the global economic crisis are in contravention of states' international legal obligations under ICESCR. Reviewing the Committee's more recent work, however, she suggests that that body may have abandoned the language of 'retrogressive measures', while finally proving willing to apply that concept in practice. With regard to private actors, Nolan argues that, although the Committee has not ignored such actors with regard to the realisation of ESR, it has proven reluctant to move beyond consideration of the need for state regulation of such actors under the auspices of the obligation to protect. She argues that the other key state duty with regard to privatisation is the obligation to fulfil—and that the Committee's failure to acknowledge this and to engage critically with privatisation models and processes is a key gap in its work from a budget perspective. She concludes by emphasising the importance that the Committee should be prepared to play a leadership role in terms of conceptualising and applying a strong and coherent framework of budget-related ESR obligations.

Concentrating on the causes and responses to the economic crisis more broadly, Paul O'Connell (chapter three) argues that the undermining of ESR protection and enjoyment associated with the current age of austerity is not an anomaly, but rather the necessary fate of ESR in the current social and economic order. According to O'Connell, in the context of an economic and social system which invariably privileges small, elite groups within society, commitments to ESR are only ever formal and honoured in the most grudging and limited of ways. In focusing on the impact of austerity on ESR in a number of countries, he argues that the recent push for austerity is motivated not by objective, economic necessity, but is driven by an ideological and political project to further entrench neoliberal capitalism. He critiques the portrayal of austerity as a broad 'pain-sharing' exercise. He highlights how, in practice, it benefits the economic elites who were responsible for causing the crisis, while adversely affecting millions of poor and working people. O'Connell notes that the language of human rights has been absent both from post-economic crisis governmental justifications and proposals and oppositional discourses. Furthermore, he asserts, the so-called 'free market'—a key element of neoliberal policy—operates in way that is inherently inegalitarian, resulting in inequalities and structural denials of ESR. The author emphasises the danger of the view of macroeconomic decisions as 'value neutral' or 'technocratic' and highlights how existing budgetary processes need to be opened up to broad-based participation and contestation (ie, democratised and politicised). In doing so, he advances the claim that participatory budgeting processes could constitute an important counter to the undemocratic and technocratic tendencies of neoliberal orthodoxy, as well as developing a (potentially ESR-centred) alternative to the limited language of existing processes.

The arguments made in the final contribution to Part I bring together the themes of fiscal policy, ESR obligations, the financial and economic crises and austerity that have already been explored by the first three authors. In chapter four, Saiz focuses on the need (and potential) to combat tax injustice from a human rights perspective. Like Elson et al, he regards taxation as one of the most important policy instruments that states can deploy to generate the resources necessary to realise the full range of human rights. He outlines three central functions of taxation from a human rights perspective: its role in generating the 'maximum available resources' to finance human rights-related expenditure; its potential role in redistributing resources in order to mitigate and redress social inequalities; and its role in cementing the bonds of accountability between state and citizen. He argues for the particular need to bring taxation under the lens of human rights scrutiny given the impact of the crises and the non-fulfilment of many of the Millennium Development Goals (MDGs). He bases his claims firmly on 'real world' examples of the application of human rights to domestic tax policy: (1) the link between inadequate revenue generation and poor human development outcomes in Guatemala; and (2) the human rights impacts of the failure to put in place equitable tax policies in response to the fiscal deficits created by the economic crises in Ireland and Spain. The conclusion of Saiz's chapter outlines current opportunities for linking human rights and the emergent tax justice advocacy movement, arguing in favour of the introduction of a global financial transaction tax and the clamping down on tax havens.

II. Governance

This volume is part of a scholarly and practitioner-driven trend of exploring how human rights, including ESR, might be more effectively integrated in governance, law, policy and practice. The major actors considered in this book are politicians, public servants and civil society, with their role in realising ESR the work's key focus. As such, the book seeks to assist in deepening knowledge on the part of both those who have responsibility for implementing ESR obligations (including elected government, public servants) and those who monitor such implementation (for instance, activists, national human rights institutions, academics). Reflective of this concern, the chapters in Part II consider the challenges that are inherent in integrating human rights analysis with governance, law and policy in a public finance context.

Chapter five sees Rory O'Connell review the history of human rights law and examine the role of the public finance in the early understanding of human rights. He highlights how concerns with revenue and expenditure formed part of early debates about rights, identifying elements common to both historic and current debates with regard to the interrelationship (and, indeed, sometimes hierarchy) between emerging human rights protections and public finance issues. O'Connell discusses the deeply political nature of early debates about human rights; unlike much current discussion of ESR, those debates were not simply limited to a consideration of the respective roles of existing branches of government but were bound up in wider questions about the legitimacy of the political system as a whole. O'Connell emphasises that a key aspect of human rights work in the area of public finances and budgets is its focus on the political rather than the judicial arena. He argues strongly that effective human rights work on public finances is not simply a question of ensuring that politicians speak the language of human rights; rather it also entails attending to the wider political system and shortcomings in democratic processes and structures relating to public finance. The author thus echoes Paul O'Connell's emphasis on democracy and participation.

In chapter six, Rooney and Harvey provide a critical appraisal of mainstreaming theory in relation to ESR, considering the issue of the 'transformation' of government through the absorption of rights-based discourse into state practice, procedures and policies. In keeping with the volume's focus, they concentrate primarily on the role of the legislative and executive branches of government. They argue, however, that legal culture and institutions cannot be allowed to remain exempt from mainstreaming if such activity is truly to result in the comprehensive promotion of rights within law and policy. Highlighting the procedural elements of mainstreaming, together with its 'soft law' nature and the importance that it should be 'good faith' in character (as opposed to tokenistic), the authors discuss the prospects of these conditions being met in the contemporary 'neoliberal' social and economic circumstances. In doing so, they explore the interrelationship between and the compatibility (or not) of ESR and markets. Focusing on theories of change and power, Rooney and Harvey assert that mainstreaming has the potential to produce some change—even in an environment in which neoliberal economic theory predominates. Ultimately, they argue that mainstreaming provides a vocabulary and mentality for thinking about governance along human rights lines. However, they contend that there are serious risks in relation to ownership and co-option of ESR discourse, and the subsequent interpretation thereof in a governance context, depending on whether such activity is 'integrationist' or 'transformative' in nature.

III. Group-Specific Work

Having considered the key conceptual issues arising in relation to human rights and public finance, in terms of both standards and governance structures, the collection turns to consider the use of human rights budget work both in shaping and evaluating budgetary decisions. Part III of the book centres on group-specific budget work, with contributions from Ganguly Thukral and Quinn focusing on children and women, respectively.

Ganguly Thukral (chapter seven) writes about the disaggregation and analysis of budgets from a child-rights perspective. Having described children's particular 'invisibility' in terms of the processes that determine budgets, she outlines the crucial linkages between resources, budgets and the implementation of children's rights as reflected both in the United Nations Convention on the Rights of the Child (CRC) itself, and in the work of the Committee on the Rights of the Child. The author explores the connections between budgets, child citizenship and the inclusion of children in governance, and details the role of budget analysis as a financial performance and political accountability tool in relation to state implementation of children's human rights. In discussing comparative national efforts to track budgetary allocation and expenditure on children's rights, Ganguly Thukral highlights the importance of ensuring that child rights budget work is participatory, and thereby consistent with the CRC and understandings of children as rights-bearing agents in budget processes, rather than simply as passive objects of such. Advocating for child citizenship and participation is thus presented as a key element of child rights budget work. Ganguly Thukral provides numerous examples of child rights-based budget analysis advocacy that have had positive impacts in terms of budgetary allocation and expenditure with regard to child rights; in India, for instance, child rights-based budget analysis work has affected the design and presentation of budgets, resulting in increases in the national budget in certain child-specific sectors. The author concludes that the ultimate (and thus far unachieved) indicator of success of child rights budget work would be the mainstreaming of children's rights as an indicator in all planning initiatives and actions of the government.

Concern with prospective—and not just reactive—integration of human rights into budgetary mechanisms and decisions also emerges in Quinn's contribution (chapter eight), which focuses on working with budget processes to better progress equality outcomes. Quinn demonstrates how gender responsive budgeting (ie, the application of gender mainstreaming in the budgetary process) can be adapted and applied to the broader equality agenda. She advances her arguments in the context of the Northern Ireland budgetary process which takes places against the backdrop of the 'Section 75' statutory duty. This duty requires public authorities to have due regard to the need to promote equality of opportunity between a range of different groups when carrying out their functions.[4] Having discussed the well-established and extensive body of work on gender responsive budgeting globally, as well as the constituent elements of the methodologies employed in relation to such, Quinn outlines how we can move from a single to a multiple equality ground approach to budgets. In arguing strongly for the legitimacy of

[4] s 75 Northern Ireland Act 1998.

using the budget to advance equality, she outlines modifications of the concepts, methodologies and tools that have been employed in gender responsive budgeting processes so as to render equality responsive budget work for the purposes of Section 75 possible.

IV. Analysis in Action

Part IV of the book moves from group-focused to thematic human rights-based budget analysis. Building on earlier discussion of global trends in human rights-based budget analysis, as well as the budget-related obligations arising out of ICESCR, chapter nine by Rooney and Dutschke focuses on the implementation of the right to adequate housing in Northern Ireland. Using a framework based on the right to adequate housing under Article 11(1) ICESCR, they evaluate a number of elements of the social housing budget in Northern Ireland. Like many jurisdictions, Northern Ireland has seen a shift from public provision of housing towards great reliance on home-ownership, a growing employment of public/private partnership models for financing housing, and an ever more extensive reliance on the private rented sector to meet housing needs.[5] Like many countries, Northern Ireland has experienced increases in homelessness and a lack of affordability of housing, and has been negatively affected by the economic crisis in terms of public spending. As such, Rooney and Dutschke's analysis of the extent to which such developments comply with international human rights law ESR obligations like those of 'progressive realisation' and the use of 'maximum available resources' have resonance far beyond the UK.

Harrison and Stephenson (chapter ten) also engage directly with the post-financial and economic crises situation, arguing that the legal standards in equality and human rights legislation can be the basis for examination of the impact of public spending decisions. Having asserted that cuts to public spending will disproportionately affect the most vulnerable in society due to those people's greater reliance on welfare benefits and public services, the authors emphasise the importance of gauging the multifaceted, cumulative impacts of multiple cuts. They present equality and human rights impact assessments (EHRIAs) as a key policy instrument for doing so. Using the example of an EHRIA assessing the impact of cuts on women in Coventry in the UK, Harrison and Stephenson focus in particular on the situation of victims and survivors of violence and abuse. The authors discuss the potential of EHRIAs but also highlight serious problems with the state conducting such processes as superficial, rushed 'tick-box' exercises,

[5] For more, see eg, R Rolnik, 'Report of the Special Rapporteur on the Right to Adequate Housing as a Component of the Right to an Adequate Standard of Living, and the Right to Non-discrimination in this Context: Promotion and Protection of all Human Rights, Civil, Political, Economic, Social and Cultural Rights, including the Right to Development' (UN Doc A/HRC/10/7 2009).

resulting in equality and human rights principles having little real impact on decision-making. They therefore outline how current practice should be improved so as to render EHRIAs effective and meaningful policymaking tools. In doing so, they emphasise issues relating to guidance, shared evidence bases and the use of an ESR-specific approach. Harrison and Stephenson caution, however, that a balance must be struck between rigour and usability. Ultimately, they make a strong case that, just as EHRIAs are carried out by a range of national and international state and non-state actors, the responsibility for developing such goes beyond public authorities to encompass academics.

V. Bringing It All Together

While coming at the topic of public finance and human rights from a wide range of perspectives, a number of common themes emerge strongly from this collection. All of these contribute, both individually and in tandem, to a multifaceted understanding of the interrelationship—both real and/or desired—between human rights and public finance.

All the contributors emphasise the importance of the rights framework and argue in favour of it playing a central role in relation to analysis, methodology and advocacy. Similarly, concern with effective operationalisation of ESR is a key element of every chapter. While some authors focus on the employment of human rights analysis in considering public finance decisions from a post facto monitoring perspective (for example, Nolan, Rooney and Dutschke), a key message emerging from most chapters is the need for prospective—as well as retrospective—integration of ESR concepts and analysis into national and supranational law and policymaking (for example, Harvey and Rooney, Harrison and Stephenson, Quinn, and Ganguly Thukral). These contributors are not so much concerned with the questions that judges address (have legal standards been breached?). Rather, they are concerned with incorporating a human rights perspective into the thinking and actions of politicians, public servants, civil society and rights-bearers (how might the transformative and emancipatory potential of human rights law be realised in tangible ways)?

Ultimately, all of the authors are concerned with state accountability for human rights obligations in the area of public finance, whether in relation to specific policy instruments such as tax (for example, Saiz) or policymaking tools (for example, Quinn and Harrison and Stephenson) or with regard to macroeconomic policy more broadly (Elson et al, Paul O'Connell and Rory O'Connell). It is recognised clearly, however, that responsibility for ensuring that ESR are achieved does not lie solely with the state; the role of private actors and privatisation processes (Nolan) and civil society (Saiz, Ganguly Thukral, Quinn and Harrison and Stephenson) with regard to ESR realisation are also subject to scrutiny. Academics are identified as having a key function in relation to the development and operationalisation of human rights assessment methodologies, as well as in relation to the elaboration and deepening of the conceptual framework (Nolan, Quinn, Harrison and Stephenson). Contributors emphasise the importance that budgetary decision-making processes should be inclusive and participatory (Paul O'Connell, Rory O'Connell, Rooney and Harvey, Ganguly Thukral, Saiz). In this sense, an inclusive approach must specifically include the experiences and concerns of vulnerable or disadvantaged groups (Quinn, Ganguly Thukral), and must provide for genuine and not merely formal, democratic engagement (Paul O'Connell, Rory O'Connell, Rooney and Harvey).

The impact of the economic and financial crises is a central theme of the volume, as is the dominance of neoliberal economic policy, both before, during and after the recent crises. The challenges posed by neoliberalism with regard to ESR realisation—both potential and in fact—are raised by numerous authors (Elson et al, Paul O'Connell, Harvey and Rooney, Rooney and Dutschke), with concern repeatedly being expressed with regard to the inequalities and structural biases in terms of ESR enjoyment that neoliberal economic policies frequently cause.

Bringing together critical voices to highlight global and local perspectives on the state of law, policy and practice, this volume is the first edited collection that directly addresses the question of how public finance decisions can—and should—affect the effective implementation of ESR. It is thus the editors' hope that the contributions to this book will enrich the global dialogue on human rights by serving as a basis for research and practice, thereby stimulating a wider academic and popular debate on budgets, economic policy and human rights.

I

Foundations

1

Public Finance, Maximum Available Resources and Human Rights

DIANE ELSON, RADHIKA BALAKRISHNAN AND JAMES HEINTZ

I. Introduction

Human rights cannot be realised without resources. As an irreducible minimum, the apparatus of justice requires public money to fund lawmakers, judges and magistrates and their courts, police, ombudsmen etc. However, substantial progress towards a full realisation of human rights—economic, social and cultural as well as civil and political—makes demands on public finance well beyond what is required for the basic administration of justice. This is recognised in Article 2(1) of the International Covenant on Economic, Social and Cultural Rights (ICESCR):

> Each State Party to the present Covenant undertakes to take steps, individually and through international assistance and co-operation, especially economic and technical, to the maximum of its available resources, with a view to achieving progressively the full realisation of the rights recognised in the present Covenant by all appropriate means, including particularly the adoption of legislative measures.

This chapter explores how 'maximum available resources' has been clarified by the human rights community (section II) and discusses how the human rights understanding of the concept could be enriched by consideration of the concepts of fiscal and monetary space used by economists (section III). We then discuss how 'maximum available resources' is related to five components of public finance: government expenditure (section IV), government revenue (section V), official development assistance (section VI), borrowing and debt (section VII) and monetary policy and financial regulation (section VIII). Particular attention is paid to the clarification of 'maximum available resources' in contexts of economic crisis; and the discussion focuses on economic and social rights (ESR).[1]

[1] This chapter draws on R Balakrishnan, D Elson, J Heintz and N Lusiani, *Maximum Available Resources and Human Rights: Analytical Report* (New Jersey, Center for Women's Global Leadership, Rutgers University, 2011).

We argue that other dimensions of public finance besides expenditure are also important: monetary policy, including financial regulation; and government borrowing. The concept of maximum available resources, we argue, implies that the role of the state is not only as an efficient administrator of existing resources, but as an institution that mobilises additional resources. These are not only financial. We also think it is important to recognise that public finance mobilises other resources: human; technological; organisational; natural and information resources—not only in the public sector but also through its impact on the activities of businesses and households. In particular, public finance influences the levels of unemployment and underemployment in an economy. An economy with high levels of unemployment and underemployment is not making maximum use of available human resources.

II. Clarification of 'Maximum Available Resources' by the Human Rights Community

There has been further discussion of the meaning of 'maximum available resources' by the UN Committee on Economic, Social and Cultural Rights (the Committee) and the UN Committee on the Rights of the Child. In addition, several Special Rapporteurs and Independent Experts have referred to the relevance of government expenditure and taxation for the realisation of economic and social rights. Here we note some of the key points they have made.

In 2007, the UN Committee on Economic, Social and Cultural Rights made a statement entitled 'An Evaluation of the Obligation to Take Steps to the "Maximum of Available Resources" Under an Optional Protocol to the Covenant'.[2] However, the statement did not define what constitutes 'available resources' beyond stating that it refers to 'both the resources existing within a state, as well as those available from the international community through international cooperation and assistance'.[3] It does state, in paragraph 7, that:

> The obligation to protect and, to a greater extent, the obligation to fulfill … often require positive budgetary measures in order to prevent third parties from interfering with the rights recognised in the Covenant (obligation to protect) or to facilitate, provide and promote the enjoyment of these rights (obligation to fulfil).

In considering a claim that 'resource constraints' explain a failure to either make progress, or to take retrogressive steps, in terms of the realisation of Covenant rights, the Committee would, inter alia, examine the existence of other serious claims on States Parties' limited resources (which implies a consideration

[2] ComESCR, 'An Evaluation of the Obligation to Take Steps to the "Maximum of Available Resources" under an Optional Protocol to the Covenant', UN Doc E/C.12/2007/1 (2007).

[3] Ibid para 5.

of priorities);[4] and whether a State Party had tried to get more development assistance.[5] The statement did not mention other methods of resource mobilisation such as changes in tax policy, financial sector reform and monetary policy.

The UN Convention on the Rights of the Child (CRC) explicitly refers to States Parties' obligations to take steps to use the maximum available resources to ensure realisation of economic, social and cultural rights.[6] The Committee on the Rights of the Child has clarified this further in General Comment No 5,[7] which calls for identifying and analysing resources for children in national budgets:

> No State can tell whether it is fulfilling children's economic, social and cultural rights 'to the maximum extent … of available resources', as it is required to do under article 4, unless it can identify the proportion of national budget and other budgets allocated to the social sector, and, within that, to children, both directly and indirectly.[8]

In 2007, the Committee held a Day of General Discussion on the topic 'Resources for the Rights of the Child—Responsibility of States: Investments for the Implementation of Economic, Social and Cultural Rights of Children and International Cooperation'. The keynote speaker for the day argued that 'available resources' refers not only to financial resources, but also to human and organisational resources; he commented, inter alia, on the factors which may affect the availability of resources, emphasising the 'strength and efficacy of the taxation system, including whether there is a progressive tax policy'.[9] The Concluding Recommendations affirmed that resources should be understood to include not only financial resources, but also human, technological, organisational, natural and information resources.[10] However, the Committee did not take up the issue of taxation. The contribution of international development assistance to resources was highlighted, and the Committee recommended that States Parties meet the UN target that international development assistance should be at the level of 0.7 per cent of Gross Domestic Product (GDP).

Several UN Special Rapporteurs and Independent Experts have also addressed the meaning of 'maximum available resources'. Magdalena Sepúlveda, the former Independent Expert, now Special Rapporteur on the Question of Human Rights and Extreme Poverty, has examined the obligation of governments to use the 'maximum of available resources' to realise economic social and cultural rights

[4] Ibid para 10(d).

[5] Ibid para 10(f).

[6] See Art 4: 'States Parties shall undertake all appropriate legislative, administrative, and other measures for the implementation of the rights recognised in the present Convention. With regard to economic, social and cultural rights, States Parties shall undertake such measures to the maximum extent of their available resources and, where needed, within the framework of international co-operation'.

[7] ComRC General Comment No 5 on general measures of implementation of the convention on the rights of the child (arts 4, 42 and 44, para 6), UN Doc CRC/GC/2003/5 (2003).

[8] Ibid para 51.

[9] Committee on the Rights of the Child, 'Day of General Discussion—Resources for the Rights of the Child: Responsibility of States', 46th Session (2007), Mr Kamal Siddique, a member of the Committee on the Rights of the Child, para 6.

[10] Ibid para 24.

and concluded that governments must mobilise resources within the country to their utmost ability.[11] Government expenditures must be efficient and effective. Failure to curb corruption is a failure to comply with the obligation.[12] Funds earmarked in the budget for economic, social and cultural rights (ESCR) must not be diverted to non-ESCR areas.[13] Funds earmarked for ESCR must be fully expended for that purpose.[14] Governments that introduce regressive measures, such as cuts in expenditure on ESCR, must show that they have used the maximum of available resources to avoid taking such a step.[15] Governments must do all they can to secure international assistance where national resources are inadequate to realise ESCR. Her conclusions point to the importance of domestic resource mobilisation, as well as of expenditure policy and international assistance.

The Special Rapporteur on the Realisation of Economic, Social and Cultural Rights, Danilo Türk, referred to taxation in his work, noting that

> [p]rogressive (as opposed to regressive) measures of taxation can, if supported by adequate administrative machinery and enforcement mechanisms, lead to gentle and gradual forms of income redistribution within States without threatening economic stability or patterns of growth, thereby creating conditions that enable a larger proportion of society to enjoy economic, social and cultural rights.[16]

The Special Rapporteur on the Right to Education has noted that, 'It is hard to imagine how any state would raise the revenue to finance health, education, water, and sanitation, or assistance for those too young or too old to work, were it not for taxation'.[17]

As a final example, Olivier de Schutter, the Special Rapporteur on the Right to Food, in his 2009 report on Brazil, draws attention to the role of taxes in fulfilling the obligation to using the 'maximum available resources':

> The tax structure in Brazil remains highly regressive. Tax rates are high for goods and services and low for income and property, bringing about very inequitable outcomes ... while the social programmes developed under the 'Zero Hunger' strategy are impressive in scope, they are essentially funded by the very persons whom they seek to benefit, as the regressive system of taxation seriously limits the redistributive aspect of the programmes. Only by introducing a tax reform that would reverse the current situation could Brazil claim to be seeking to realise the right to adequate food by taking steps to the maximum of its available resources.[18]

[11] M Sepúlveda, *The Nature of the Obligations under the International Covenant on Economic, Social and Cultural Rights* (Antwerp, Intersentia, 2003).

[12] Ibid.

[13] Ibid.

[14] Ibid.

[15] Ibid.

[16] D Türk, 'Report of the Special Rapporteur on the Realisation of Economic, Social and Cultural Rights' (UN Doc E/CN.4/Sub.2/1992/16).

[17] K Tomasevski, 'Background Paper submitted by Special Rapporteur on the Right to Education, Committee on Economic, Social and Cultural Rights' 19th Session (UN Doc E/C.12/1998/18) 5.

[18] O De Schutter, 'Report of the Special Rapporteur on the Right to Food—Mission to Brazil' (UN Doc A/HRC/13/33/Add.6, 2009), para 36.

It is thus clear that the human rights community has recognised the importance of government revenues, including taxation and official development assistance, as well as public expenditure, to the concept of maximum available resources.

To understand in more detail how far a government faces resource constraints in progressively realising human rights, it is helpful to consider the concepts of fiscal space and monetary space used by economists.

III. Fiscal Space and Monetary Space

When economists talk about fiscal space, they are concerned with the question of whether it is possible to expand public expenditure on programmes that will support desired outcomes in terms of human well-being (such as health and education and job creation) and/or in terms of economic development (such as economic growth and structural change). For example:

> The idea is that fiscal space must exist or be created if extra resources are to be made available for worthwhile government spending (International Monetary Fund 2005).[19]

> [In the context of the Millennium Development Goals] the focus has shifted to an assessment of how fiscal space for scaling up public investments can be amplified (UNDP 2010).[20]

> The concept of 'fiscal space' refers to the flexibility (or 'room') available to a government to adjust elements of its budget in order to increase spending, either overall or in some priority area such, as for example, basic social services for children.[21]

All economists agree that more fiscal space may be created by: reallocating public spending towards the desired goals and improving its efficiency and effectiveness; increasing tax revenue, through changes to the tax code and improvements in the effectiveness of tax collection; obtaining more official development assistance; and appropriate borrowing from private domestic or international sources.[22] But mainstream neoclassical economics, as exemplified for instance, in the policy focus of the International Monetary Fund (IMF) and World Bank, has a much more restricted view of the scope for increasing fiscal space by these

[19] P Heller, 'Back to Basics Fiscal Space: What It is and How to Get It' (2005) 42(2) *Finance and Development*: www.imf.org.

[20] 'The Fiscal Space Challenge and Financing for MDG Achievements' in United Nations Development Programme (UNDP), *Beyond the Midpoint: Achieving the Millennium Development Goals* (New York, UNDP, 2010) 82: content.undp.org/go/cms-service/stream/asset/?asset_id=2223965.

[21] United Nations Children's Fund (UNICEF), 'Fiscal Space and Public Expenditure on the Social Sectors' (February 2009) Briefing Paper, 2: www.unicef.org/wcaro/wcaro_08_UNICEF_OPM_briefing_paper__Fiscal_Space.pdf.

[22] For a more systematic overview of perspectives on fiscal resource mobilisation among economists, see R Roy and A Heuty (eds), *Fiscal Space: Policy Options for Financing Human Development* (New York, Earthscan and UNDP, 2009).

means than does Keynesian and human development economics. For example, neoclassical economics theorises that government spending, financed through either taxes or debt, will 'crowd-out' private spending, producing no net effect on economic activity.[23] The neoclassical approach asserts that debt-financed government spending will have little effect on overall demand in the economy, since individuals will adjust their current consumption behaviour to account for the costs of paying back debt in the future.[24] In contrast, Keynes argued that government spending could stimulate economic activity in the context of unemployment and excess productive capacity.[25] The founder of human development economics, Nobel laureate Amartya Sen, argues that 'anti-deficit radicalism' undermines human development.[26]

Neoclassical economists espouse a theory of how economies work which assumes that market economies tend to full employment equilibrium through decentralised decisions of consumers and producers guided by prices.[27] Such an equilibrium represents an efficient use of resources, in which more of one thing cannot be produced without producing less of something else. Government activity is regarded with suspicion because it may 'distort' the decisions of producers and consumers away from the 'efficient' market-based decisions they would otherwise make. As a result, neoclassical economists are inclined to suggest that private sector provision is more efficient than public sector provision.[28] This general assertion can give rise to a number of specific implications: that increasing government spending and tax rates reduces private sector investment, consumption and effort thereby having zero net effect on the economy; that governments of developing countries may not have the capacity to manage extra inflows of aid effectively or may reduce their tax effort if they obtain more aid; and that public sector borrowing and investment displaces private sector borrowing and investment.

Keynesian economists and many development economists espouse a theory of how economies work that assumes there is no tendency towards a full employment equilibrium, that disequilibrium is inherent in market economies and that, instead of leading to social optimums, unmanaged markets, particularly

[23] For a recent exposition of this argument, cast in terms of the effectiveness of stimulus spending to address the 2008 global financial crisis, see R Barro and C Redlick, 'Stimulus Spending Doesn't Work' *The Wall Street Journal* (New York, 1 October 2009).

[24] R Barro, 'Are Government Bonds Net Wealth?' (1974) 82 *Journal of Political Economy* 1095.

[25] JM Keynes, *The General Theory of Employment, Interest, and Money* (San Diego, Harcourt Brace & Company, 1964).

[26] AK Sen, 'Human Development and Financial Conservatism' (1998) 26 *World Development* 742.

[27] The classical exposition of the neoclassical model of market clearing prices is the Arrow-Debreu model. K Arrow and G Debreu, 'Existence of an Equilibrium for a Competitive Economy' (1954) 22 *Econometrica* 265.

[28] Milton Friedman represents a proponent of this line of reasoning. For specific examples involving a critical evaluation of government policies on education, discrimination, the licensing of occupations, and social welfare programs, among other issues, see M Friedman, *Capitalism and Freedom* (Chicago, University of Chicago Press, 2002).

financial markets, produce conditions of fragility and crisis.[29] In particular, such economists recognise the possibility that employment and economic activity can be limited by a lack of sufficient aggregate demand: consumption, private investment, government expenditure, or exports can be too low to allow the economy to function at full capacity. They also stress that public investment can be complementary to private investment and create a supportive environment that encourages private investment. They agree that government economic policy will tend to change behaviour of consumers and producers from what they would otherwise be, but argue that this effect should not be condemned as a 'distortion' but assessed in terms of how far it supports the realisation of desirable economic and social goals. Markets themselves are rarely perfect and interventions are needed to improve social well-being.[30]

With respect to fiscal space, there are disagreements are about how far the creation of fiscal space should be limited by concerns about the sustainability of the government's financial position (defined in terms of specific limits to budget deficits as a share of GDP and to public debt as a share of GDP).[31] Neoclassical economists tend to place great emphasis on balanced budgets and low debt/GDP ratios, and these fiscal policy rules are increasing reflected in policy decisions. For example, the European Fiscal Compact (within the Treaty on Stability, Coordination, and Governance), adopted by 25 Member States of the European Union in March 2012, would limit budget deficits to 0.5 per cent of GDP, or 1 per cent of GDP for countries with debt/GDP ratios below 60 per cent.[32] In contrast, human development and Keynesian economists argue that the appropriate targets for deficits and debts and inflation have to be judged in light of the state of the economy (recession calls for different targets than periods of rapid growth); how the financial resources are used (for instance, for long-term public investment or current expenditures) and of other objectives (the extent to which reductions in spending harm future economic performance).[33]

[29] See eg, Keynes above n 25; H Minksy, *Stabilizing an Unstable Economy* (New York, McGraw Hill, 2008); M Kalecki, *Essays in the Theory of Economic Fluctuations* (New York, Russell & Russell, 1972).

[30] Numerous economists have studied imperfect and incomplete markets which yield socially sub-optimal outcomes. These theories have been applied to: labour markets (C Shapiro and J Stiglitz, 'Equilibrium Unemployment as a Worker Discipline Device' (1984) 74 *American Economic Review* 433 and S Bowles, 'The Production Process in a Competitive Economy: Walrasian, Neo-Hobbesian, and Marxian Models' (1985) 75 *American Economic Review* 16); credit markets (J Stiglitz and A Weiss, 'Credit Rationing in Markets with Imperfect Information (1981) 71 *American Economic Review* 753); and product markets (G Akerlof, 'The Market for Lemons: Quality Uncertainty and the Market Mechanism'(1970) 84 *Quarterly Journal of Economics* 488).

[31] For a more complete discussion of the setting of fiscal rules within the context of mainstream economics, see IMF, *Fiscal Monitor: Balancing Fiscal Policy Risks* (Washington DC, IMF, 2012).

[32] Treaty on Stability, Coordination and Governance in the Economic and Monetary Union (Fiscal Compact), adopted by the Council of the European Union, 2 March 2012. Note, the deficit targets in the Treaty refer to structural deficits. Cyclical deficits may be greater in the event of an economic downturn.

[33] Roy and Heuty above n 22.

Such economists also emphasise the interconnection between public expenditure and mobilisation of tax revenue. Cuts in government spending in an economic downturn lead to falls in tax revenue, as people spend less, and lose their jobs.[34] Increases in government spending in a downturn lead to increases in tax revenue if jobs and household incomes are boosted. In contrast, neoclassical economists place great faith in deregulation of markets as a way of creating jobs, on the basis of their theoretical position, that market economies, if left to themselves, are full-employment economies, that ensure the mobilisation and efficient use of all available resources.[35]

Fiscal space is connected to what we might call 'monetary space', the issue of how far it is possible to expand access to credit in an economy, to fund public and private investment and public and private consumption without creating macroeconomic instability. The central bank can influence supply of credit in an economy through the rules it sets for commercial banks, and the interest rates that it charges to government and to commercial banks for borrowing from the central bank. The central bank also influences the exchange rate between a country's currency and those of other countries, by maintaining foreign exchange reserves and buying and selling foreign currency.

Neoclassical and Keynesian/human development economists have profoundly different views about the appropriate role of central banks, monetary policy and financial regulation and define macroeconomic stability in different ways. For neoclassical economists, macroeconomic stability means keeping inflation rates at a stable, low level;[36] Keynesian/human development economists provide evidence that very low rates of inflation come at the cost of expansion of output and jobs, and argue for a broader understanding of macroeconomic stability that includes not only avoidance of excessive inflation, but also expansion of output and jobs.[37] They argue that widespread underemployment and unemployment is clearly a waste of resources and a waste of lives. In many developing countries, inflationary pressures are not monetary in character, but arise from pressures on global food or energy prices. Under these conditions, using monetary policy to reduce inflation can make the negative economic consequences of price shocks worse.[38]

[34] There are many books and articles by Keynesian economists that explain this point. Two recent examples are V Chick and A Pettifor, 'The Economic Consequences of Mr Osborne': www.debtonation.org, and T Palley, *The Fiscal Austerity Trap* (Washington DC, New American Foundation, 2009).

[35] See eg, Friedman above n 28.

[36] R Billi and GA Kahn, 'What is the Optimal Rate of Inflation?' (2008) Second Quarter *Economic Review of the Federal Reserve Bank of Kansas City* 5. Billi and Kahn argue that inflation rates should be kept low, but above zero. The reasons for low, yet positive, inflation rates include reducing the risks of deflation, the presence of nominal price rigidities, the zero lower bound on nominal interest rates and concerns over debt deflation.

[37] G Epstein, 'Central Banks as Agents of Employment Creation' in JA Ocampo and KS Jomo (eds), *Towards Full and Decent Employment* (London, Zed Books, 2007).

[38] J Heintz and N Léonce, 'Is There a Case for Formal Inflation-targeting in sub-Saharan Africa?' (2010) 20 *Journal of African Economies* 67.

The neoclassical economists, in conjunction with banks and other financial sector businesses, and international financial institutions such as the IMF, have successfully pushed for central banks to be quasi-independent of governments and to focus exclusively on targets for low inflation, implying higher interest rates for the private sector (which in turn tends to reduce investment in job creation) and for the public sector (which increases the costs of servicing public debt). They have also supported deregulation of financial markets. The financial crisis of 2008 and the subsequent recession in many countries have led to some questioning of this orthodoxy, but there have not been any fundamental policy changes. Human development and Keynesian economists have pressed for more flexibility. UNICEF, for instance, has argued for a 'more accommodating macroeconomic framework', which permits higher budget deficits and higher levels of inflation in the short run to permit vital investments in basic services for children and prevent irreparable harm.[39]

Neoclassical economists dominate economic policy advice at the national and international levels. The human rights community needs to be aware that there are alternative policies and to push for open and transparent discussion of alternatives before any decision is made. As the Committee on Economic, Social and Cultural Rights has made clear, while human rights obligations do accord States Parties a 'margin of appreciation' to 'take steps and adopt measures most suited to their specific circumstances', the Committee will take into account 'where several policy options are available, whether the State adopts the option that least restricts Covenant rights'.[40] If measures are deliberately introduced that lead to retrogression in enjoyment of human rights then the state has to show that they have been 'introduced after consideration of all alternatives and are fully justifiable by reference to totality of rights provided for in the Covenant and in context of the full use of the maximum of available resources'.[41]

It is important to bear in mind that the judgements made by governments on the extent to which they have additional fiscal and monetary space, and the policies they adopt, are constrained by the policies of other governments, both directly and through their role in international institutions such as the IMF, the World Bank and the European Union. In particular, the policies adopted and supported by governments of the rich countries have enormous impact on many other countries, including via the creation of channels for tax evasion and avoidance, conditions attached to official development cooperation assistance and failure to enforce

[39] See I Ortiz, J Chai and M Cummins, 'Identifying Fiscal Space: Options for Social and Economic Development for Children and Poor Households in 184 Countries' (2011) Social and Economic Policy Working Paper (New York, UNICEF).

[40] ComESCR, 'An Evaluation of the Obligation to Take Steps to the "Maximum of Available Resources"' above n 2, paras 8 and 12.

[41] ComESCR General Comment No 3 on the nature of States parties' obligations (art 2 (1)), UN Doc E/1991/23 (1990), para 9; ComESCR General Comment No 12 on the right to adequate food (art 11), UN Doc E/C.12/1999/5 (1999), para 45; ComESCR General Comment No 14 on the right to the highest attainable standard of health (art 12), UN Doc E/C.12/2000/4 (2000), para 32; ComESCR General Comment No15 on the right to water (arts 11 and 12), UN Doc E/C.12/2002/11 (2003), para 19).

adequate regulation of the financial sector. Extraterritorial obligations must be borne in mind as well as obligations to those living in the jurisdiction of a state.

In the following discussion of the components of 'maximum available resources', we keep in mind the different views on alternatives put forward by neoclassical and Keynesian/human development economists, and the issue of extraterritorial as well as territorial obligations. In turn we consider public expenditure, taxation, official development assistance, budget deficits, borrowing and debt and monetary policy and financial regulation.

IV. Public Expenditure

In considering whether it is possible for a government to allocate more funding to programmes related to the realisation of economic and social rights, it is relevant to examine the distribution of public expenditure between different uses. For instance, to examine the allocation of spending to particular targeted programmes that support the realisation of specific rights, for example, spending on health, education and social security programmes, and compare this with areas of spending which may not support human rights, for instance military spending. Information about both the level of such expenditure (for example, real per capita expenditure on health) and its share of GDP (for example, the ratio of public expenditure on health to GDP) is useful in terms of evaluating, at a general level, whether budgetary spending reflects priorities with regard to economic and social rights. However, in our view such indicators should be thought of as providing broad benchmarks for assessing government policy rather than prescriptive targets. There may be valid reasons why government expenditure as a share of GDP will vary from the benchmark. We counsel against an attempt to specify precise targets (for example, that 5 per cent of GDP must go to health). Instead, such indicators should be used to judge whether there is cause for concern about compliance with obligations of conduct, in comparison with similar countries and with past performance of the same country.

Nevertheless, it is important not to limit the analysis of public expenditures to social sector spending (such as health, education and social security), since the realisation of economic and social rights often also depends on public investment in basic infrastructure. Consider a case in which efforts to realise children's rights have been exclusively focused on spending on health and education and not on infrastructure investments, such as building all-weather roads and providing public transport. Though the spending on health and education can have some positive human rights outcomes, the lack of spending on infrastructure may deny some children access to clinics and schools. Thus, defining what constitutes an expenditure in support of economic and social rights should not be limited to social sectors alone, but also include consideration of investments in economic sectors, such as transport and energy. Expenditure in economic sectors is also important for the realisation of the right to work and the right to an adequate standard of living. Expenditure targeted to job creation is an obvious example.

The growing practice of subcontracting the private sector to provide public services further complicates the picture. In these circumstances, states have a duty to monitor and regulate the private provision of these services to ensure that human rights obligations are met. The increasing privatisation of water supply and distribution is one such example. Effective regulation itself requires public resources to finance the costs of operating regulatory institutions, although not in expenditure categories typically associated with economic and social rights.

Government spending must also be evaluated in terms of the distribution of benefits among households and individuals. To comply with principles of non-discrimination, public spending should not be allocated in ways which reinforce existing inequalities or which fail to deliver benefits to vulnerable and marginalised populations. For example, public health expenditure that primarily supports hospitals and medical facilities which serve the ethnic majority, and to which ethnic minorities have limited or no access, will not support the realisation of economic and social rights to the same extent as an alternative, more equitable, allocation of funding.

Of course, the extent to which public expenditure supports the progressive realisation of human rights does not just depend on the allocation of finance, but also on how efficiently and effectively it is used. Efficiency in this context is often defined in terms of the *financial costs of the inputs* required to produce a particular outcome—greater efficiency implies that more can be produced with a given amount of financial resources; or that the same can be produced with less finance. For example, the efficiency of education expenditures may be measured in terms of the average cost per student.

However, care must be taken when evaluating efficiency. Are all inputs adequately accounted for or are there important resources which are ignored (for example, unpaid work contributed by volunteers or by family members)? For example, in the health sector, efficiency is typically judged in terms of the financial cost per treatment.[42] This can be reduced by shortening the time that patients spend in hospital. However, typically patients still need further care at home after discharge from hospital, and frequently this is provided, unpaid, by family members, most often women and girls.[43] Therefore, efficiency, narrowly defined, in financial terms, may appear to improve as the cost of providing treatment for each patient drops, but there are hidden costs for their relatives who have to cut back on time spent on other activities (for example, sleep, leisure, paid work) to care for a family member. In terms of human resources, there may be no reduction

[42] See eg, H Oxley and M MacFarlan, 'Health Care Reform: Controlling Spending and Increasing Efficiency' (1995) 24 *OECD Economic Studies* 7.

[43] See eg, M Luxton, 'Friends, Neighbours, and Community: A Case Study of the Role of Informal Caregiving in Social Reproduction' in K Bezanson and M Luxton (eds), *Social Reproduction* (Montreal, McGill-Queen's University Press, 2006).

in inputs required to deliver the same health outcome; merely a change in the proportion of the care that is provided unpaid. What looks like an increase in efficiency in use of financial resources is instead revealed as a transfer of costs in terms of human resources, with a disproportionate impact on women and girls.

Efficiency, understood narrowly, may also appear to improve if the costs of providing a service are cut, by reducing the wages and social benefits of those who provide it. However, in these cases, we must consider whether the cuts in employment costs are achieved at the expense of the economic and social rights of employees. Does the job continue to provide an adequate standard of living and the right to social security? A reduction in the wages and benefits of those who are already on low incomes (for example, those who clean public buildings) is not the same as cutting the wages and benefits of those who are already on very high incomes (for example, those who are high level officials).

A further type of apparent increase in efficiency is when the workforce is reduced but the output is maintained by workers having to work more intensively, for instance, to work faster, or perform more than one task at the same time. Again we must consider the implications for economic and social rights. Are rights at work and the right to health compromised by additional stress? Or are the workers affected those that were previously enjoying a lot of 'on the job' leisure? And is the *quality,* as well as the *quantity* of output maintained? For example, reducing expenditures per student in the educational system would often be associated with poorer quality education, rather than a gain in efficiency.

These are the questions that need to be asked when a government claims that efficiency will be increased by contracting out the service to the private sector. The for-profit provider may be able to deliver the service at lower financial cost but is it transferring costs to unpaid work in households, which will be disproportionately borne by women and girls? Is it denying workers an adequate standard of living, rights at work and the right to social security etc? Is it reducing the quality of the service?

This links to the question of the effectiveness of spending in achieving positive impact on enjoyment of rights. As previously mentioned, it is the *quality* as well as the quantity of outputs that matters. Services must be delivered in ways that respect the individual's dignity, and this may require more time to interact with people and give them personal attention; a faster service is a worse service in many forms of interpersonal care.[44] Effectiveness of spending requires good training for public employees, including on how to treat people with respect, especially poor people, people from minority groups and women.[45]

[44] For examples, see W Sykes and C Groom, *Older People's Experiences of Home Care in England,* Equality and Human Rights Research report no 79 (Manchester, Equality and Human Rights Commission, 2011).

[45] See eg, Equality and Human Rights Commission, *From Safety Net to Springboard: A New Approach to Care and Support for All Based on Equality and Human Rights* (London, Equality and Human Rights Commission, 2009).

One strategy to increase efficiency and effectiveness of public services is through partnerships in which communities are asked to provide unpaid services to complement provision of public money. For example, a government may provide a grant to cover materials and the community must contribute the labour to provide a service or construct a facility, such as a school or clinic. This may result in a better quality product at lower financial cost through harnessing the self interest of those who will use the service. Such partnerships are not necessarily antithetical to human rights, but we must consider who in the community bears the burden of carrying out these new tasks, and whether the labour is voluntarily provided. Communities are often highly unequal. Perhaps it is the most disadvantaged who provide the unpaid work, and the most advantaged who reap the benefits.

We can all agree that more efficiency and effectiveness in spending public money is desirable, but it is important to probe how far there are truly gains in efficiency and effectiveness and whether any retrogression in enjoyment of economic and social rights are involved.

The risk of retrogression must also be at the forefront of examination of austerity policies. Retrogression is often manifested in the form of cuts to public expenditure. Finance ministers and international financial institutions, such as the IMF, often recognise that cuts to government expenditures slow economic activity during a downturn. However, they are prone to argue that, in the context of declining revenues and slower growth, public expenditure must be cut to reduce unsustainable budget deficits and protect medium-term fiscal stability, especially in contexts of financial and economic crisis. For example, the April 2012 issue of the IMF publication, *Fiscal Monitor*, states 'short-term caution should not be an excuse to slow or delay efforts to put public finances on a sounder footing over the medium term, as this remains a key requirement for sustainable growth'.[46]

Arguments that government spending should be cut to maintain fiscal stability must first be scrutinised in light of how far they have mobilised other resources, such as tax revenue, development cooperation assistance and loans; and what instructions and targets they have given to central banks to guide the conduct of monetary policy.[47] We will return to this point at the end of this chapter, when these other dimensions of public finance have been considered. However, we agree that even after consideration of all other resource mobilisation strategies, it may be necessary to cut public expenditure. In this case avoidance of retrogression in the realisation of human rights must be at the forefront of the design of the size and scope of expenditure cuts. Governments have an immediate obligation to provide the minimum core of ESCRs to safeguard the most deprived.[48] This suggests two questions must be answered. First, is the fiscal austerity plan based on an

[46] IMF, *Fiscal Monitor* above n 31, ix.

[47] Many organisations contribute to such scrutiny, from international organisations such as UNICEF, which reports regularly on the implications of austerity plans for the rights of the child (see: www.unicef.org), to small NGOs, such as the UK Women's Budget Group, which reports on the implications of UK austerity plans for UK women's rights, see: www.wbg.org.uk.

[48] ComESCR General Comment No 3 above n 41, para 10.

appropriate balance between cutting expenditures and increasing taxes? Second, what are impacts on the poorest and most deprived of the cutbacks, and how can the rights of these groups be safeguarded?

In May 2012, these considerations were drawn to the attention of States Parties to the ICESCR in a letter from the Chair of the Committee,[49] which says that any proposed policies to adjust the implementation of Covenant rights, in context of financial and economic crisis, must meet the following requirements:

> First, the policy is a temporary measure covering the period of crisis only; second the policy is necessary and proportionate, in the sense that the adoption of any other policy, or failure to act, would be more detrimental to economic, social and cultural rights; third, the policy is not discriminatory and comprises all possible measures, including tax measures, to support social transfers to mitigate inequalities that can grow in times of crisis and to ensure that the rights of disadvantaged and marginalised individuals and groups are not disproportionately affected; fourth, the policy identifies the minimum core content of rights, or a social protection floor, as developed by the International Labour Organisation, and ensures the protection of this core content at all times.

This specifically mentions tax measures, to which we now turn, and implies the importance of considering a range of alternative polices, to which we will return at the end of this chapter.

V. Taxation

Governments obtain revenue from several sources, including taxation, royalties paid for the utilisation of natural resources and profits from public enterprises. Here we focus on taxation as this is typically the most important source of revenue. The process of mobilising tax revenue and using those resources to provide goods, services and social transfers is widely accepted as a central responsibility of a well-functioning government.[50] Nevertheless, many mainstream economists and business interests refer to 'tax burdens' and 'distortions' caused by tax policy, using as a benchmark an economy functioning without taxes. For example, in neoclassical theory, a payroll tax implemented to finance social protection programmes will reduce employment since it raises the costs of labour and therefore lowers the demand for labour on the part of employers and firms. In our view, this is not an appropriate way of framing the issues (since no real world economy is able to function without taxation), and we suggest it is better to refer to 'tax contributions' and tax 'incentives/disincentives'.

To analyse the adequacy of tax revenue mobilisation, it is useful to refer to the share of tax revenue in GDP, in comparison to similar countries. Low-income

[49] AG Pillay, 'Letter from ComESCR Chairperson to States Parties in the context of the economic and financial crisis', CESCR/48th/SP/MAB/SW, 16 May 2012: www2.ohchr.org/english/bodies/cescr/docs/LetterCESCRtoSP16.05.12.pdf.

[50] For further discussion of taxation, see Saiz's contribution to this volume.

countries, for example, tend to have lower tax–GDP ratios than high-income countries, reflecting their different economic and social structures; but if a particular low income country has a tax–GDP ratio which is lower than that of other low income countries, this suggests it is not doing enough to collect tax revenue. Raising the amount of revenue collected may require a combination of increasing tax rates, introducing new taxes and improving tax collection. Among the new taxes that could be considered is a financial transactions tax on trading of bonds, shares and financial derivatives. The volume of such transactions is so large that a very low rate (less than 1 per cent) could raise a very large amount of revenue.

To see what scope there is for improving tax collection, it is useful to measure tax effort (ie, actual tax revenue compared with potential tax revenues). Potential tax revenues can be defined in different ways. One approach is to define potential revenues as the total value of tax revenue which would be raised under the prevailing tax code if 100 per cent of taxes due were actually collected. Tax effort can be used to assess how much additional revenue could be mobilised, without changing any tax laws, if the effectiveness of collection were improved and tax evasion and avoidance reduced. For example, in a number of sub-Saharan African countries, the efficiency of revenue collection has been enhanced through institutional reforms in the way that taxes are administered and collected, independent of changes in tax policy.[51] These indicators have a number of limitations but they are useful as benchmarks in considering whether there is cause for concern about the extent to which governments are making the maximum use of available resources.

Tax avoidance and evasion lead to substantial loss of revenue for governments. Bribery and corruption of tax officials are also common problems in many countries.[52] It is vital to strengthen tax collection processes to support progressive realisation of rights. Cutting the budgets of tax collection offices is a false economy, as it means that fewer people are available to curtail avoidance and evasion.

The existence of tax havens, with very low tax rates, facilitates tax avoidance and evasion. Multinational corporations take advantage of tax havens to reduce tax payments. By setting up headquarters in a tax haven, then manipulating the price of imports purchased from and exports shipped to other divisions and affiliates of the same company operating in different countries, corporations can show their profits as accruing in a tax haven rather than in a country with higher taxes. Estimates of the annual tax revenue lost to developing countries due to this kind of tax avoidance and evasion amount to US$98 billion to US$106 billion.[53] This compares to total overseas development assistance in 2009 from OECD countries

[51] OECD and ADB, *African Economic Outlook 2010* (Paris, Organisation for Economic Co-operation and Development and African Development Bank, 2010).

[52] This issue is further explored by Transparency International: www.transparancy.org and Tax Justice Network: www.taxjustice.net/cms/front_content.php?idcatart=2&lang=1.

[53] A Hollingshead, *The Implied Tax Revenue Loss from Trade Mispricing* (Washington DC, Global Financial Integrity, 2010).

of US$83.5 billion.[54] Cooperation among states is vital to reduce the scope for cross-border tax avoidance strategies.

As well as raising adequate levels of revenue, tax policy needs to comply with principles of non-discrimination and equality. Consider the case of increasing VAT rates. This will increase prices of goods and services to households and have a disproportionate impact on lower-income households. This is because low-income households spend a larger share of their income on goods and services than high-income households, who can afford to save part of their income.[55] The result is that VAT payments account for a larger share of the income of lower-income households relative to high-income households. This can be mitigated by exempting basic goods and services from VAT.

Incidence analysis looks at the tax contributions of different households in relation to their income. This analysis can be used to analyse tax contributions by household, either by looking at individual taxes (sales tax, VAT, income tax, etc) or by amalgamating them all and determining what share of income goes in tax payments. This type of analysis can show how much low-income households pay in taxes, as a percentage of their income, relative to richer households. It can also throw light on the interaction between other forms of disadvantage and tax, such as what share of their income is paid by households with differing gender characteristics (for example, sex of head of household, sex of primary earner, etc).[56] Regressive taxation regimes, which require the poor and disadvantaged to pay a bigger share of their income than the rich, are questionable from the perspective of non-discrimination, while progressive tax regimes, which make more use if income and wealth taxes, are generally more able to mobilise domestic revenue equitably.

One common concern is that higher taxes on businesses and wealthy households will reduce investment and, hence, growth and employment.[57] Such an impact could conceivably limit the generation of resources available for realising economic and social rights. However, lower tax rates and various kinds of tax allowances may just be windfall gains for businesses and wealthy households who would have invested anyway. The primary reasons companies invest (for example, market access, the availability of an educated labour force, strategic export platforms, or the presence of natural resources) tend to have little to do with tax levels.

[54] Estimates are from OECD data: stats.oecd.org. The member countries of the Development Assistance Committee (DAC) include Australia, Austria, Belgium, Canada, Denmark, Finland, France, Germany, Greece, Ireland, Italy, Japan, Luxembourg, Netherlands, New Zealand, Norway, Portugal, South Korea, Spain, Sweden, Switzerland, the United Kingdom and the United States.

[55] This is a standard finding across countries. See eg, C Grown and I Valodia (eds), *Taxation and Gender Equity* (London, Routledge, 2010).

[56] Ibid.

[57] E Engen and J Skinner, 'Taxation and Economic Growth' (1996) 49 *National Tax Journal* 617. Engen and Skinner provide a summary of why taxes would affect economic growth using a standard neoclassical Solow growth model. They also present empirical findings which show a modest impact of taxes on growth.

Mobilising tax revenues to invest in economic and social infrastructure can do more to generate robust economic growth in the long term than low tax rates. The existence of a highly-educated, productive workforce and quality economic infrastructure (for example, energy, transportation) can provide a much stronger incentive for the private sector to invest than lower taxes. Prosperity and high rates of tax to GDP certainly go together in the higher-income countries that are members of the Organisation for Economic Co-operation and Development (OECD). The average tax to GDP ratio in these countries rose from 30.1 per cent in 1970 to 35.5 per cent in 2000. In developing countries, the average tax ratio did not change very much, rising from 16.2 per cent in the 1970s to 17.0 per cent in 2000.[58]

To uphold the principle of non-retrogression, any human rights-centred tax policy must be able to manage the 'booms' and 'busts' of modern capitalist economies in ways which reduce the negative consequences of drastic revenue shortfalls in downturns. One option is to create a reserve fund, sometimes called 'rainy day fund', into which the additional revenues during good times are placed. These funds can then be used to maintain spending, and prevent retrogression, during bad times. In the United States, most states are bound by a balanced budget requirement and many state governments maintain a 'rainy day fund' to help protect spending in the case of a revenue shortfall.[59]

Of course, in severe downturns, such as recessions, it is appropriate to introduce stimulus programmes which offset the lack of demand in the private sector. The design of such programmes—including the balance between tax cuts and extra spending—should take into account human rights principles and obligations. Tax cuts that put more purchasing power into the hands of the poor and middle class—through a cut in VAT for example—are more compatible with a human rights perspective than reducing income taxes for the richest groups.

VI. Official Development Assistance

Official development assistance (ODA) at first sight appears to be a win-win form of resource mobilisation. It appears to be an addition to resources available for realisation of human rights for governments that receive this assistance, and a way of discharging their extraterritorial obligations for governments that provide it. Obligations with respect to international development cooperation between governments are explicitly referred to in Article 2 ICESCR, and are underlined in specific provisions in Article 11 (right to an adequate standard of living). Articles 22

[58] R Bird, 'Taxation and Development, *Economic Premise, No 34* (Washington DC, World Bank, 2010).

[59] For more on 'rainy day funds', see Tax Policy Center, 'State and Local Tax Policy: What are rainy day funds and how do they work?': www.taxpolicycenter.org/briefing-book/state-local/fiscal/rainy-day.cfm.

and 23 specifically refer to the need for international measures. In 1990 the Committee's General Comment No 3 explicitly stated that 'international co-operation for development ... is an obligation of all States'.[60]

ODA is provided both bilaterally, government to government; and by multilateral institutions such as the World Bank, the regional development banks and the EU, to which donor governments make contributions. A starting point for assessing how far governments extend international assistance is the value of ODA as a proportion of GDP. A widely used benchmark is that high-income countries should provide ODA amounting to 0.7 per cent GDP. In 2010, net official ODA flows from members of the OECD reached US$128.7 billion, representing an increase of 6.5 per cent over 2009.[61] This is the highest real ODA level ever, surpassing even the volume provided in 2005 which was boosted by exceptional debt relief.[62] Net ODA as a share of the GDP of members of the OECD was 0.32 per cent, equal to 2005 and higher than any other year since 1992.[63] Though this is an increase, it is not half way to the target of 0.7 per cent.[64]

In 2010, the largest donors by volume were the United States, the United Kingdom, France, Germany and Japan.[65] Only Denmark, Luxembourg, the Netherlands, Norway and Sweden met the United Nations' ODA target of 0.7 per cent of GDP.[66] The largest increases in real terms in ODA between 2009 and 2010 were recorded by Australia, Belgium, Canada, Japan, Korea, Portugal and the United Kingdom.[67]

Countries were reminded in May 2012 about the importance of ODA in the context of financial and economic crisis in the letter from the Committee on Economic, Social and Cultural Rights, mentioned in section IV above. The Chairperson emphasised that 'States Parties to the Covenant should respect their obligations in relation to economic, social and cultural rights when making decisions, including decisions on official development assistance'.[68] However, some large European donors have cut back on ODA as part of their austerity plans.

In judging the extra resources it provides to recipients, it is important to recognise that ODA takes the form of loans, as well as grants. Interest has to be paid on loans and the loan has eventually to be repaid. These payments of debt service and amortisation of loans mean that not all of the ODA that flows into a country in any one year is a net addition to the resources available to the government. It is

[60] Subsequently several scholarly works have been published on this topic by human rights lawyers. See eg, S Skogly, *Beyond National Borders: States' Human Rights Obligations in their International Cooperation* (Antwerp, Intersentia, 2006).

[61] OECD, 'Development aid reaches an historic high in 2010': www.oecd.org/document/35/0,3746,en_2649_34447_47515235_1_1_1_1,00.html.

[62] Ibid.

[63] Ibid.

[64] Ibid.

[65] Ibid.

[66] Ibid.

[67] Ibid.

[68] Letter from ComESCR Chairperson above n 49.

important to distinguish between gross inflows of ODA and net inflows of ODA. Even the net inflows can overstate the amount of new resources being made available, since debt relief is counted as part of the new ODA. However, debt forgiveness simply writes off debt; it does not make any new resources available.

Moreover, an increasing share of ODA does not go to governments but to private sector companies. It is estimated that by 2014 the amount of ODA flowing to the private sector will be more than US$10 billion, amounting to almost one-third of ODA to developing countries.[69] Of course, this may contribute to the realisation of economic and social rights if it provides funding to developing country companies that would not be able to obtain it from purely commercial channels, and that use the funds to create decent jobs for low-income people, and pay taxes on the profits they make. However, research by the European Network on Debt and Development has found that there is reason for concern that this is not happening; for example, most of the funding is not going to developing country firms but to companies based in OECD countries or tax havens.[70]

ODA may be tied to specific projects, such as the building of a hospital or a bridge, but increasing amounts of ODA are not tied to a specific project; they are provided to augment the budget of specific ministries (sector support) or to the Ministry of Finance to support the budget as a whole (budget support). ODA which is not tied to a project generally has policy conditions attached to it, such as trade liberalisation, an increasing role for the private sector in service provision or ceilings on public sector pay. These conditions may have negative impacts on the realisation of economic and social rights. For instance, trade liberalisation entails a reduction in taxes on trade, reducing tax revenue, making it harder to finance spending on economic and social rights and further realise the Millennium Development Goals.[71] A study of 25 low-income African countries, covering the period from the early 1990s to the early 2000s, found that as a share of tax revenue, trade taxes dropped about 5 per cent; and rises in other taxes were insufficient to raise sufficient revenue.[72]

The impact of ODA on available resources in recipient countries will be reduced if ODA is tied to purchases of imports from donor countries that cost more than goods and services available locally or on the international market. The proportion of bilateral aid that is formally untied rose from 46 per cent in 1999–2000 to 76 per cent in 2007; however, research has found that in most investment projects, the main contract and technical assistance is still procured from donor countries,

[69] J Kwakkenbos, *Private Profit for Public Good? Can Investing in Private Companies Deliver for the Poor?* (Brussels, Eurodad, 2012): eurodad.org/wp-content/uploads/2012/05/Private-Profit-for-Public-Good.pdf.

[70] Ibid.

[71] The Millennium Development Goals (MDGs) were adopted by the UN General Assembly in 2000 to assist in guiding development cooperation and monitoring development achievements.

[72] T McKinley, *Why Have Tax Reforms Hampered MDG Financing?* (Brasilia, UNDP International Poverty Centre, 2007).

so some of the ODA that has flowed into a recipient country, almost immediately flows back out again to the donor.[73]

There are a number of arguments that can be made against increasing ODA. For instance, recipient countries may not be able to absorb additional amounts of ODA because they lack the capacity to spend it effectively. However, if this is the case, ODA can be directed towards increasing this capacity. A further argument is that if countries spend their additional ODA, it will lead to inflation rather than mobilisation of real resources. The IMF, for instance, has argued that low-income countries in Africa should keep much of their additional ODA in their foreign exchange reserves rather than spend it, unless they have very low rates of inflation.[74] Another concern is that ODA may flow out of recipient countries rather than augment available resources. A study of sub-Saharan African countries for the period between 1965 and 2006 found that 35 per cent of ODA flowed out of the recipient countries.[75]

Effective use of ODA to support economic and social rights depends on the actions of both donors and recipients in supporting development that is compliant with human rights. UN agencies such as the United Nations Development Programme (UNDP), UNICEF, the World Health Organization (WHO) and the Food and Agriculture Organization of the United Nations (FAO) now seek to mainstream human rights in their policies and programmes.[76] The World Bank has recognised that

> [t]he Articles of Agreement permit, and in some cases require, the Bank to recognise the human rights dimensions of its development policies and activities, since it is now evident that human rights are an intrinsic part of the Bank's mission.[77]

However, the Bank tends to have a limited understanding of the implications of human rights, seeing them as having legal implications but not implications for economic policy. The Bank General Counsel, Ana Palacio, recognises that

> [t]he Bank's analytical work can benefit from a systematic inclusion of human rights considerations and the broadened range of legal analysis these require. Areas such as governance or the legal empowerment of the poor are particularly relevant in this respect.[78]

[73] E Clay, M Geddes, and L Natali, *Aid Untying: Is it Working?* (London, Overseas Development Institute, 2009).

[74] T McKinley, *Why is Africa Constrained from Spending ODA?* (Brasilia, UNDP International Poverty Centre, May 2007).

[75] See J Serieux and T McKInley, *Why Does Aid Not Increase Savings Rate in Sub-Saharan Africa?* (Brasilia, UNDP International Poverty Centre, 2009).

[76] There is a wealth of information on how human rights are mainstreamed in the practice of these organisations on their websites: www.undp.org; www.unicef.org; www.who.org; www.fao.org.

[77] R Danino, 'Legal Opinion on Human Rights and the Work of the World Bank' (2006) 3 *Development Outreach* 30.

[78] A Palacio, 'The Way Forward: Human Rights and the World Bank' (2006) *Development Outreach*: web.worldbank.org/WBSITE/EXTERNAL/TOPICS/EXTLAWJUSTICE/0,,contentMDK:21106614~menuPK:445673~pagePK:64020865~piPK:149114~theSitePK:445634,00.html.

This approach does not, however, take into account the possibility that the conditions attached to loans by the World Bank may make it harder for governments to fulfil their obligations to realise economic and social rights. The Office of the High Commission for Human Rights has stated that human rights must be taken into account in the Poverty Reduction Strategies that governments have to agree with the World Bank before loans are provided; they have also issued guidelines on how this may be done.[79] Bilateral donors have increasingly promoted a rights-based approach to development, including the Governments of the United Kingdom, Sweden, Switzerland, Canada and Germany.[80]

Nevertheless, there is concern that there may be drawbacks to a rights-based approach to development, if it is developed as another set of conditions that rich countries impose on poorer countries, without any reciprocal understanding of obligations. Some of the donor governments that press aid recipients to adopt a rights-based approach to development, are themselves engaged in activities (such as the promotion of arms sales and the failure to adequately regulate banks) that may undermine the capability of recipient governments to fulfil their obligations.[81]

There have been calls for more genuine partnerships in development cooperation assistance. For example, the NGO BetterAid argues for reforms in development cooperation including: a new international legal framework to enforce a harmonisation of respective policies, efforts and approaches in promoting international development cooperation; relevant UN charter bodies, treaty bodies and various specialised agencies to be key actors in the system; and IMF and World Bank programmes and policies to be monitored and reviewed by an inclusive and democratic body under UN auspices.[82]

VII. Budget Deficits, Borrowing and Debt

When government spending exceeds total government revenue there is a budget deficit and governments must borrow to make up the difference. Governments borrow by taking loans from other governments, commercial banks and international financial institutions like the IMF and World Bank; and by selling bonds to a wide range of private sector investors.

[79] See UN Office of the High Commissioner for Human Rights, *Principles and Guidelines for a Human Rights Based Approach to Poverty Reduction Strategies* (Geneva, UN, 2006).

[80] For a discussion of bilateral development agencies and rights-based approaches to development, see LH Piron, 'Rights-Based Approaches and Bilateral Aid Agencies: More than a Metaphor?' (2001) 36 *IDS Bulletin* 19.

[81] The UK Government is one example.

[82] For more information, see Better Aid, 'Policy Papers': www.betteraid.org/en/betteraid-policy/betteraid-publications/policy-papers.html.

A bond specifies the size of the payments to the bondholders and the length of time over which the bond must be repaid. These conditions of repayment are fixed for each bond. Short-term bonds are paid back quickly, often within a few months, while long-term bonds are repaid over a much longer period, often many years. Bonds are bought and sold in the bond market, and once the government issues a bond, it can be traded among investors in global markets. The price of the bonds varies with conditions in the bond market. If a government has difficulty finding investors willing to hold its bonds, the price of the bonds falls until they are sold. From the government's point of view, lower bond prices mean that borrowing has become more expensive (the implicit rate of interest is higher), since the sale of bonds generates fewer resources. From the investor's point of view, lower prices mean a higher rate of return, since the investor has to pay less money initially in exchange for the future payments the government must make as stipulated by the bond. The price of the bonds is influenced by the ratings they are given by international credit rating agencies (which are private firms): the lower the rating, the lower the price of the bond and the higher the implied rate of interest.

In some cases, formal limitations exist that constrain the ability of governments to borrow. These restrictions may come from laws or constitutional restrictions and may only apply to a particular level of government, for example, state, provincial or local governments. Or the limitations may exist because donors place restrictions on the government's ability to borrow as a condition associated with their financial support. At the national level, restrictions are often expressed in terms of a maximum permitted debt to GDP ratio. Neoclassical economists tend to argue for such limitations,[83] but Keynesian/human development economists tend to argue for more discretion, so that governments can take into account the investment opportunities and the overall state of the economy, such as whether it is a boom or a downturn.[84]

Borrowing makes more resources available in the short run, but it creates a future charge on government budgets, as debt has to be serviced and repaid. In deciding whether borrowing can contribute to or hinder the realisation of human rights, it is critical to consider whether the government is using the debt to finance the creation of assets that will both help in the realisation of economic and social rights and generate future streams of revenue with which the debt can be serviced and repaid. Well chosen public investments in education, health, nutrition and infrastructure help to realise human rights and can generate future revenues via raising the productivity and amount of private investment. Enhanced productivity and investment supports faster growth and higher incomes which, in turn, increase tax revenues and allows governments to pay back the initial borrowing over time. Public investments in education, health and infrastructure can

[83] See eg, A Fedolino and D Zakharova, 'Reflections on Quantitative Fiscal Conditionality in African PGRF–Supported Programs' (2006) IMF Working Paper No 118.

[84] The classic statement of this argument is Keynes above n 25.

stimulate, rather than displace, private sector investment.[85] Borrowing to fund these kinds of investments supports long-run growth and generates the resources needed to meet future debt obligations, as well as supporting the realisation of human rights, provided there is a well-functioning tax system. Rich countries can borrow in their own currencies, but poor countries have to borrow in foreign currencies, such as the US dollar. This complicates servicing the debt because, not only is a strong tax system required, but strong exports are also necessary so as to ensure that sufficient foreign exchange is earned to cover the debt service.

Unfortunately, governments have often misused borrowing and left behind an accumulation of debt that reduces the resources available for the realisation of human rights. The concepts of onerous, odious and illegitimate debt provide tools with which to analyse the implications of accumulated debt.[86] Onerous debt generally refers to a situation in which the obligations attached to the debt—for example, debt servicing payments—significantly exceed the benefits which have been derived from taking on the debt. In these circumstances, the cost of servicing the debt can greatly limit the ability of the state to progressively realise rights. Odious and illegitimate debt refers to situations in which debt was incurred by a government and used for purposes that do not serve the interests of the people.[87] For example, borrowed funds were invested in ways that served only to enrich an elite who secreted their gains in overseas tax havens, or were used to finance war or repression. When money is borrowed and used in ways that do not advance human rights, the interest that has to be paid on this accumulated debt also hinders progress towards realising human rights in the future. Public debt audit commissions have been created in some countries to assess the legitimacy of a country's accumulated debt and consider if there is a case for repudiation (or forgiveness) of some of the debt. This alone will not reduce the accumulated debt burden, and Keynesian/human development economists are calling for the setting up of a legal system for sovereign debt default and restructuring (just as there are bankruptcy laws that cover firms and households).[88]

The payments that governments have to make to service their debts vary with prevailing interest rates and exchange rates. In addition, the types of bonds that governments issue, and the nature of the bond market, have a direct influence on the costs of borrowing. Some governments rely primarily on short-term bonds. In these cases, governments must continually issue new bonds when existing bonds come due, and debt management is more burdensome and uncertain. When new

[85] For a recent empirical study, see E Atukeren, 'Politico-Economic Determinants of the Crowding-in Effects of Public Investments in Developing Countries' (2010) 13 *Journal of Money, Investment and Banking Issue* 55.

[86] For more information, see the reports of the UN Independent Expert on the Effects of Foreign Debt on Human Rights: www2.ohchr.org/english/issues/development/debt/index.htm.

[87] For a discussion of odious debt, see R Howse, 'The Concept of Odious Debt in Public International Law' (2007) UNCTAD Discussion Paper No185.

[88] See R Jolly, GA Cornia, D Elson, C Fortin, S Griffith-Jones, G Helleiner, R van der Hoeven, R Kaplinsky, R Morgan, I Ortiz, R Pearson and F Stewart, *Be Outraged: There are Alternatives* (2012): policydialogue.org/files/events/Be_Outraged-finalhi_rez_1.pdf.

bonds are issued, they may not generate the same resources as the older bonds because of changing conditions in the bond market. In addition, the composition of buyers and sellers in bond markets affects the cost of servicing the debt. For example, in many low-income countries, the domestic banking sector purchases the vast majority of bonds. This gives the banks a great deal of power to influence the price at which governments can sell their bonds.

An important consideration in judging the contribution that borrowing can make to resource mobilisation is the overall state of the economy. Government revenues fall and budget deficits rise during recessions. Without the ability to borrow to finance a deficit, governments may have to cut spending in response to declining revenues, making the recession worse. During periods of stable growth and high employment, debts can be repaid and deficits reduced as government revenues recover. The use of deficit financing to support government spending during downturns, and then paying back this borrowing when growth and employment has recovered, is referred to as 'counter-cyclical fiscal policy'. However, the ability to pursue such a policy depends on the views and expectations of creditors. Austerity measures that some European governments have been forced to undertake in 2010/11, as a result of pressure from the EU and the IMF, are part of an attempt to restore the confidence of bondholders in order to convince them to continue holding the bonds. Nevertheless, bondholders have been demanding higher rates of return in exchange for agreeing to hold the debt of some governments (including Ireland, Portugal, Greece and Spain). This raises the payments governments must make to service the debt. In the context of an economic downturn, when government revenues are already under pressure, higher debt servicing payments squeeze other areas of spending. There is a danger that obligations to creditors overwhelm the obligation to progressively realise human rights.[89] International cooperation is necessary to deal with a crisis of this kind, which has its roots in inadequate financial regulation.

VIII. Monetary Policy and Financial Regulation

Monetary policy, conducted by central banks, directly affects the resources available for the realisation of economic and social rights. It does this by influencing interest rates, exchange rates and the amount of credit available in the economy. Higher interest rates discourage borrowing and make credit more expensive—as a consequence, economic activity slows when central banks raise interest rates, and there

[89] For further discussion on economic crisis, austerity policies and human rights, see Center for Economic and Social Rights, 'Fiscal Fallacies: 8 Myths About the 'Age of Austerity' and Human Rights Responses' Rights in Crisis Series Briefing Paper: www.cesr.org/downloads/CESR-FiscalFallacies.pdf.

is less job creation.[90] Indeed, very high interest rates may lead to unemployment, as firms can no longer afford the working capital necessary to keep employing and producing. Exchange rates affect exports and imports. For example, if the domestic currency is devalued relative to other currencies (ie, it takes more of the domestic currency to purchase one dollar, one euro etc), exports become less expensive (and more competitive) while imports become more expensive. This may create more jobs in export industries, but may also raise the price of imported food. The amount of credit available and its distribution is influenced by the way in which the central bank regulates the financial sector. Inadequate regulation may lead to a lack of finance for some sectors; or to the financial sector taking too many risks in the provision of credit, paving the way for financial crises, as was the case with the sub-prime mortgage crisis in the US economy.

Today central banks are, in most countries, quasi-independent institutions, free to make their own decisions on interest rates and exchange rates provided they meet objectives set by the government that appoints the governor of the bank. Several central banks have a strict mandate under law to maintain the rate of inflation at a specified low rate; for example, the European Central Bank. Those that are not bound by statute have, nevertheless, in many cases formally adopted a policy of 'inflation-targeting' and announced the target rate.[91] The extent to which the mandate and practices of the central bank are consistent with human rights obligations is rarely considered. However, there is no reason why central banks should not be held accountable to the same human rights principles as other government agencies.[92]

A key issue in relation to maximum available resources is the impact of central bank policy on the level of output and employment. If a low rate of inflation is the only objective, this is likely to lead to higher rates on interest than would otherwise be the case, as central banks raise interest rates to depress demand, guided by neoclassical economic theory which considers inflation as primarily caused by excessive aggregate demand. The result is to keep unemployment higher than it otherwise would be.

As noted above, Keynesian/human development economists argue for relaxing inflation targets and making employment creation a target too, as it was in the 1950s and 1960s in the high-income economies of the industrialised north. If a low inflation rate means that there are not enough job opportunities, then the conditions for an adequate standard of living are not fulfilled. A counter-argument is

[90] E Braunstein and J Heintz, 'Gender bias and Central Bank Policy: Employment and Inflation Reduction' (2008) 22 *International Review of Applied Economics* 173. Braunstein and Heintz show, for low and middle-income countries, that in periods of inflation reduction in which employment decreased, real interest rates were kept above their long-run trend in most cases. They also document differential impacts on men and women of central bank policy.

[91] G Epstein and E Yeldan, 'Inflation Targeting, Employment Creation, and Economic Development: Assessing the Impacts and Policy Alternatives' (2008) 22 *International Review of Applied Economics* 131.

[92] See J Heintz, 'Central Banks: Do They Have Human Rights Obligations' (2012): www.coc.org/rbw/central-banks-do-they-have-human-rights-obligations-january-2012.

that that price stability is necessary to prevent the erosion of an adequate standard of living. However, it is possible to index the minimum wage and welfare benefits to the rate of inflation so that their real value is maintained.

Moreover, inflation is not necessarily the result of a monetary policy which is too lax. In many countries, inflation is not a problem of excessive credit leading to too much demand, but rather a problem of poor infrastructure, low productivity, and/or the monopoly power of some businesses which have sufficient market power to raise prices. Increasing prices in global markets for essential goods, such as food and energy, can also contribute to inflation through the cost of imports. Monetary policy could do more to mobilise resources in countries where there is high unemployment and underemployment if central banks had regard to job creation as well as to inflation.

To shield themselves against global economic shocks, many central banks in low-income countries hold reserves of foreign currencies. Foreign exchange reserves are typically denominated in a major international currency, such as the dollar or euro. In recent decades, the rapid mobility of finance across international borders has increased the risks of financial crises. Short-term inflows of capital—to buy stocks, bonds, and other financial products—can quickly reverse themselves, putting pressure on a country's currency, its financial sector and the domestic economy. This kind of reversal of capital flows was evident in a number of recent financial crises, including the East Asian crisis (1997) and the Argentinean crisis (1999–2002). In the event of this kind of rapid outflow of capital, a country can draw on its foreign reserves in order to protect its currency and to provide some insulation against the negative consequences of such a crisis. Many countries began to accumulate large stocks of foreign exchange after the East Asian financial crisis.

In many respects, these large stocks of foreign exchange reserves represent idle resources. There are real costs associated with diverting resources towards the accumulation of foreign exchange reserves, instead of being used to finance development.[93] From a human rights perspective, the accumulation of reserves could be justified in terms of insuring against a financial crisis which could lead to budget cuts that affect economic and social rights. However, it is important to question whether such safeguards could be secured in other ways, in which case idle reserves could be mobilised for the realisation of rights, ie, they would contribute to the maximum available resources. Explicit restrictions on short-term capital inflows and outflows, often called capital controls, represent one alternative to the accumulation of foreign reserves. By limiting the free movement of capital, particularly financial flows that are speculative in character, countries can open up space to pursue policies that facilitate the realisation of basic rights.

As well as setting the rate of interest, monetary policy influences the amount of credit created by the financial sector. How these resources are used—and the

[93] M Cruz and B Walters, 'Is the Accumulation of International Reserves Good for Development?' (2008) 32 *Cambridge Journal of Economics*, 665.

extent to which they support the realisation of economic and social rights—depends on the nature of financial institutions and how the financial sector is regulated. Central banks frequently have a key regulatory role, setting out the rules and incentives and determining how the financial sector channels and allocates its resources. By changing these rules, central banks can help mobilise financial resources and channel them to uses which support the realisation of rights. For example, central banks could strengthen the regulatory requirements on commercial banks which fail to extend a certain amount of credit to priority areas, for instance, housing, job-creating investments or small-scale loans to the informal self-employed. Positive incentives could also be put in place. If banks are not lending because of perceived risk, government guarantees could be extended on ESR-priority areas. Public development banks could also be created, which could be more accountable and interested in facilitating investments which improve the public welfare. Governance problems, such as corruption and cronyism, can emerge and undermine the effectiveness of such institutions. However, the problem is not with the concept that public banks or financial regulations can be used to support human rights. Instead, the challenge is to design effective institutions for mobilising and directing a country's financial resources to socially productive ends, so that finance serves to support the realisation of economic and social rights, rather than to undermine such realisation.

IX. Conclusion

In times of economic and financial crisis, the issue of whether a government is undertaking steps to realise economic and social rights 'to the maximum of its available resources' is particularly important. Resources include human, technological, organisational, natural, informational and financial resources, both public and private. Public finance is critical in mobilising other resources; for instance, in avoiding the waste of resources and lives through unemployment and underemployment, as well as in mobilising finance to support public expenditure on health and education. Public finance in this context includes expenditure, taxation, overseas development assistance, borrowing and monetary policy. We have used the concepts of fiscal and monetary space to discuss how these aspects of public finance are related to one another and to show that governments do have alternatives, singly and together, which must be considered before decisions are taken.

2

Putting ESR-Based Budget Analysis into Practice: Addressing the Conceptual Challenges

AOIFE NOLAN

I. Introduction

Interest in the use of economic and social rights (ESR) standards to analyse and evaluate budgets and economic policy more generally has ballooned. This reality is evidenced by the growing number of advocacy organisations and national human rights institutions that have either developed, or expressed an intention to develop, their activities and capacities with regard to such activity.[1] In the last few years such work has been promoted by leading human rights actors including the Office of the High Commissioner for Human Rights (OHCHR)[2] and the UN Special Procedures with ESR-related thematic mandates.[3] Intergovernmental organisations such as the Food and Agricultural Organization of the United

[1] For an overview of key examples of existing work on ESR-based budget analysis, see the QUB Budget Analysis Project, *Budget Analysis and Economic and Social Rights: A Review of Selected Case Studies and Guidance* (Belfast, Queen's University Belfast, 2010). For further instances of rights-based budget analysis, as well as other human rights-related budget work, see A Blyberg, 'The Case of the Mislaid Allocation: Economic and Social Rights and Budget Work' (2009) 11(6) *SUR—International Journal on Human Rights* 123. For further discussion of a variety of groups that have carried out such work, see chapters in M Robinson (ed), *Budgeting for the Poor* (Basingstoke, Palgrave MacMillan, 2008). For an example of an IGO employed ESR-based budget analysis, see FAO, *Budget Work to Advance the Right to Food: Many a Slip…* (Rome, FAO, 2009). For an example of an effort by a national human rights institution to analyse a national budget from an ESR perspective, see South African Human Rights Commission & Studies in Poverty and Inequality Institute, 'How Much are We Spending on Transforming Our Society? A Rights-based Analysis of the 2011 Annual Budget' (February 2011): www.spii.org.za/agentfiles/434/file/Analysis%20of%20the%202011%20National%20Budget.pdf

[2] See OHCHR, 'Report of the High Commissioner for Human Rights on Implementation of Economic, Social and Cultural Rights' (UN Doc E/2009/90).

[3] See eg, the consideration of budgetary allocations in the context of discussions of 'process indicators' for various ESR in the following special procedure reports: P Hunt, 'Report of the Special Rapporteur on the right of everyone to the enjoyment of the highest attainable standard of physical and mental health' (UN Doc E/CN.4/2006/48), para 23; Annex 2 of Annual Report of the Special Rapporteur on the right to adequate housing as a component of the right to an adequate standard of living (UN Doc A/HRC/4/18), paras 27–28.

Nations (FAO) are increasingly promoting the use of budget work to advance the implementation of ESR.[4] The (now former) Council of Europe Commissioner for Human Rights, Thomas Hammarberg, has described budget analysis as 'a potent instrument in the struggle for human rights' and has emphasised that the current economic crisis has made it particularly important to screen state budgets for their compliance with human rights.[5]

However, despite the significant developments with regard to ESR-based budget analysis that have already taken place, as well as the important actual and potential function(s) of such work with regard to evaluating the extent of state implementation of ESR, key issues and challenges remain. These must be addressed if ESR-based budget analysis is to contribute effectively to improved achievement and enjoyment of ESR.

The challenges can be broken down into three key areas. First, there are those that will constitute the key focus of this chapter: namely, conceptual challenges that result from the current condition of the international ESR framework as set out in the International Covenant on Economic, Social and Cultural Rights (ICESCR) and interpreted by the Committee on Economic, Social and Cultural Rights (the Committee). The second set of challenges addressed is those of a practical or logistical nature—obstacles that are faced by practitioners seeking to carry out budget analysis in the performance of such work. The final category of challenges relates to efforts to use budget analysis outputs for advocacy purposes. While the latter two sets of challenges have significant implications for, respectively, (a) the ability to carry out ESR-based budget analysis and (b) the efficacy of such methodology as an advocacy tool, the former goes to the heart of the integrity of ESR-based budget analysis as a monitoring tool.[6]

The chapter opens by outlining what 'ESR-based budget analysis' methodology actually is. I then address the framework that is most commonly employed by ESR-budget analysis practitioners, ICESCR. In doing so, I focus in particular on two key elements of that framework: namely, (i) retrogressive measures and (ii) the issue of private (or non-state) actors. The reason for my attention on (i) is the impact that the post-2008 financial and economic crises and the responses thereto have had in terms of progressing (or not) ESR goods and service delivery. The concern with privatisation is attributable to the fact that neoliberal economic processes have resulted in private actors assuming ever greater power and responsibility vis-a-vis ESR provision; a situation that is potentially problematic in terms of attribution of accountability for such rights, given the state-centric nature of ICESCR. The chapter will conclude with some brief proposals with regard to how

[4] See eg, FAO above n 1.

[5] T Hammarberg, 'State Budgets Reveal whether Governments are Committed to Human Rights' *Viewpoint* (3 August 2009).

[6] For a more extensive discussion of the second and third set of challenges, see A Nolan, 'Budget Analysis and Economic and Social Rights' in G Giacca, C Golay and E Riedel (eds), *Contemporary Issues in the Realisation of Economic, Social and Cultural Rights* (Oxford, Oxford University Press, forthcoming 2014).

issues surrounding the ICESR framework from an ESR-based budget analysis perspective can be addressed.

II. Defining ESR-Based Budget Analysis

Human rights budget analysis is a sub-category of human rights budget work. This latter broader field of activity has been defined as 'work that seeks to relate human rights to government budgets, and budget work to human rights'.[7] As Blyberg notes, human rights budget work has been described as 'human rights budgeting', 'budgeting or budget work from a human rights perspective' and 'budget analysis and ESC rights'.[8] This abundance of terms renders it important to clarify at the outset what is understood by ESR-based budget analysis for the purposes of this chapter. I define such activity as the analysis of budgetary decisions using a framework premised on substantive ESR protections set out in international or domestic human rights instruments (for example, in human rights treaties, constitutions, domestic legislation). Ultimately all such analysis seeks to determine the impact of budgetary decisions on the implementation and enjoyment of ESR.[9]

Approaches to ESR-based budget analysis vary considerably. First, such analysis may be rights-thematic, group-based or both. While some practitioners analyse budgets from the perspective of a particular ESR such as housing,[10] education[11] or health,[12] others focus on the impact of budget decisions on the ESR of a particular group, for instance children.[13]

ESR-based budget analysis builds on the relatively longer-established equality (and particularly gender) budget analysis, which employs equality and non-discrimination protections or a specific equality schema, as the primary framework through which to analyse budgetary decisions.[14] Given the interdependence

[7] Blyberg, 'The Case of the Mislaid Allocation' above n 1, 125.

[8] Ibid.

[9] For more on ESR-based budget analysis in practice, see Rooney and Dutschke in this volume.

[10] See eg, QUB Budget Analysis Project, *Budgeting for Social Housing in Northern Ireland: A Human Rights Analysis* (Belfast, QUB, 2010).

[11] For an example of guidance on how right to education-based budget analysis might be carried out, see IHRIP/International Budget Project, *Reading the Books: Government Budgets and the Right to Education* (Washington, IHRIP/IBP, 2010).

[12] See eg, Fundar, *Healthcare: A Question of Rights, Not Charity* (Fundar, Mexico, 2002).

[13] See eg, Ganguly Thukral's contribution to this volume on the work of the Indian-based HAQ: Centre for Child Rights which produces analyses of the impact of national and state budgets from a child-rights perspective, including ESR: www.haqcrc.org/.

[14] For an example of an explicitly equality rights-based approach to gender budget analysis, see D Elson, *Budgeting for Women's Rights: Monitoring Government Budgets for Compliance with CEDAW* (New York, UNIFEM, 2006). For an example of a non-rights-based gender budget analysis, see the work of the UK-based Women's Budget Group which analyses budgets in order to establish the impact of resource allocation on gender equality. For more on gender budgeting, see Quinn's contribution to this volume.

and interrelationship between ESR and equality protections, as well as the fact that the duty of states to ensure non-discrimination in access and enjoyment of ESR is an immediate obligation imposed by all ESR, it is unsurprising that there is significant overlap between ESR-based budget analysis and that premised on equality rights.[15] Indeed, ESR-based budget analysis will frequently incorporate equality budget analysis to some degree.[16]

ESR-based budget analysis may either be static or dynamic: 'static analysis evaluates a given budget by itself. Dynamic analysis compares the evolution of budgets over time, looking at variations in allocations and spending over different periods'.[17] Dynamic analysis is particularly important when practitioners are seeking to evaluate the extent to which states are giving effect to their obligations to progressively realise ESR to the maximum extent of available resources in terms of Article 2(1) ICESCR.

Such work will also vary in terms of the 'budget' being analysed. Budgetary allocation, expenditure, revenue and international and domestic macroeconomic policy all have implications for the enjoyment of ESR. ESR-based budget analysis may thus focus on a range of different budgetary aspects. Most practitioners have focused on the first two budgetary issues, however.[18] This is demonstrated by a study carried out by the QUB Budget Analysis Project of a range of key case stud ies and guidance on ESC-based budget analysis. The study's authors found that practitioners examined numerous dimensions of budgets:

> All documents refer to allocation of resources and past expenditure is discussed by 13 out of the 14 documents. Budget outcomes (the impact that the budget has on the enjoyment of ESR) are considered in 12. Budget outputs (the goods and services produced by the budget) are identified in nine reports, while budget revenue streams were cited in eight. Only four papers discuss the macroeconomics of the budget.[19]

There is also variety within ESR-based budget analysis work in terms of the 'kind' of budget being considered, with actors focusing on national, sub-national or local government level budgets.[20]

[15] For an example of a discussion of the interaction of equality/non-discrimination protections under a 'non-discrimination treaty' with the 'substantive rights' set out ICESCR and other human rights treaties, see Elson above n 14, especially 13–17.

[16] See eg, QUB Budget Analysis Project, *Budget Analysis and Economic and Social Rights: A Review of Selected Case Studies and Guidance* (Belfast, Queen's University Belfast, 2010) 10, 12, which highlighted that 11 out of the 14 documents examined addressed the equality/non-discrimination obligations imposed by ICESCR.

[17] OHCHR above n 2, 14.

[18] For an example of a recently developed methodology designed to evaluate macroeconomic policies from an ESR perspective, see R Balakrishnan, D Elson and R Patel, *Rethinking Macroeconomic Strategies from a Human Rights Perspective (Why MES with Human Rights II)* (New York, Marymount Manhattan College/ US Human Rights Network 2009).

[19] QUB Budget Analysis Project, *Budget Analysis and Economic and Social Rights* above n 1, 6.

[20] A useful South African example of an organisation carrying out ESR-based analyses of both national and sub-national budgets was IDASA, which has produced 'Budgetbriefs' analysing both national and provincial budgets from an ESR perspective.

Thus, while efforts to employ ESR-based budget analysis methodologies share the employment of a framework premised on substantive ESR protections in analysing budgetary decisions, the specific ESR framework at issue, the budgetary decisions under consideration, and the way in which those decisions are approached, vary from case to case.

III. Engaging with the Framework

While, as highlighted above, not all ESR-based budget analysis practitioners premise their work on ICESCR, many do so. Of those that do not, many employ frameworks that are strongly influenced by that instrument and use the jurisprudence of the Committee on Economic, Social and Cultural Rights to support their arguments.[21] It is therefore logical to focus on this—the most celebrated and developed of ESR frameworks—when considering the conceptual challenges faced by practitioners.

The first issue faced by practitioners is that the substantive content of ESR duties such as 'maximum available resources' and 'minimum core obligation' is complex and subject to contestation.[22] Questions include: what resources come within the scope of Article 2(1)? How can/should one determine whether the state is making the fullest possible use of the wide range of resources available to it?[23] Is the minimum core an obligation of conduct or result? Is it relative or absolute?[24] Similarly, the tripartite typology of 'respect, protect and fulfil', which has been

[21] Of the 14 studies considered by the QUB Budget Analysis Project in its review of existing guidance and case studies on ESR budget analysis, 11 referred to ICESCR and the General Comments of ComESCR as points of reference (QUB Budget Analysis Project, *Budget Analysis and Economic and Social Rights* above n 1, 5). The three IDASA-authored studies that did not do so instead premised their analysis on the South African Constitution, the formulation and the interpretation of the ESR under which have been heavily influenced by ICESCR. On the role of international instruments in the formulation of the ESR provisions under the South African Constitution, see S Liebenberg, 'Socio-Economic Rights' in M Chaskalson et al (eds), *Constitutional Law of South Africa* (Cape Town, Juta, 1996) 41–44.

[22] A discussion of the many debates surrounding these obligations is beyond the scope of this chapter. For a discussion of 'maximum available resources', see Elson Balakrishnan and Heintz in this volume. For a more general discussion of the debate surrounding ESR obligations and their interrelationship with budgetary processes, see QUB Budget Analysis Project, *Budgeting for Economic and Social Rights: A Human Rights Framework* (Belfast, QUB, 2010).

[23] For more the issues surrounding the obligation of 'maximum available resources' and other elements of Art 2(1) ICESCR from a 'budget perspective', see A Nolan and M Dutschke, 'Article 2(1) ICESCR and States Parties' Obligations: Whither the Budget?' (2010) 3 *European Human Rights Law Review* 280. For a useful discussion of how fiscal and monetary policy decisions influence the resources available for realising rights, see R Balakrishnan, D Elson, J Heintz and N Lusiani, *Maximum Available Resources and Human Rights: Analytical Report* (New Jersey, Center for Women's Global Leadership, Rutgers University, 2011).

[24] For more on the contested nature of the minimum core, see K Young, 'The Minimum Core of Economic and Social Rights: A Concept in Search of Content' (2008) 33 *Yale Journal of International Law* 113.

used by the Committee as an analytical tool in all its General Comments on substantive ESR since its 1999 General Comment on the Right to Adequate Food,[25] has been criticised for its indeterminacy and the overlap between the respective levels of obligation.[26] There are undoubtedly definite advantages to having ESR and the obligations they impose phrased or conceptualised sufficiently broadly to ensure that they should be capable of general application to a variety of individual circumstances and different contexts over time.[27] However, where obligations are vague and overlapping this will have implications for the efficacy of budget analysis as a human rights monitoring methodology. How can one evaluate budgetary compliance with ESR standards if those standards are not clear?

Until recently, relatively little work had been done to link these different categories of obligation directly with budgetary processes. While there has been an increase in the literature on this issue,[28] important questions remain. In particular, as previously suggested, there are two issues relevant to the current economic and policy context that have yet to be addressed adequately by the Committee in such a way as to provide guidance to practitioners: 'retrogressive measures' and the issue of private (or non-state) actors.

A. Retrogressive Measures

As Dutschke and I have noted elsewhere:

> Implicit in the duty to progressively realise ESR is a prohibition on taking deliberately retrogressive measures,[29] which Sepulveda has defined as backwards steps in the level of ESR enjoyment as a consequence of an intentional decision(s) by the state[30] ... in budgetary terms, this includes unjustified reductions in public expenditure devoted to

[25] ComESCR General Comment No 12 on the right to adequate food (art 11), UN Doc E/C.12/1999/5 (1999). For more on the evolution of the tripartite typology and its application by the ComESCR, see A Nolan, 'Addressing Economic and Social Rights Violations by Non-state Actors through the Role of the State: A Comparison of Regional Approaches to the "Obligation to Protect"' (2009) 9(2) *Human Rights Law Review* 225; I Koch, 'Dichotomies, Trichotomies or Waves of Duties?' (2005) 5 *Human Rights Law Review* 81, 84–87.

[26] QUB Budget Analysis Project, *Budgeting for Economic and Social Rights* above n 22, 48.

[27] A Nolan, M Langford and B Porter, 'The Justiciability of Social and Economic Rights: An Updated Appraisal' (2007) NYU Center for Human Rights and Global Justice Working Paper Series No 15, 14.

[28] Notable examples include R O'Connell, A Nolan, C Harvey, E Rooney and M Dutschke, *Applying an International Human Rights Framework to State Budget Allocations: Rights and Resources* (London, Routledge, 2014) chs 3 and 4. International Human Rights Internship Program (IHRIP), 'Government Human Rights Obligations and Budget Work' (IHRIP, 2008); A Blyberg, 'Notes from an International Roundtable Discussion on the Obligation to Use 'Maximum of Available Resources' (Washington DC, IBP/IHRIP, 2008).

[29] ComESCR General Comment No 3 on the nature of States parties' obligations (art 2 (1)), UN Doc E/1991/23 (1990), para 9.

[30] M Sepulveda, *The Nature of the Obligations under the International Covenant on Economic Social and Cultural Rights* (Antwerp, Intersentia, 2003) 323.

the implementation to ESR in the absence of adequate compensatory measures for the protection of injured individuals.[31,32]

In the same piece, we highlighted that apparent retrogressive measures have been commented upon by the Committee in its consideration of state reports submitted under ICESCR in a number of instances. These range from the steady decline in expenditure on the health care system in Algeria,[33] to budgetary cutbacks in the educational sector in Senegal,[34] to the successive restrictions on social security benefits introduced by Canada.[35] In none of these cases, however, did the Committee explicitly use the term 'retrogressive measures'.

The Committee has provided some limited guidance on the approach that it will adopt in evaluating the acceptability of retrogressive measures.[36] In a statement on 'An Evaluation of the Obligation to Take Steps to the "Maximum of Available Resources" under an Optional Protocol to the Covenant', the Committee highlighted that, should a State Party use 'resource constraints' as an explanation for any retrogressive steps taken, the Committee would consider such information on a country-by-country basis in the light of 'objective criteria'.[37] Such criteria would include: the country's level of development; the severity of the alleged breach (in particular whether the situation concerned the enjoyment of the minimum core content of the Covenant); the country's current economic situation (in particular whether the country was undergoing a period of economic recession); the existence of other serious claims on the State Party's limited resources (for example, resulting from a recent natural disaster or from recent internal or international armed conflict); whether the State Party had sought to identify low-cost options; and whether the State Party had sought cooperation and assistance or rejected offers of resources from the international community for the purposes of implementing the provisions of the Covenant without sufficient reason.[38] The Committee did not, however, use this statement as an opportunity to define what a retrogressive measure actually is, apparently regarding the term as self-explanatory.

The conception of a retrogressive measure has thus remained nebulous. Among other things, the Committee has never addressed the difference between retrogressive measures that are 'deliberate' and those that are not. Nor has the Committee consistently engaged with, or attempted to delineate, the circumstances in which

[31] Ibid 324.
[32] Nolan and Dutschke above n 23, 282, 285.
[33] ComESCR, 'Concluding Observations: Algeria', UN Doc E/C.12/1/Add.71 (2001), para 20.
[34] ComESCR, 'Concluding Observations: Senegal', UN Doc E/C.12/1993/18 (1994), para 7.
[35] ComESCR, 'Concluding Observations: Canada', UN Doc E/C/12/1/Add.31 (1998), para 20.
[36] For more on the Committee's approach to retrogressive measures, see C Courtis, 'The Prohibition of Retrogression in the Area of Economic, Social and Cultural Rights: An Introductory Outline' in A Nolan (ed), *Economic and Social Rights after the Global Financial Crisis* (Cambridge, CUP, forthcoming 2014).
[37] ComESCR, 'An Evaluation of the Obligation to Take Steps to the "Maximum of Available Resources" under an Optional Protocol to the Covenant', UN Doc E/C.12/2007/1 (2007), para 10.
[38] Ibid.

such a measure might be permissible in terms of concrete examples. This is significant given that the prohibition of retrogressive measures is not absolute; in its General Comment No 3 on the nature of States Parties obligations, the Committee states that

> any deliberately retrogressive measures in that regard would require the most careful consideration and would need to be fully justified by reference to the totality of the rights provided for in the Covenant and in the context of the full use of the maximum available resources.[39]

This language is echoed in a number of other General Comments,[40] some of which also set out the requirement to ensure 'there has been the most careful consideration of all alternatives'.[41] A number of other General Comments have highlighted that the adoption of any retrogressive measures incompatible with the 'core obligations' under the Covenant would be impermissible.[42] In only one General Comment, however, has the Committee delineated detailed examples of retrogressive measures.[43] Furthermore, it was only in General Comment No 19 in the context of the right to social security that the Committee proceeded to outline in detail some of the key factors it would employ in considering whether a retrogressive measure was justifiable in terms of the Covenant.[44]

[39] ComESCR General Comment No 3, para 9.

[40] ComESCR General Comment No 21 on the right of everyone to take part in cultural life, UN Doc E/C.12/GC/21 (2009), para 65; General Comment No 19 on the right to social security, UN Doc E/C.12/GC/19 (2008), para 42; ComESCR General Comment No 18 on the right to work (art 6), UN Doc E/C.12/GC/18 (2006), para 21; ComESCR General Comment No 17 on the right of everyone to benefit from the protection of the moral and material interests resulting from any scientific, literary or artistic production of which he or she is the author, UN Doc E/C.12/GC/17 (2006), para 27; ComESCR General Comment No 15 on the right to water (arts 11 and 12), UN Doc E/C.12/2002/11 (2003), para 19; ComESCR General Comment No 14 on the right to the highest attainable standard of health (art 12), UN Doc E/C.12/2000/4 (2000), para 32; and ComESCR General Comment No 13 on the right to education (art 13), UN Doc E/C.12/1999/10 (1999), para 45.

[41] ComESCR General Comment No 19, para 42; ComESCR General Comment No 18, para 21; ComESCR General Comment No 17, para 27; ComESCR General Comment No 15, para 19; ComESCR General Comment No 14, para 32; and ComESCR General Comment No 13, para 45.

[42] See ComESCR General Comment No 15, para 42; ComESCR General Comment No 14, para 48.

[43] See ComESCR General Comment No 18, para 34: 'As for all other rights in the Covenant, there is a strong presumption that retrogressive measures taken in relation to the right to work are not permissible. Such retrogressive measures include, inter alia, denial of access to employment to particular individuals or groups, whether such discrimination is based on legislation or practice, abrogation or suspension of the legislation necessary for the exercise of the right to work or the adoption of laws or policies that are manifestly incompatible with international legal obligations relating to the right to work. An example would be the institution of forced labour or the abrogation of legislation protecting the employee against unlawful dismissal. Such measures would constitute a violation of States parties' obligation to respect the right to work'.

[44] ComESCR General Comment No 19, para 42. Here, the Committee stated that with regard to the justifiability of retrogressive measures in the area of social security, it would look carefully at '(a) there was reasonable justification for the action; (b) alternatives were comprehensively examined; (c) there was genuine participation of affected groups in examining the proposed measures and alternatives; (d) the measures were directly or indirectly discriminatory; (e) the measures will have a sustained impact on the realization of the right to social security, an unreasonable impact on acquired social security rights or whether an individual or group is deprived of access to the minimum essential level of social security; and (f) whether there was an independent review of the measures at the national level' (ibid).

The Committee has also failed to consider the notion of limitations on Covenant rights in terms of Article 4 ICESCR. According to that provision, States Parties may only subject the rights set out in that instrument to such limitations 'as are determined by law' and 'only in so far as this may be compatible with the nature of these rights and solely for the purpose of promoting the general welfare in a democratic society'. Not only has the Committee failed to outline the scope of such limitations in any detail, it has also failed to address the relationship (if any) between Article 4 limitations and retrogressive measures. Leckie, for instance, has argued that any deliberately retrogressive measure would limit the enjoyment of rights found in ICESCR and thus require justification with due regard for the limitations provisions of Article 4.[45] However, in the context of differentiating between Article 2(1) and Article 4, it has been suggested by other commentators that there is a distinction between formal limitations of rights on the one hand and 'a general level of attainment' of those rights on the other.[46] If one accepts that the latter is just a reflection of resource availability, then it seems probable that a resource-motivated reduction in the level of enjoyment/attainment of a particular right would not constitute a 'limitation' in terms of Article 4.[47]

Given the ongoing spending cuts and austerity measures impacting on ESR enjoyment globally, the Committee's historic failure to delineate clearly the parameters of permissible retrogressive measures or limitations in terms of ESR has proved problematic in the post-financial/economic crises era. In her 2011 annual report, the UN Independent Expert (now Special Rapporteur) on the Question of Human Rights and Extreme Poverty highlighted that a number of economic 'recovery measures' taken by states, such as cuts to social protection systems, may violate the prohibition of retrogressive measures.[48] It was not, however, until May 2012 that the Committee finally engaged to any degree with the crises and their implications for Covenant rights. That month saw the Chairperson of the Committee address a letter to States Parties 'in relation to the protection of Covenant rights in the context of the economic and financial crisis'.[49] In it, he stated that 'economic and financial crises, and a lack of growth, impede the progressive realisation of economic, social and cultural rights and can

[45] S Leckie, 'Another Step Towards Indivisibility: Identifying the Key Features of Violations of Economic, Social and Cultural Rights' (1998) 20 *Human Rights Quarterly* 81, 98.

[46] P Alston and G Quinn, 'The Nature and Scope of State Parties' Obligations under the International Covenant on Economic, Social and Cultural Rights' (1987) 9 *Human Rights Quarterly* 156, 205.

[47] Alston and Quinn, ibid. For an argument that the ComESCR does not regard retrogressive measures as limitations in terms of Art 4, see A Müller, 'Limitations to and Derogations from Economic, Social and Cultural Rights' (2009) 9(4) *Human Rights Law Review* 557.

[48] M Sepúlveda Carmona, 'Report of the Independent Expert on the question of human rights and extreme poverty on the human rights based approach to recovery from the global economic and financial crises, with a focus on those living in poverty' (UN Doc A/HRC/17/34), paras 44, 47.

[49] AG Pillay, 'Letter from ComESCR Chairperson to States Parties in the context of the economic and financial crisis', CESCR/48th/SP/MAB/SW, 16 May 2012: www2.ohchr.org/english/bodies/cescr/docs/LetterCESCRtoSP16.05.12.pdf.

lead to retrogression in the enjoyment of those rights'[50] and highlighted that the Covenant provides 'certain important guideposts which can help States Parties to adopt appropriate policies that deal with the economic downturn while respecting economic, social and cultural rights'.[51] This letter undoubtedly represented progress on the part of the Committee in terms of addressing the issue of retrogression.

The most important part of the letter centres on the requirements that 'any proposed policy change or adjustment' in response to the crises has to meet: first, the policy must be a *temporary* measure covering only the period of the crisis; second, the policy must be *necessary and proportionate*, in the sense that the adoption of any other policy, or a failure to act, would be more detrimental to economic, social and cultural rights; third, the policy must not be *discriminatory* and must comprise all possible measures, including tax measures, to support social transfers and mitigate inequalities that can grow in times of crisis and to ensure that the rights of disadvantaged and marginalised individuals and groups are not disproportionately affected; and, finally, the policy should identify the *minimum core content of rights*, or a social protection floor, as developed by the International Labour Organization (ILO), and ensure the protection of this core content at all times.[52] The Chairperson also highlighted the obligations of States Parties vis a vis decision-making in the context of overseas development assistance, in international financial institutions and regional integration organisations, and expressed hope that governments would be guided by their Covenant obligations when developing international and regional programmes to overcome the crises.[53]

This letter certainly constitutes a useful step on the part of the Committee with regard to delineating state responsibilities in the wake of the global financial meltdown—particularly in relation to austerity measures. However, it is notable that the words 'retrogressive measures' are not mentioned in it. Nor is there reference to the language of General Comment No 3 with regard to the need for such measures to be 'fully justified by reference to the totality of the rights provided for in the Covenant and in the context of the full use of the maximum available resources'. Furthermore, while the letter is written on behalf of the Committee as a whole, it is not a General Comment. Indeed, it is highly unlikely that it has the status of even soft law.[54] As we will see below, however, the Committee's approach

[50] Ibid 1.

[51] Ibid 2.

[52] For more on the concept of a 'social protection floor', see ILO Recommendation Concerning National Floors of Social Protection, adopted by International Labour Conference on 14 June 2012: www.ilo.org/wcmsp5/groups/public/---ed_norm/---relconf/documents/meetingdocument/wcms_183326.pdf, and M Sepulveda and C Nyst, *The Human Rights Approach to Social Protection* (Finland, Finland Ministry for Foreign Affairs, 2012) 9–10: www.cdp-hrc.uottawa.ca/uploads/HumanRightsApproachToSocialProtection.pdf.

[53] Letter from ComESCR Chairperson above n 49, 2.

[54] I am grateful to Professor Michael O'Flaherty for his useful insights on this point (in conversation with the author, 16 November 2012).

to the test in recent work suggests that it may be well on its way to assuming such status.[55]

At this point, therefore, it remains to be seen to what extent the Committee will explicitly engage with retrogressive measures in its practice in the post-crises era. It is notable that in its recent consideration of the Spanish periodic report,[56] the Committee focused on a range of backward steps in terms of ESR enjoyment in that country, recommending that 'the State party ensure that all the austerity measures adopted reflect the minimum core content of all the Covenant rights'[57] and drawing the State Party's attention to the Chairperson's letter.[58] The Committee also expressed concern about 'the constant rise in unemployment and long-term unemployment rates'[59] and recommended that 'the State party avoid any step backwards in the field of employment, including with regard to the protection of workers' labour rights'.[60] The Committee recommended that the State Party should review the reforms adopted in the context of the economic and financial crises to ensure that all the austerity measures introduced uphold the level of the protection attained in the realm of economic, social and cultural rights and that, in all cases, such measures are temporary and proportionate and do not negatively impinge on such rights.[61] The Committee also urged the State Party to assess the impact of any proposed cuts on the access of the most disadvantaged and marginalised individuals and groups to health services.[62] Even here, however, the Committee did not use the language of 'regression' or 'retrogressive measures'. This was despite the fact that two civil society groups had submitted a joint submission focusing particularly on those rights most affected by the economic crisis and the country's responses to it, including explicit references to retrogression in ESR enjoyment.[63]

A similar approach was adopted by the Committee in its Concluding Observations on the Icelandic periodic state report. In this instance, having expressed concern that 'despite measures taken by the State party, the national financial and economic crisis has had a negative impact on the realisation of economic, social and cultural rights', the Committee proceeded to 'remind' the state of the requirements that any proposed policy change or adjustment by the State Party in reaction to the economic crisis must meet.[64] In doing so, it reiterated

[55] For a useful overview of the features and effects of 'soft law' in the area of international law, see D Thürer, 'Soft Law' in R Wolfrum (ed), *Max Planck Encyclopedia of Public International Law*: www.mpepil.com.

[56] For more on the Spanish periodic report process, see Saiz's contribution in this volume.

[57] ComESCR, 'Concluding Observations: Spain', UN Doc E/C.12/ESP/CO/5 (2012), para 8.

[58] Ibid.

[59] Ibid para 12.

[60] Ibid.

[61] Ibid para 17.

[62] Ibid para 19.

[63] See Center for Economic and Social Rights and Observatori DESC, Spain Pre-session Working Group Submission, 1 April 2011: cesr.org/downloads/Spain%20Presessional%20Working%20Group%20Submission%20-%20CESCR%20Observatori%20DESC%20_%20CESR.pdf, 2, 3.

[64] ComESCR, 'Concluding Observations: Iceland', UN Doc E/C.12/ISL/CO/4 (2012), para 6.

the conditions highlighted in the Chairperson's letter.[65] Again, the language of 'retrogression' was avoided. This set of Concluding Observations is notable from a budgetary perspective as, when making recommendations as to the steps that the State Party should take to address the negative impact of financial crisis, the Committee criticised cuts made by Iceland to its budgets for public health care and the public education system and explicitly recommended that the budgets in these areas be increased.[66]

A significant positive feature of the Spanish and Icelandic Concluding Observations is that the Committee appears to apply the requirements outlined in the Chairperson's letter to specific country situations. Taking these together with the May 2012 letter, the Committee has advanced in terms of providing examples and standards to advocates who hope to evaluate and criticise retrogression on the part of States Parties to address specific cuts. However, the Committee appears to remain reluctant to engage with the language of 'retrogressive measures' used in its earlier General Comments.[67]

A commendable exception to this reluctance is provided in the Committee's Concluding Observations on New Zealand, which were issued two weeks after the Chairperson's letter to States Parties. Here the Committee expressed 'concern about the *retrogressive nature* and possible discriminatory impact of welfare reforms ... particularly in light of the State party's recovery from an economic downturn'.[68] The Committee proceeded to urge New Zealand to ensure that welfare reforms protect the rights to social security and to an adequate standard of living in respect of disadvantaged and marginalized individuals and groups, drawing New Zealand's attention to General Comment No. 19 on the social security, and the Chairperson's letter.[69]

The Committee's failure to engage convincingly with the concept of retrogressive measures until recently has limited the capacity of anti-poverty and human rights campaigners to argue authoritatively that specific budgetary responses to the global economic crisis are in contravention of states' international legal obligations under ICESCR. However, as we have already seen in the New Zealand, Spanish and Icelandic cases, there will undoubtedly be scope for the Committee to assess austerity measures and other steps backwards in state implementation of Covenant rights over the coming years, perhaps most notably in its Concluding Observations on States Parties periodic reports that include post-2008 data. Language matters when it comes to delineating international human rights obligations and it is hoped that the Committee will continue to prove willing to 'call a spade a spade' if it is to address, rather than simply duck, the reality of retrogression.

[65] Ibid.

[66] Ibid paras 17 and 18.

[67] While the Committee explicitly criticised 'regressive measures' with regard to education in the form of increased university tuition fees (para 28), this appears to be a direct 'borrowing' of language from the ComESCR's General Comment No 11 on plans of action for primary education (art 14), UN Doc E/C.12/1999/4 (1999), para 7 (which makes no reference to 'retrogressive measures') rather than a 'shorthand' for 'retrogressive measures'.

[68] ComESCR, 'Concluding Observations: New Zealand', UN Doc E/C.12/NZL/CO/(2012), para 17 (emphasis added).

[69] Ibid.

B. Engaging with the Private Sphere

Another highly problematic example of the Committee failing to provide adequate elaboration of ICESCR arises in the context of the role of private actors and privatisation.[70] Given the increasing tendency globally towards the privatisation of ESR-related services that have traditionally been delivered by states, it is vital that the Committee should engage adequately with this issue.[71] Indeed, in its 1998 'Statement on Globalisation and its Impact on the Enjoyment of Economic, Social and Cultural Rights',[72] the Committee made specific reference to privatisation highlighting that

> [globalisation] has become associated with a variety of specific trends and policies including an increasing reliance upon the free market, a significant growth in the influence of international financial markets and institutions in determining the viability of national policy priorities, a diminution in the role of the state and the size of its budget, *the privatisation of various functions previously considered to be the exclusive domain of the state*, the deregulation of a range of activities with a view to facilitating investment and rewarding individual initiative, *and a corresponding increase in the role and even responsibilities attributed to private actors*, both in the corporate sector, in particular to the transnational corporations, and in civil society (emphasis added).[73]

In terms of budgetary processes, resources are paid by the state to private actors for the provision of ESR-related services in a range of different ways. One example, considered in the Northern Irish context by Rooney and Dutschke in chapter nine of this volume, is the growing dependence of the state in many countries on the private rented sector as a result of a lack of social housing. This involves the subsidisation of low-income tenants' rent by the state through housing-related benefit payments, meaning that the government is effectively funding the private rented sector to realise the right to adequate housing. Such a model is prima facie acceptable in terms of delivery of the right to adequate housing as the Committee has made it clear that the private sector may have a role to play in relation to the implementation of that right.[74] However, this situation clearly raises issues in relation to the employment of maximum available resources as housing benefit paid to state social housing providers is reinvested in social housing services while that paid to private landlords will not be. As such, the question must be asked whether the use of the private rented sector to house tenants who require social housing and are

[70] By privatisation, I mean 'a shift towards provision by nongovernmental organisations of certain classes or goods and services, or performance by those organisations of certain classes of functions, for the provision or performance of which, individuals have been accustomed to relying exclusively or mainly on government offices and agencies'. (F Michelman, 'Constitutionalism, Privatisation and Globalisation: Whither the Constitution?' (2000) 21 *Cardozo Law Review* 1063, 1063).

[71] For an example of a nuanced discussion of the role of non-state actors and privatisation models and processes in the context of a specific ESR (the right to safe drinking water and sanitation), see C de Albuquerque, 'Report of the Special Rapporteur on the Human Right to Safe Drinking Water and Sanitation' (UN Doc A/HRC/15/31).

[72] Eighteenth session, UN Doc E/1999/22-E/C.12/1998/26; Chapter VI, section A, para 515.

[73] Ibid para 2.

[74] See ComESCR General Comment No 4 on the right to adequate housing, UN Doc E/1992/23 (1991), paras 8(a), 14 and 17.

in receipt of housing benefit constitutes a failure to use the maximum resources available for the progressive realisation of the right to adequate housing.

Another way in which the private sector is involved in the provision of ESR-related goods and services is through the increasing use in many jurisdictions of public–private partnerships (PPP) for the delivery of social housing[75] and health services.[76] PPPs are contractual arrangements between government and private sector entities for the purpose of providing traditionally public services or infrastructure.[77]

Balakrishnan et al, however, have highlighted that, while PPPs may seem advantageous in the short run as the borrowing is not included as part of public sector debt, in general, private companies face higher rates of interest than the governments, so the costs of the investment are higher.[78] Furthermore, PPP contracts generally transfer risks to the government, so that if the enterprise is mismanaged or delivery is poorly implemented, the public sector is forced to assume the burden of correcting the problem—together with the budgetary implications of such.[79]

The Committee has not ignored the role of private actors with regard to the realisation of ESR. Indeed, seven General Comments contain chapters explicitly addressing 'obligations of actors other than states'.[80] However, when focusing on the state's duty with regard to private actors, in the context of the tripartite typology, the Committee has generally based its analysis on the obligation to protect; that is the state's duty to prevent third parties from interfering with ESR.[81] In a similar vein, much of the Committee's discussion of the role of the state vis-a-vis the satisfaction of ESR-related needs by private actors has centred on the issue of

[75] For a discussion of such mechanisms in the context of the provision of social housing in Northern Ireland, see QUB Budget Analysis Project, *Budgeting for Social Housing in Northern Ireland* above n 10, and Rooney and Dutschke in this volume.

[76] For information on a range of European examples of PPP in a health care context, see I Nikolic and H Maikisch, 'Public–Private Partnerships and Collaboration in the Health Sector: An Overview with Case Studies from Recent European Experience, Health, Nutrition and Population' (HNP) Discussion Paper (Washington, The World Bank, 2006).

[77] This definition is derived from the United Nations Development Programme (UNDP) Public–Private Partnerships for the Urban Environment 'PPP Definitions': www.google.co.uk/url?sa=t&rct=j&q=public%20private%20partnership%20definition&source=web&cd=6&cad=rja&ved=0CE4QFjAF&url=http%3A%2F%2Feuropeandcis.undp.org%2Ffiles%2Fuploads%2FMilan%2Fhandout%2520PPP%2520definitions.doc&ei=3C4ZUbbGHs6a0QXAgIHoDw&usg=AFQjCNHNCnlzmgzz0d4q4jAQ8VKxdpo8gg.

[78] Balakrishnan et al above n 23, 9. For an example of this in the Northern Irish housing context, see Rooney and Dutschke in this volume.

[79] Ibid.

[80] See, ComESCR General Comment No 13, Chapter III; ComESCR General Comment No 14, Chapter V; ComESCR General Comment No 15, Chapter VI; ComESCR General Comment No 17, Chapter VI; ComESCR General Comment No 18, Chapter VI; ComESCR General Comment No 19, Chapter VI; ComESCR General Comment No 21, Chapter IV.

[81] See, ComESCR General Comment No 12, paras 15, 27; ComESCR General Comment No 13, para 50; ComESCR General Comment No 16 on the equal right of men and women to the enjoyment of all economic, social and cultural rights (UN Doc E/2005/3 art 3), paras 19–20; ComESCR General Comment No 17, para 32; ComESCR General Comment No 18, para 25; ComESCR General Comment No 19, paras 45–46; ComESCR General Comment No 20 on non-discrimination in economic, social and cultural rights (art 2), para 11; and ComESCR General Comment No 21, para 50(b).

the regulation of such actors—again, primarily in the context of discussion of the obligation to protect.[82]

While the regulatory role of the state is certainly very important with regard to preventing, controlling and punishing violations by non-state actors, the other key element of the tripartite typology with regard to privatisation is the state's obligation to fulfil. That is, the duty which requires states to adopt appropriate legislative, administrative, budgetary, judicial, promotional and other measures towards the full realisation of ESR.[83] Indeed, the only two times that the Committee has addressed the issue of privatisation specifically in the context of a discussion of the obligation to *fulfil* ESR took place in General Comment No 12 on the right to the highest attainable standard of health and General Comment No 15 on the right to water. Here, the Committee stressed 'further obligations include the provision of a public, private or mixed health insurance system which is affordable for all'[84] and that states must ensure that water services, 'whether privately or publicly provided, are affordable for all'.[85]

The furthest that the Committee has gone in terms of considering the issue of resources and privatisation in its General Comments is its statement in its General Comment No 4 on the right to adequate housing that,

> [w]hile in some states public financing of housing might most usefully be spent on direct construction of new housing, in most cases, experience has shown the inability of Governments to fully satisfy housing deficits. The promotion by States parties of 'enabling strategies', combined with a full commitment to obligations under the right to adequate housing, should thus be encouraged. In essence the obligation is to demonstrate that, in aggregate the measures being taken as sufficient to realise the right for every individual in the shortest possible time in accorded with the maximum of available resources ... Many of the measures that will be required will involve resource allocations and policy initiatives of a general kind.[86]

[82] See eg, ComESCR General Comment No 7 on the right to adequate housing: forced evictions (art 11(1)), UN Doc E/1998/22, annex IV (1997), para 9; ComESCR General Comment No 12, paras 27 and 19 (in the context of discussing violations caused by the direct action of states 'or other entities insufficiently regulated by states'); ComESCR General Comment No 13, para 59 (in the context of discussing 'acts of omission'); ComESCR General Comment No 14, paras 26 (in the context of discussing the requirement of states to ensure that private health providers comply with the principle of non-discrimination) and 49 (in the context of discussing 'acts of omission'; ComESCR General Comment No 15, para 44(b); ComESCR General Comment No 16, para 20; ComESCR General Comment No 17, para 32 and 55; ComESCR General Comment No 19, para 46; ComESR General Comment No 18, para 35.

[83] Paraphrased from ComESCR General Comment No14, para 33. This focus on the 'obligation to protect' is also reflected in the Committee's 'Statement on the obligations of States Parties regarding the corporate sector and economic, social and cultural rights', UN Doc E/C.12/2011/1, 20 May 2011, which is discussed below.

[84] ComESCR General Comment No 14, para 36.

[85] ComESCR General Comment No 15, para 27. The Committee has made similar statements in other General Comments (see above n 82) but not expressly in relation to the obligation to fulfil. See eg, ComESCR General Comment No 5, para 11.

[86] ComESCR General Comment No 4, paras 14, 15.

Given that such measures can be understood to include privatisation, the Committee's statement here can be taken as recognition that such a model will have resource implications. However, while this is a useful general guidance statement, models of privatisation vary widely in terms of their form and the extent to which they result in the effective realisation of ESR. Different models will have different implications for budgetary decisions. Thus far, however, the Committee has failed to engage in any extensive discussion of privatisation and ESR, whether in its General Comments or in Concluding Observations. It is particularly striking that Committee's 2011 'Statement on the Obligations of States Parties Regarding the Corporate Sector and Economic, Social and Cultural Rights' did not even mention the issue of privatisation[87]—despite its acknowledgement of 'the growing role played by non-state actors'[88] and the 'primary obligation' of States Parties to 'respect, protect and fulfil the Covenant rights of all persons under their jurisdiction in the context of corporate activities, undertaken by state-owned or private enterprises'.[89] If anything, this is a step backwards from the Committee's stance in its 1998 Statement in terms of level of engagement with privatisation.

As with retrogressive measures, the role of private actors is an issue that the Committee must address properly if its work is to be relevant and convincing to those seeking to hold the state to account with regard to its obligations under ICESCR.

IV. Conclusion

We are at a crucial time in terms of ESR-based budget analysis. On the one hand, it has never been so widely practised. On the other hand, the financial and economic crises mean that such work is arguably now more necessary than it has ever been since the establishment of the international human rights framework.[90]

In terms of practice, it is crucial that those carrying out ESR-based budget analysis work face the conceptual challenges caused by gaps and confusions in the ICESCR framework head-on. This certainly does not mean abandoning such work. Rather, where an element of the ICESCR framework being employed is ambiguous and the practitioner has settled on a particular interpretation, this should be expressly recognised and the chosen approach justified, rather than merely elided over. While it is inevitable that there will be some degree of divergence in interpretation of rather broad standards, it is notable that there has been relatively little consistency in the application of ICESCR principles and concepts

[87] UN Doc E/C.12/2011/1, 20 May 2011.
[88] Ibid para 1.
[89] Ibid para 3.
[90] The first step in the international human rights framework was the adoption of the Universal Declaration of Human Rights by UN General Assembly on 10 December 1948.

to budgets by practitioners.[91] Furthermore, there is frequently a failure to explain and justify the specific understandings of ESR concepts that are being employed in different analyses.[92] In addition to impacting negatively on the quality of the analysis presented in specific cases, this may have the effect of limiting the transferability of frameworks employed by practitioners to different contexts.

There is, however, a broader issue with regard to the expertise of the Committee and its willingness to engage with complicated concepts that are central both to states' efforts to realise ESR and to those of advocates seeking to hold states to account. It is vital that the Committee be prepared to play a leadership role in terms of conceptualising and applying a strong, coherent and flexible framework of budget-related ESR obligations. This extends to highlighting and addressing gaps and inconsistencies in the international ESR framework as it stands. A failure by the Committee to do so would risk setting its mandate to oversee the progress of state adherence to ICESCR at nought.

[91] For examples of this, see, QUB Budget Analysis Project, *Budgeting for Economic and Social Rights* above n 22.

[92] See ibid.

3

Let Them Eat Cake: Socio-Economic Rights in an Age of Austerity

PAUL O'CONNELL*

> The global crisis is being tackled by a massive transfer of wealth from poor to rich ... (this process) suggests a return to nineteenth-century beliefs in the principle and practice of natural inequality. On this view, it is not poverty that needs to be eradicated; the problem is the poor people themselves, who lack the ability to pull themselves up out of their misery. Handicapped by all kinds of defects, they constitute a useless residue and an unnecessary burden. How to get rid of this ballast?[1]

I. Introduction

It may well be axiomatic, but an important truism worth restating is that 'the realisation of human rights, especially economic and social rights, requires resources as well as laws'.[2] Or, to put it another way, the formal recognition of rights—and for present purposes of socio-economic rights—is fundamentally undermined if such formal recognition is not matched by the substantive commitment of

* Reader in Law, University of Leicester. My thanks to Ben Fine, Cosmo Graham, Colm O'Cinneide, Ellie Palmer, Joe Wills and the editors of the present volume for reading and commenting on earlier drafts of this chapter. While this work has no doubt benefited from their input, responsibility for all remaining errors and shortcomings rests solely with the author.

[1] J Breman, 'Myth of the Global Safety Net' (2009) 59 *New Left Review* 29, 35–36. Similarly, and in keeping with the title of this chapter, Robin Blackburn argues that the current global conjuncture (with entrenched and quasi-'natural' wealth inequalities, and the new aristocracy in the form of corporate CEOs and bondholders) is increasingly coming to resemble the French *ancien regime*: R Blackburn, 'Economic Democracy: Meaningful, Desirable, Feasible?' (2007) 136 *Daedalus* 36, 44.

[2] R Balakrishnan and D Elson, 'Auditing Economic Policy in the Light of Obligations on Economic and Social Rights' (2008) 5 *Essex Human Rights Review* 1, 1. Or, as Audrey Chapman puts it, the 'question of resources and how to evaluate the sufficiency of investment is central to implementing and monitoring the realisation of economic, social and cultural rights': AR Chapman, 'The Status of Efforts to Monitor Economic, Social and Cultural Rights' in S Hertel and L Minkler (eds), *Economic Rights: Conceptual, Measurement and Policy Issues* (Cambridge, Cambridge University Press, 2007) 143, 156.

resources. And while the last 20 years has certainly seen a global 'boom' in the nominal acceptance of socio-economic rights *qua* rights,[3] such formal commitment has all too often lacked the requisite substantive, material commitment.[4] There are a number of reasons for the relegation of socio-economic rights to this 'Cinderella' status within the human rights corpus,[5] but chief among them is the fact that there are irreducible tensions between the system of social and economic reproduction that now prevails on a global scale, and the meaningful protection of socio-economic rights.[6] In the wake of the 'Great Financial Crisis'/'Great Recession' that began in 2007, and in the context of ongoing stagnation in the most developed capitalist countries,[7] this routine neglect (or under-resourcing) of socio-economic rights has now been exacerbated by the mantra of austerity and conscious and explicit cuts to numerous social programmes, as well as to the social wage, which ensure people enjoy such rights.

The argument advanced here, in a nutshell, is that this current age of austerity should not be viewed, as it is often cast, as exceptional, but should instead be understood as the natural order with respect to government attitudes to socio-economic rights. To put it slightly differently: in the context of an economic and social system which invariably privileges numerically small, elite groups within society, both at the domestic and global level,[8] commitments to socio economic rights are only ever formal, and honoured in the most grudging and limited of ways. Returning to the title of this chapter, in an economic and political order premised on the privileging of the few at the expense of the many, governments

[3] As Taunya Lovell Banks has recently argued, the last 20 years have seen socio-economic 'regaining currency' at both domestic and international levels: T Lovell Banks, 'A Few Random Thoughts About Socio-Economic "Rights" in the United States in Light of the 2008 Financial Meltdown' (2009) 24 *Maryland Journal of International Law* 169, 169. Similarly, Kristin Henrard has recently argued that 'the recognition of the justiciability of economic, social and cultural rights is growing and becoming stronger by the day': K Henrard, 'Introduction: The Justiciability of ESC Rights and the Interdependence of All Fundamental Rights' (2009) 2 *Erasmus Law Review* 373, 377.

[4] On this disjuncture, see H Steiner, P Alston and R Goodman, *International Human Rights in Context: Law, Politics, Morals*, 3rd edn (Oxford, Oxford University Press, 2008) 263–64; D Olowu, 'Human Rights and the Avoidance of Domestic Implementation: The Phenomenon of Non-Justiciable Constitutional Guarantees' (2006) 69 *Saskatchewan Law Review* 39, 41.

[5] S Fredman, *Human Rights Transformed: Positive Rights and Positive Duties* (Oxford, Oxford University Press, 2008) 2.

[6] As CB Macpherson put it: 'Those who are concerned to protect the right of private capital accumulation are quite correct in seeing that that right is threatened by [socio-economic] rights claims. Implementation of [socio-economic rights] in the advanced countries would clearly reduce the rate of accumulation there … Thus the position of human rights (specifically socio-economic rights) in the West seems to be due to the type of economic system. *The capitalist system necessarily works against [socio-economic] rights*' (emphasis added): CB Macpherson, *The Rise and Fall of Economic Justice and Other Essays* (Oxford, Oxford University Press, 1985) 26.

[7] For analysis of the genesis and likely consequences of the current crisis, see J Bellamy Foster and F Magdoff, *The Great Financial Crisis: Causes and Consequences* (New York, Monthly Review Press, 2009).

[8] See eg, EO Wright, *Envisioning Real Utopias* (London, Verso, 2010) 47; R Plant, 'Social and Economic Rights Revisited' (2003) 14 *Kings College Law Journal* 1, 14.

are happy to agree to allow everyone to 'eat cake',[9] so long as each atomistic market actor is ready to secure it for his or herself.[10]

One important consequence of this state of affairs, is that the language of socio-economic rights, and consequently the various interests related to and protected by them, tends not to feature in decision-making processes about the size and share of the national resources cake. Therefore, in seeking to take what silver lining there may be from the current crisis, we need to look at ways of democratising such decision-making processes, to provide at least the possibility that socio-economic rights, and the interests associated with them, will figure in the calculus.

The first substantive section of this chapter frames the argument with a discussion of the current age of austerity. In particular it sketches out the adverse consequences which the great austerity drive is having for socio-economic rights in the UK, Ireland and Greece.[11] In the context of this discussion, it is argued that the push for austerity has little or nothing to do with objective, economic necessity, but instead is driven by an ideological and political project to further entrench neoliberal capitalism.[12] In the subsequent section it will be argued that existing budgetary decision-making processes are,[13] from the perspective of the meaningful protection of socio-economic rights, fundamentally flawed in two important respects: first, insofar as the normative and ideological presuppositions upon which such processes rely are fundamentally in tension with the protection of socio-economic rights; and second, because of their generally undemocratic and opaque nature.

Following on from this it will be argued, in the penultimate section, that if we are serious about the protection of socio-economic rights, then we need to not only develop technical and analytical tools for budget analysis, important though this is, but we must also raise fundamental questions about the nature of existing

[9] Even allowing for the fact that the infamous phrase attributed to Marie Antoinette was not actually uttered by her, the apocryphal story stands as a monument to the arrogance and insularity of ruling elites, who are more than happy to accord their subjects the same life chances they enjoy, but are just not willing to do anything to facilitate such enjoyment. On this misattribution of the famous phrase to Marie Antoinette, see NN Barker, '"Let Them Eat Cake" The Mythical Marie Antoinette and the French Revolution' (1993) 55 *The Historian* 709.

[10] On this see L Philipps, 'Taxing the Market Citizen: Fiscal Policy and Inequality in an Age of Privatisation' (2000) 63 *Law and Contemporary Problems* 111.

[11] For discussion of the politics of the austerity drives in these three countries, and in the United States, see G Albo and B Evans, 'From Rescue Strategies to Exit Strategies: The Struggle Over Public Sector Austerity' in L Panitch, G Albo and V Chibber (eds), *Socialist Register 2011: The Crisis This Time* (London, Merlin Press, 2010) 283.

[12] As Robert Wright has noted, at times of economic crises and downturns 'governments can to a large extent decide which parties will bear crisis costs' and in the present crisis the majority of governments around the world are choosing to socialise the costs and punish poor and working people. RE Wright, 'Hybrid Failures and Bailouts: Social Costs and Private Profits' in RE Wright (ed), *Bailouts: Public Money, Private Profit* (New York, Columbia University Press, 2010) 18.

[13] For the purposes of this chapter, the term 'budgetary decision-making processes' is used as a catchall for all aspects of fiscal, and to a lesser extent monetary and regulatory, policy. In effect the term is used to cover all significant processes that affect decisions about how revenue will be raised, and how it will be distributed within a given country.

budgetary decision-making processes, and the normative principles that inform them. This point is made well by David Harvey, who argues that '[to] propose different rights to those held sacrosanct by neoliberalism carries with it ... the obligation to specify alternative social processes within which such alternative rights can inhere'.[14] In the current crisis, then, the obligation upon us is to think big and look beyond received orthodoxies. This will enable us to make strides, both theoretical and practical, towards a sustainable society, in which the enjoyment of socio-economic rights can be a genuine taken-for-granted, and not an empty, rhetorical promise.

II. Swinging the Axe, and Sharing the Pain

In a truly astounding sleight of the proverbial invisible hand of the market,[15] a crisis created by the structural contradictions inherent within neoliberal capitalism,[16] has now been turned to the advantage of the same class of people who were central in causing it, through a seamless transition to an age of seemingly perpetual austerity. As Robin Blackburn notes:

> Bail-out measures adopted during the early phase of the crisis between 2007–09 saw the US, UK and Eurozone authorities increase public indebtedness by 20–40 per cent of GDP, with larger current account deficits ... Before long, the bond markets were demanding plans to cut these deficits by slashing public spending and shrinking social protection. The centre left and centre right were already persuaded that the welfare state was too expensive and bureaucratic, and needed to be downsized and handed over to private suppliers.[17]

Similarly William Mitchell argues that '[what] began as a problem of unsustainable private growth, driven by an out-of-control financial sector aided and abetted by government deregulation, has mysteriously morphed into an alleged sovereign debt crisis'.[18] In effect, then, the massive public debt of governments around the

[14] D Harvey, *A Brief History of Neoliberalism* (Oxford, Oxford University Press, 2005) 204.

[15] Peter Burnham notes the seamless transition from 'a *discourse of financial crisis* to one of a *crisis of sovereign debt* to the current phase of the *politics of austerity and cuts*' [original emphasis]. P Burnham, 'Towards a Political Theory of Crisis: Policy and Resistance Across Europe' (2011) 33 *New Political Science* 493, 493.

[16] The current crisis was not simply, as mainstream commentary would have it, the consequence of 'bad bankers' losing the run of themselves, or of regulators momentarily taking their eyes off the ball, but rather a consequence of inherent, structural contradictions that the global capitalist system is unable to resolve. As Callinicos puts it '[the] economic and financial crisis of the late 2000s was not an accident nor the mere result of a banking system that had escaped control. It was a moment of revelation, one that exposed the systemic contradictions with which global capitalism has been struggling for decades': A Callinicos, *Bonfire of Illusions* (Cambridge, Polity Press, 2010) 94; Bellamy Foster and Magdoff above n 7.

[17] R Blackburn, 'Crisis 2.0' (2011) 72 *New Left Review* 33, 33.

[18] W Mitchell, 'Beyond Austerity' *The Nation* (4 April 2011): www.thenation.com/article/159288/beyond-austerity.

world, which is the target of the champions of austerity, primarily results from the socialisation of the losses made by banks and bondholders during the halcyon days of neoliberal casino capitalism.[19] In spite of this, throughout both the initial period of the crisis, and now in the incipient age of austerity, the costs of this crisis are falling disproportionately on the poor and on working people.[20] Now, in the post-bank bailout climate, austerity is posited as a necessary evil to compensate for the profligacy of the past.

In this environment it is argued that cuts to public spending, and consequently to myriad programmes and schemes which impact on the protection of socio-economic rights, are necessary as part of a broad 'pain sharing' exercise to get the public finances back in order.[21] There are, however, two crucial problems with this narrative: the first is that the purported necessity of austerity is very much open to question,[22] with the concomitant drive to roll back the state looking less like a neutral economic necessity, and more an ideologically driven project.[23] But, even if we were to allow for the need for cutbacks, the second major shortcoming is that the rhetoric of pain sharing is just that: rhetoric in the most pejorative and debased sense of that term, as the pain of the cuts to public spending is invariably concentrated on those who can least afford to bear it.[24]

A few examples will serve to demonstrate the human costs of austerity, and also to show how the various cuts, changes to welfare regimes and regressive

[19] As Phillips argues 'government accounts were not pushed so far into the red by public sector profligacy, but rather by the wholesale transfer of private, speculative debt on the part of banks and developers to the public purse': L Phillips, 'The Creaking European Austerity Machine' (2011) 176 *Red Pepper* 46, 46; and see A Storey, 'They Make a Desert and They Call It Peace': politico.ie/crisisjam/7148-they-make-a-desert-and-they-call-it-peace.html.

[20] See Breman above n 1; and Albo and Evans above n 11.

[21] As Serwotka notes 'large-scale public sector cuts, have become the accepted wisdom of our age', M Serwotka, 'There is an Alternative to Public Spending Cuts' *The Guardian* (London, 13 September 2010).

[22] See G Irvin, D Byrne, R Murphy, H Reed and S Ruane, *In Place of Cuts: Tax Reform to Build a Fairer Society* (London, Compass, 2009); WI Robinson, 'The Global Capital Leviathan' (2011) 165 *Radical Philosophy* 2; H Radice, 'Cutting Government Deficits: Economic Science or Class War?' (2010) 35 *Capital & Class* 125. Indeed, Mitchell goes so far as to argue that the case for austerity, on a global scale, is 'built on a lie': Mitchell above n 18.

[23] For an insight into the overarching ideological vision driving the British Conservative-led Government's cuts agenda, see D Cameron, 'How We Will Release the Grip of State Control' *The Telegraph* (London, 20 February 2011); J Harris, 'The Coalition Has Sneaked a *Coup* on a Sleeping Public' *The Guardian* (London, 27 February 2011); G Monbiot, 'For the Conservatives, This is Not a Financial Crisis But a Long-Awaited Opportunity' *The Guardian* (London, 18 October 2010). See also *Open Public Services* (White Paper, Cm 8145, 2011).

[24] See M Sepúlveda Carmona, 'Report of the Independent Expert on the question of human rights and extreme poverty on the human rights based approach to recovery from the global economic and financial crises, with a focus on those living in poverty' (UN Doc A/HRC/17/34). For examples in the UK context, see L Elliot, 'A Brand of Austerity About as Progressive as Thatcher's' *The Guardian* (London, 25 August 2010); P Curtis, 'Council Budgets Cuts Hit the Most Deprived Areas, Says Study' *The Guardian* (London, 11 December 2010); P Curtis, 'Poorest Councils Will Face Biggest Cuts' *The Guardian* (London, 13 December 2010); P Butler, 'Councils Say Poorest Areas Will Be Worst Hit By Cuts' *The Guardian* (London, 14 January 2011).

tax changes are adversely affecting the entire gamut of socio-economic rights.[25] To begin with, in the United Kingdom, it is anticipated that as many as 90,000 individual council housing tenants, and up to 82,000 families, could face eviction and homelessness due to cuts in housing benefit.[26] It is also expected that cuts, or to use the euphemism of the day 'efficiencies', in the National Health Service (NHS), coupled with the drive towards further marketisation and privatisation,[27] will invariably work to benefit the well off, and result in decreasing standards of care for those in poor and marginalised areas.[28] We see similar cuts in many other countries around the world, both in the global north and south, some of which have been imposed by international financial institutions.

As in Ireland, where, in compliance with requirements negotiated (demanded may well be the more accurate term) by the European Union (EU) and International Monetary Fund (IMF) in exchange for aid, the Irish Government slashed €2.8 billion from the national welfare budget, €1.4 billion from the national health budget and cut the national minimum wage by €1 an hour as well as introducing a slew of regressive taxes,[29] all such measures will impact most on the poor and on working people. These initial cuts were then followed by the adoption of a four-year 'national recovery plan',[30] which contains a combination of cuts and tax increases to balance the national budget. These wide-reaching cuts include reducing the number of people employed in the public service, as well as further cuts to health, education and social welfare spending.[31] On the tax front, 'most of the proposals hit low and average-income earners rather than

[25] The instances adumbrated here are a partial, and almost meaningless, illustration of the suffering being caused by the austerity drive, for a fuller picture see UN Department of Economic and Social Affairs, *The Global Social Crisis: Report on the World Social Situation 2011* (New York, United Nations, 2011).

[26] J Hari, 'David Cameron's Assault on the Homeless is Dickensian' *The Independent* (London, 4 March 2011); and see Crisis, 'Crisis Fears Drastic Benefit Cut Risks Rise in Rough Sleeping as Charity Publishes Damning New Survey Evidence' (March 2011): www.crisis.org.uk/pressreleases.php/442/crisis-fears-drastic-benefit-cut-risks-rise-in-rough-sleeping-as-charity-publishes-damning-new-surve.

[27] On this see C Leys and S Player, *The Plot Against the NHS* (London, Merlin Press, 2010).

[28] See R Ramesh, 'NHS Plans Will Penalise Poor, Says BMA Doctor' *The Guardian* (London, 25 January 2011); P O'Connell, 'The Human Right to Health and Privatisation of Irish Health Care' (2005) 11 *Medico-Legal Journal of Ireland* 76. Indeed, in the UK indications are that already the cuts—or 'efficiencies' as the Government would have it—to the NHS are already adversely affecting patient treatment, particularly in poorer areas: see D Campbell, 'NHS Chiefs Ration Healthcare to Meet Cuts Target' *The Guardian* (London, 11 April 2011).

[29] For discussions of some of the austerity measures adopted in Ireland since 2008, including those imposed by the EU–IMF, see Center for Economic and Social Rights, *Mauled by the Celtic Tiger: Human Rights in Ireland's Economic Meltdown* (Madrid, CESR, 2012); P Barkham, 'The Victims of Ireland's Economic Collapse' *The Guardian* (London, 26 May 2010); S Collins, H McGee and M Minihan, 'Welfare and Pensions Hardest Hit in €15bn Package of Cuts and Taxes' *Irish Times* (Dublin, 25 November 2010); D Finn, 'Ireland on the Turn?' (2011) 67 *New Left Review* 5.

[30] Finn above n 29.

[31] See P Kirby, 'When Banks Cannibalise the State: Responses to Ireland's Economic Collapse' in L Panitch, G Albo and V Chibber (eds), *Socialist Register 2012: The Crisis and the Left* (London, Merlin Press, 2011) 249, 243.

high-income earners'.[32] A recent report from the Center for Economic and Social Rights has concluded that the measures adopted in Ireland represent a clear disregard of the state's human rights obligations, and have 'severely reduced enjoyment of a range of economic and social rights'.[33]

Similarly in Greece, we see a savage assault on the living standards and rights of ordinary Greek citizens,[34] with massive cuts in public sector salaries, cuts to public sector jobs in the hundreds of thousands, reductions in pensions, myriad cuts to social benefits, as well as the introduction of a slew of new taxes (including the impressively Orwellian 'solidarity levy') which will impact on poor and working people the most, as well the wholesale privatisation of vast swathes of public infrastructure.[35] All these measures are being imposed on the Greek people, notwithstanding the fact that polls show up to 80 per cent of Greeks are opposed to them.[36] And as with Ireland, and far too many countries before it, Greece is being fed this toxic combination of 'aid' and austerity, so that it can bail out banks and bondholders.[37] Commenting on the slew of measures being adopted by Greek governments, under the guidance of the IMF and EU, the UN Independent Expert on Foreign Debt and Human Rights argued that these measures could pose very serious threats to human rights.[38] A collation of European human rights organisations went even further and argued that 'the austerity measures imposed on Greece lead the society to a dramatic and suicidal situation'.[39]

It is depressingly unsurprising that at the very same time we see millions of people pushed further into penury through conscious state policy (with all the rights-denying effects that this has), we also see the number of wealthy people around the world steadily increasing,[40] as well as governments introducing 'business friendly' tax regimes (which necessarily increase the wealth of the already

[32] Ibid.

[33] Center for Economic and Social Rights above n 29, 24.

[34] For a harrowing account of the Greek experience see N Burgi, 'Greece in Chaos' *Le Monde Diplomatique*, (Paris, December 2011): mondediplo.com/2011/12/03greece.

[35] For discussions of the austerity drive in Greece, see G Wearden, 'Greece Austerity Plan: What Is Being Voted On' *The Guardian* (London, 29 June 2011); 'The Labours of Austerity: Greece's Economic Woes' *The Economist* (London, 7 April 2011); Albo and Evans above n 11, 299–301.

[36] Editorial, 'Greece and Austerity: Brussels v The People' *The Guardian* (London, 29 June 2011).

[37] As the above editorial in *The Guardian* puts it 'Greece is being pumped with cash so as it can repay its debts to German and French banks. The financiers are being bailed out, while the economy craters, society is pushed to breaking point and Greek politics becomes ever more combustible', ibid.

[38] UN News Centre, 'Greek Austerity Measures Could Violate Human Rights, UN Expert Says': www.un.org/apps/news/story.asp?NewsID=38901&Cr=austerity&Cr1.

[39] European Association for the Defence of Human Rights, Hellenic League for Human Rights and the French League of Human Rights, 'Greece: A Suicide of "Increasing Austerity"': www.hlhr.gr/detailsen.php?id=638.

[40] On this see Capgemini and Merrill Lynch, *World Wealth Report 2011* (New York, 2011): www.ml.com/media/114235.pdf; J Treanor, 'World's Wealthiest People Now Richer than before the Credit Crunch' *The Guardian* (London, 22 June 2011); J Copping, 'Sunday Times Rich List 2010: Britain's Richest See Wealth Rise by One Third' *The Telegraph* (London, 24 April 2010).

wealthy)[41] and foregoing billions in potential wealth tax revenues.[42] In view of this, the rhetoric of pain sharing rings particularly hollow, and it can be seen that the costs of the economic crisis induced by neoliberal capitalism are now being paid for predominantly by ordinary working people, with the net effect being the increased and systematic undermining of the entire gamut of socio-economic rights, from the right to housing, health care, education, social welfare through to the right to work and to organise in trade unions.[43]

Instead, therefore, of representing a necessary response to the wild and carefree public spending of the past, one can view the push for austerity on a global scale as representing a third phase in the embedding of neoliberal capitalism.[44] In this latest phase, the processes of immiseration and subjugation that have been tried and tested by transnational economic elites and their political agents throughout the global periphery over the past 30 years,[45] are now being imposed with renewed vigour on the poor and working people of the advanced capitalist countries, as well as throughout the periphery.[46] As Hugo Radice notes, behind arguments of economic necessity,

> the real reason for the cuts is twofold. On the one hand, the business, financial and political elites—in short, the ruling classes—were obliged in 2008 to summon the interventionist state back onto the stage to avoid a total collapse of global finance, and now want to banish it once more to a merely supportive role. On the other hand, the cuts in state spending and increases in taxes are being structured in such a way as to transfer income and wealth from working people to the rich and powerful.[47]

Consequently, the current age of austerity is not so much an exceptional and objectively necessary response to bloated public finances; instead the growth of public debt caused by the inherent instability of neoliberal capitalism now provides

[41] See Elliot above n 24; Irvin et al above n 22.

[42] Mark Serwotka argues that the UK forgoes an estimated £70bn a year through tax evasion (or avoidance, as the politer term may be) by the wealthy, and under-enforcement of the tax code: Serwotka above n 21.

[43] See UN Department of Economic and Social Affairs above n 25.

[44] Accepting Ben Fine's and Dimitris Milonakis' argument that, up to now, 'neoliberalism might best be seen as falling roughly into two phases—the first as the shock-therapy associated with Reagan and Thatcher, Latin America, and the Soviet bloc, and the second with the social market, Third-Wayism and the post-Washington consensus': B Fine and D Milonakis, '"Useless But True": Economic Crisis and the Peculiarities of Economic Science' (2011) 19 *Historical Materialism* 3, 6. See also R Hendrikse and J Sidaway, 'Neoliberalism 3.0' (2010) 42 *Environment and Planning* 2037.

[45] For an excellent discussion of past sovereign debt crises, connecting them to the current conjuncture, and showing how such 'crises' are in fact functional to the maintenance of the neoliberal global economic order, see T Mahmud, 'Is it Greek or *Déjà Vu* All Over Again?: Neoliberalism and Winners and Losers of International Debt Crises' (2011) 42 *Loyola University Chicago Law Journal* 629; Storey above n 19.

[46] See G Albo, S Gindin and L Panitch, *In and Out of Crisis: The Global Financial Meltdown and Left Alternatives* (Oakland CA, PM Press, 2010) 23. As Robinson puts it 'Transnational capital and its political agents are attempting to resolve the current structural crisis by a vast shift in the balance of class and social forces worldwide—in effect, to deepen many times over and to consummate the "neoliberal counterrevolution" that began in the 1980s': Robinson above n 22, 4.

[47] Radice above n 22, 126.

a pretext for a more brutal and extensive application of the inegalitarian logics inherent within neoliberal capitalism.

III. The Myopia of the Handmaidens[48]

Inevitably the various cuts, as well as regressive changes to national tax systems to encourage growth, will have the net effect of adversely affecting the socio-economic rights of millions of poor and working people,[49] and in particular members of discreet and politically powerless groups.[50] There is, therefore, a very strong case for arguing that cuts such as those being implemented in the UK and elsewhere would implicate, and quite likely be found to be in breach of, established international human rights standards and obligations.[51] Notwithstanding this, the language of human rights has been, for all intents and purposes, absent from both governmental justifications and proposals, and from oppositional discourses.[52]

For Ignacio Saiz, the absence of references to socio-economic rights in governmental and intergovernmental responses to the crisis, and in proposed austerity programmes, indicates that these rights

> are seen as derogable in times of crisis, a luxury only permissible in times of plenty. For all the progress made in normative recognition of (socio-economic rights), the response to the crisis reveals that these rights are still treated by many if not most governments as mere rhetorical aspirations rather than binding principles of public policy.[53]

On this, Saiz is at least half right. For where he appears to see the current conjuncture as exceptional, in truth the current crisis has simply exposed the reality that, for the vast majority of governments (irrespective of political stripe),

[48] This phrase is borrowed from P Alston, 'The Myopia of the Handmaidens: International Lawyers and Globalisation' (1997) 3 *European Journal of International Law* 435. It is applied here in a different context.

[49] See Robinson above n 22, 5.

[50] In the UK, for example, The Fawcett Society unsuccessfully sought judicial review of the Government's planned cuts, on the basis that they would have disproportionately adverse effects on women, contrary to the Government's obligations under the Equality Act 2010; see A Grice, 'Osborne in Court Fight Over "Anti-Women" Cuts' *The Independent* (London, 6 December 2010). Similarly, cuts, and changes, to welfare programmes are expected to have particularly adverse consequences for people with disabilities and for children: see R Shields, 'The Impact of Welfare Cuts: Britons on the Breadline' *The Independent* (London, 4 July 2010); R Ramesh, 'Spending Cuts "Will See Rise in Absolute Child Poverty"' *The Guardian* (London, 16 December 2010).

[51] See A Nolan, 'Is the Government's Austerity Programme Breaking Human Rights Law?': www.opendemocracy.net/ourkingdom/aoife-nolan/is-governments-austerity-programme-breaking-human-rights-law.

[52] On this point, see A Donald, 'Austerity Opposition Needs a Coherent Narrative: Human Rights Provides One' *The Guardian* (London, 25 January 2011).

[53] I Saiz, 'Rights in Recession? Challenges for Economic and Social Rights in Times of Crisis' (2009) 1 *Journal of Human Rights Practice* 277, 280.

commitments to socio-economic rights were, in the context of neoliberal hegemony, only ever formal.

The reasons for this nominal commitment are manifold, but one crucial factor is that on a global scale the majority of governments have, for the last 30 years, been committed to a particular economic and political paradigm, generally referred to as neoliberalism.[54] As a result of which, the dominant optic in social, political and, crucially for present purposes, economic policy discourse (and in mainstream economic theory) over the last 20 to 30 years has been neoliberalism (or its various synonyms: the Washington consensus, the Chicago School or neoclassicalism).[55] Alfredo Saad-Filho spells out the assumptions on which neoliberal economic policy is premised as follows:

> Neoliberal policies are based on three premises. First, the dichotomy between markets and the state. Neoliberalism presumes that the state and the market are distinct and mutually exclusive institutions, and that one expands only at the expense of the other. Second, it claims that markets are efficient, whereas states are wasteful and economically inefficient. Third, it argues that state intervention creates systemic economic problems, especially resource misallocation, rent-seeking behaviour and technological backwardness. These premises imply that certain economic policies are 'naturally' desirable. These include, first, rolling back the state in order to institute 'free markets', for example, through privatisation and deregulation of economic activity … Second, tight fiscal and monetary policies, including tax reforms end expenditure cuts, in order to control inflation and limit the scope for state intervention.[56]

Ultimately, there are fundamental and inherent tensions between these assumptions underlying this model of economic policy analysis and prescription, and alternative perspectives that privilege the interests associated with human rights.[57]

For example, in the context of the current debate about cuts—if, indeed, it can be called a debate—neoliberal economic theory is by default suspicious of public spending, arguing that it crowds out private investment and thereby stifles economic growth.[58] Such a premise, particularly in the hands of a government ideologically committed to the rolling back of the state,[59] leads invariably to the sorts of cuts we see today. Furthermore, neoliberal economic thought values and

[54] For discussions of the genesis and nature of neoliberalism, see Harvey above n 14; R Plant, *The Neo-liberal State* (Oxford, Oxford University Press, 2010); D Miller, 'How Neoliberalism Got to Where It Is: Elite Planning, Corporate Lobbying and the Release of the Free Market' in K Birch and V Mykhnenko (eds), *The Rise and Fall of Neoliberalism: The Collapse of an Economic Order?* (London, Zed Books, 2010) 23; J Peck, *Constructions of Neoliberal Reason* (Oxford, Oxford University Press, 2010).

[55] See Radice above n 22; Fine and Milonakis above n 44; M Perelman, *Railroading Economics* (New York, Monthly Review Press, 2006).

[56] A Saad-Filho, 'Introduction' in A Saad-Filho (ed), *Anti-Capitalism: A Marxist Introduction* (London, Pluto Press, 2003) 1, 7.

[57] See Balakrishnan and Elson above n 2, 1; P O'Connell, 'On Reconciling Irreconcilables: Neo-liberal Globalisation and Human Rights' (2007) 7 *Human Rights Law Review* 483; Macpherson above n 6.

[58] R Balakrishnan, D Elson and R Patel, 'Rethinking Macro Economic Strategies from a Human Rights Perspective' (2010) 53 *Development* 27, 34.

[59] See Cameron above n 23.

valorises growth for growth's sake,[60] with the incidental sop that at some point the rising tide will lift all boats. In this way, the logic of this neoliberal system encourages tax cuts, deregulation, privatisation and myriad other activities which it is said will result in economic growth—irrespective of the consequences such policies may have for equality, sustainability and rights.[61] The fundamental problem with this approach is that in practice the functioning of the supposedly free market is inherently inegalitarian,[62] and in myriad ways leads to the growth of various forms of inequality, but in particular to wealth inequalities and to structural denials of socio-economic rights.[63]

Another of the fundamental shortcomings of existing budgetary processes is that they are inherently elitist and opaque. In relation to this point, it is important to be aware that part of the project of neoliberal globalisation over the last 30 years has been to recast private power and economic power relations as natural and neutral. One consequence of this has been a concerted effort to portray matters of macroeconomic policy as purely technical, a-political choices.[64] As Lisa Duggan points out:

> The most successful ruse of neoliberal dominance in both global and domestic affairs is the definition of economic policy, as primarily a matter of neutral, technical expertise. This expertise is then presented as separate from politics and culture, and not properly subject to specifically political accountability or cultural critique.[65]

In line with this, established budgetary processes tend to be exclusionary, and presented as neutral, technocratic exercises of expertise,[66] with political choice reduced to a minimum.[67]

[60] On this fetishisation of 'growth' in capitalist society, and hence in mainstream economics, Macpherson notes that 'As to the ideology, economic growth is so essential to capitalism that the directors of capitalist societies come to take it as an end in itself, to which everything else may appropriately be subordinated': Macpherson above n 6, 29.

[61] See Balakrishnan, Elson and Patel above n 58; and D McNally, 'Inequality, the Profit System and Global Crisis' in J Guard and W Antony (eds), *Bankruptcies & Bailouts* (Winnipeg, Fernwood Publishing, 2009) 32.

[62] See E Schutz, *Inequality and Power: The Economics of Class* (Oxford, Routledge, 2011).

[63] See P O'Connell, 'Brave New World?: Human Rights in the Era of Globalisation' in M Baderin and M Ssenyonjo (eds), *International Human Rights Law: Six Decades After the UDHR and Beyond* (Hampshire, Ashgate, 2010) 195. Such inconvenient empirical realities are, however, irrelevant to mainstream economic thinking, which prides itself on its pseudo-scientific character, and detachment from the real world: see Fine and Milonakis above n 44.

[64] For an extensive and informative account of this process, see D Milonakis and B Fine, *From Political Economy to Economics: Method, the Social and the Historical in the Evolution of Economic Theory* (Oxford, Routledge, 2008).

[65] L Duggan, *The Twilight of Equality* (Boston MA, Beacon Press, 2003) xiv.

[66] As Harvey notes, 'Neoliberal theorists are … profoundly suspicious of democracy … Neoliberals therefore tend to favor governance by experts and elites': Harvey above n 14, 66.

[67] This elitism pervades all aspects of economic and budgetary policymaking, but one glaring example has been the global move towards the creation of independent central banks in recent years: see TA Canova, 'Non-State Actors and the International Institutional Order: Central Bank Capture and the Globalisation of Monetary Amnesia' (2007) 101 *American Society of International Law Proceedings* 469.

In this way macroeconomic decisions—such as whether or not a country should run a budget deficit, and whether massive public spending cuts are 'essential'—are presented as value neutral, when nothing could be further from the truth.[68] Such decisions are inherently political,[69] and should be advanced and judged on their merits, as substantive normative positions, rather than being shrouded in the veil of technocracy. As a consequence of the combination of the normative underpinning of established budgetary processes, and their opaque and technocratic nature, many voices and perspectives are excluded from these processes (including those perspectives that give priority to human rights) and are subject to elite capture and thus to entrenching already existing power relations.[70] In such a context, we should not fall into the trap of simply valorising the role of Parliament and seek to introduce the language of human rights into parliamentary processes,[71] but instead should look to fundamentally recast both the nature of budgetary decision-making processes and the normative principles which inform them. In the next section one proposal as to how this could be done is explored.

IV. It's the Political Economy, Stupid

The essence of the foregoing discussion is that the current age of austerity is not exceptional, but instead a natural development of the system of neoliberal capitalism and that the undermining of socio-economic rights protection and enjoyment associated with the current age of austerity is not an anomaly, but rather the necessary fate of socio-economic rights in the current social and economic order. It is useful then to recall Harvey's argument that if we are serious about the protection of certain rights, or a certain conception of rights, then we must also look to develop social processes within which such rights can inhere.[72] Specifically with regard to socio-economic rights, the argument here is that their denial (or the undermining of the potential to enjoy them in a meaningful sense) is inherent within neoliberal capitalism, and that the spread and ferocity of the current cuts agenda shows that existing budgetary processes exclude genuine account being taken of socio-economic rights *qua* rights.

If this is the case—and if a commitment to the protection and realisation of socio-economic rights obliges us to envisage new social processes which could

[68] As Jim Stanford notes 'Economics is an inherently subjective, value-laden, political discipline': J Stanford, *Economics for Everyone* (London, Pluto Press, 2008) 335.

[69] Insofar as 'politics' is understood as the 'process through which human communities make decisions regarding their collective conditions and existence', see JC Myers, *The Politics of Equality: An Introduction* (London, Zed Books, 2010) 3.

[70] As Erik Olin Wright puts it 'those who occupy powerful positions in the economy invariably have a disproportionate influence on political outcomes in all capitalist societies': Wright above n 8, 84.

[71] Although for an interesting proposal on this front see M Hunt, 'Enhancing Parliament's Role in Relation to Economic and Social Rights' (2010) *European Human Rights Law Review* 242.

[72] Harvey above n 14.

contribute to the protection of such rights—then one way in which we could seek to overcome the limitations of budgetary processes could be through the development of something akin to the practice of participatory budgeting, popularised by the experience in Porto Alegre, Brazil.[73] Participatory budgeting represents an important, recent innovation in democratic practice,[74] an instance of what Erik Olin Wright and others have called 'empowered participatory governance'.[75] While participatory budgeting initiatives may take a number of institutional forms, depending on context,[76] the basic, overarching idea behind such processes are that citizens should meet regularly, to take decisions—and in this sense it is essential that they have genuine decision-making powers—about the budgetary priorities of their communities.[77] And while the Porto Alegre experience has been far from faultless or pristine, it has, taken as a whole, 'been an enormous success, both in terms of its claims as an experiment in deepening direct democracy and its effectiveness in the practical tasks of formulating budgets'.[78] For the purposes of the present discussion, one of the most noteworthy developments in the context of the Porto Alegre experience is that the process has seen a massive shift in spending towards prioritising the needs of the poorest sections of the community.[79]

Bearing in mind the critique of extant budgetary processes advanced above, there are a number of reasons as to why seeking to develop something akin to this practice in the current context of the global austerity drive would be important. The first relates to the basic principle of democracy; as Albo, Gindin and Panitch put it, if 'democracy is a kind of society and not just a form of government, the economy—which is so fundamental to shaping our lives—will eventually have to be democratised'.[80] As was argued above, neoliberal orthodoxy tends towards the prioritising of technocratic governance, and the closing off of spaces for democratic

[73] For excellent accounts of the Porto Alegre experience, see B de Sousa Santos, 'Participatory Budgeting in Porto Alegre: Toward a Redistributive Democracy' in B de Sousa Santos (ed), *Democratizing Democracy: Beyond the Liberal Democratic Canon* (London, Verso, 2005) 307; G Baiocchi, 'Participation, Activism, and Politics: The Porto Alegre Experiment' in A Fung and EO Wright (eds), *Deepening Democracy: Institutional Innovations in Empowered Participatory Governance* (London, Verso, 2003) 45. And for discussion of the diffusion of participatory budgeting, see Y Sintomer, C Herzberg and A Röcke, 'Participatory Budgeting in Europe: Potentials and Challenges' (2008) 32 *International Journal of Urban and Regional Research* 164.

[74] On this point see Y Cabannes, 'Participatory Budgeting: A Significant Contribution to Participatory Democracy' (2004) 16 *Environment and Urbanisation* 27.

[75] See Wright above n 8, 155; and RN Abers, 'Reflections on What Makes Empowered Participatory Governance Happen' in A Fung and EO Wright (eds), *Deepening Democracy: Institutional Innovations in Empowered Participatory Governance* (London, Verso, 2003) 200.

[76] See Cabannes above n 74; and Sintomer, Herzberg and Röcke above n 73.

[77] As Erik Olin Wright notes, 'the basic idea is that citizens meet in popular assemblies ... to deliberate on how the ... budget should be spent', Wright above n 8, 156.

[78] Ibid 157–58.

[79] Wright above n 8, 158. As Baiocchi notes, through participatory budgeting in Porto Alegre 'high numbers of participants from several strata of ... society have come together to share in a governance structure that has been efficient and *highly redistributive*' (emphasis added): Baiocchi above n 73, 67.

[80] Albo, Gindin and Panitch above n 46, 114.

participation.[81] In complete contrast,[82] participatory budgeting extends and deepens the dimensions of our shared social life that are subject to democratic control and contestation; and in the current global conjuncture, this contestation aspect is crucially important.

If, as has been contended here, the current age of austerity can be viewed as, in effect, the third phase of neoliberal entrenchment, in which the pretext of alleged fiscal profligacy is used as a device to further strengthen the position of global economic elites and immiserate the poor and working classes of the world, then 'the level and composition of government budgets will be a critical terrain upon which social forces will seek to advance their opposing interests'.[83] In this context, it is essential for progressives of all stripes—including those who focus on the advancement and protection of socio-economic rights—to 'start to carve out [spaces] for developing a challenge to the still-prevailing dominance of the neoliberal, pro-market, hegemonic consensus'.[84]

Throughout the world, albeit with some slight differences of emphasis, government responses to the crisis have overwhelmingly been concerned with restoring the conditions of profitable accumulation for economic elites, and at the same time effecting a transfer of wealth from poor and working people to the already rich. It is essential, therefore, that budgetary and economic decision-making is opened up to contestation and debate, and that discussions over which spending and revenue generating streams will be prioritised are made sites of struggle, in order for individuals, communities and organisations to have the potential to claim their rights in a meaningful way. As Stanford notes:

> Workers and poor people get only as much from the economy as they are able to demand, fight for, and win. There is no reason to believe that the success of capitalists will ever naturally 'trickle down' into improved living standards for the bulk of humanity. Neoclassical theories which claim that everyone gets paid according to their productivity are theoretically inconsistent and empirically false. Income distribution is determined by power, more than markets. Demanding a fairer deal from the system, and building the organisational and political power to back-up that demand … is the only way to redivide the pie.[85]

Opening up budgetary decision-making processes to broad based, democratic participation and contestation, allows at least the possibility of breaking with the debilitating rhetoric of 'There is no Alternative' to the austerity and cuts agenda.

[81] See S Amin, *The Liberal Virus* (London, Pluto Press, 2004); Duggan above n 65.

[82] Santos has gone so far as to argue that the emergence and spread of participatory budgeting, constitutes an important 'form of counter-hegemonic globalisation': Santos above n 73, 307.

[83] K Beitel, 'The Crisis, the Deficit and the Power of the Dollar: Resisting the Public Sector's Devaluation' in L Panitch, G Albo and V Chibber (eds), *Socialist Register 2011: The Crisis This Time* (London, Merlin Press, 2010) 260, 276.

[84] Ibid. As Albo and Evans note, in the context of the present austerity drive it is essential that we create new spaces that allow for 'democratic struggles over the legitimacy of the austerity programmes' and to 'contest neoliberal discourses': Albo and Evans above n 11, 303.

[85] Stanford above n 68, 338–39.

So, for example, in an open and democratic forum, it could reasonably be argued that instead of cuts to essential public services being forced through, the hundreds of billions held by large corporations should be tapped, in a number of ways, and put to useful and productive social ends, rather than being hoarded.[86] In this way, some form of participatory budgeting, with genuine decision-making power, could provide an important counter to the undemocratic and technocratic tendencies of neoliberal orthodoxy.[87]

The second reason why the adoption of some form of participatory budgeting would be useful is that it could provide space for the development of an alternative to the limited language of existing processes. Through opening up and democratising the budgetary process, we can potentially enhance the chances of ensuring sustained, long-term governmental commitment to socio-economic rights, even in times of economic contraction. In this context, empowered individuals, communities, trade unions and other organisations can utilise the language of human rights to amplify their voices in the deliberative process. As Hertel and Minkler argue:

> By invoking the normative force of human rights in defence of their own needs ... grassroots protestors can change the nature of their interaction with powerful government and private sector representatives. Instead of offering petitions for help, they can demand that rights be fulfilled—explicitly referencing documents such as the UDHR [and] the ICESCR ... which codify key [socio-economic] rights. In so doing, they transform their status from that of supplicants to claimants.[88]

Participatory budgeting, combined with the language of human rights, could therefore serve to provide a voice to the most excluded and marginalised, but, crucially, such a process also exposes the inherently political nature of budgetary decision-making and introduces a new normative discourse into it.

It also shifts the terrain from the nebulous (arguably useless) language of 'fairness', so easily appropriated by 'compassionate conservatives', and reframes claims for the resourcing of important programmes in imperative, binding language. This can fundamentally shift the terms of a debate, because 'by moving to a human rights framework, the elimination of poverty becomes more than just a desirable, charitable or even moral policy goal. It becomes [a] ... duty of states'.[89] Also, in opening up the discourse of budget analysis in a participatory way, we could then problematise and seek to address key questions for the realisation of

[86] See D Weldon, 'There is An Alternative—Unlock the Surplus' (2011) 175 *Red Pepper* 18, who notes, at 19, that at the height of the first phase of the recession in 2009 'UK non financial corporations were holding cash and bank deposits worth £652.4 billion pounds with UK banks'. See also the various alternatives to austerity and proposals for the socialisation of forgone tax revenues in Blackburn, 'Crisis 2.0' above n 17; D Whitfield, *In Place of Austerity* (Nottingham, Spokesman, 2012) 64–115.

[87] See A Marquetti, CE Schonerwald da Silva and A Campbell, 'Participatory Economic Democracy in Action: Participatory Budgeting in Porto Alegre, 1989–2004' (2012) 44 *Review of Radical Political Economics* 62.

[88] S Hertel and L Minkler, 'Economic Rights: The Terrain' in S Hertel and L Minkler (eds), *Economic Rights: Conceptual, Measurement and Policy Issues* (Cambridge, Cambridge University Press, 2007) 1, 3.

[89] Ibid 29.

socio-economic rights. For example, the oft-posited spectre of scarcity could be called into question by claiming that the states' obligation to devote the maximum available resources to the realisation of socio-economic rights,[90] is incompatible with a regressive tax system, which places a relatively light burden on the wealthy and tolerates mass tax evasion (or avoidance) by large corporations, thereby reducing the resources available to prioritise the realisation of socio-economic rights.[91]

In the same way, the various cuts which implicate a variety of international human rights principles (the individual entitlement to a minimum core enjoyment of socio-economic rights, the principle against retrogressive measures and the principle against non-discrimination),[92] could be evaluated and judged against the normative standards of such rights and not just be forced through on the basis of adherence to some ostensibly scientific economic necessity.[93] The value of adopting such an approach is that it brings to the fore the reality that, ultimately, budgetary choices are political choices. As a recent initiative by the Vermont Workers' Center, which evaluated the Vermont State budget in light of human rights standards, put it, the cuts to public spending and social programmes are 'not the inevitable by-product of a cyclical downturn, [they] are the result of deliberate budget policies that fail to prioritise the needs and rights of human beings'.[94]

It has to be stressed though, that participatory budgeting is just one proposal, and one framed particularly with the issue of socio-economic rights in mind. In truth, far more radical and thoroughgoing changes to every aspect of our societies would be necessary to move to a situation in which socio-economic rights are enjoyed as a matter of course by the majority of people. Participatory budgeting also has its limitations, one of the most important being that extant participatory budgeting processes are, for the most part, confined to decisions about the distribution of a given pot of funds, whereas truly democratic budgetary decision-making would require deliberation and decision-making about both revenue (taxes etc) and expenditure.[95] Therefore, the claim here is by no means that participatory budgeting is some form of *panacea*; to the contrary, participatory

[90] See Art 2(1) International Covenant on Economic, Social and Cultural Rights.

[91] See Balakrishnan and Elson above n 2, 5; Irvin et al above n 22, 7.

[92] For extensive discussion of the various principles implicated in this context, see QUB Budget Analysis Project, *Budgeting for Economic and Social Rights: A Human Rights Framework* (QUB, Belfast 2010); A Blyberg, 'The Case of the Mislaid Allocation: Economic and Social Rights and Budget Work' (2009) 11(3) *SUR—International Journal on Human Rights* 123; Balakrishnan and Elson above n 2.

[93] As Bellamy Foster and Magdoff argue, the current crisis represents a potentially historic turning point, but how precisely it will play out will hinge on the willingness and ability of 'the great mass of the population [to] decide that economics is really *political* economy, and hence theirs to choose': Bellamy Foster and Magdoff above n 7, 9.

[94] Vermont Workers' Center, *People's Budget Report: Preliminary Findings* (Vermont, 2010) 3: www.workerscenter.org/sites/default/files/People's%20Budget%20Report.pdf.

[95] As Blackburn argues: 'If it is to have real substance, economic democracy should be about organizing wealth production as well as disposal of the wider economic surplus': Blackburn, 'Economic Democracy' above n 1, 42.

budgeting is subject to capture and distortion, just as any other discourse or practice is in the context of existing social power relations.[96] However, at least by beginning to think about budgetary processes (about decisions as to how revenue is raised and dispersed, as to what projects to prioritise in society and, ultimately, about the proper distribution of wealth and power) we can start to break with the stranglehold of neoliberal orthodoxy and confidently assert that there is an alternative to austerity, immiseration and the undermining of socio-economic rights.

V. Conclusion

There is no denying the value added to the discourse of human rights—in particular of socio-economic rights—by an analysis of the budgetary processes that so fundamentally affect these rights. Likewise, it would be a step in the right direction if existing budgetary processes begin to take into account the interests associated with human rights.[97] However, honing one or other of these analyses, or even better again refining a combined analysis involving them both, is no substitute for substantive, normative political judgements.[98] At the end of the day, our views on issues such as tax, resource allocation and priorities for public expenditure turn on our substantive vision of the sort of society that we want to see. So, if you are persuaded by the neoliberal promise of the eventual trickle-down of wealth and self-satisfaction, then you might not be inclined towards arguments for the democratisation and politicisation of budgetary processes with a view to placing the language of socio-economic rights at the centre of them.

If, on the other hand, you are committed to a society in which the full and free development of each individual is nurtured and facilitated through democratically accountable and egalitarian social processes[99]—and you are disinclined to accept that 'the magic of *laissez-faire*' is likely to deliver this[100]—then you will be more open to proposals for radical democratic and egalitarian institutional reforms, which seek to institute an alternative social vision, more in tune with the

[96] The recent example of local residents in the UK being given the choice as to which of their public services should be cut, and which should be spared, is just one example of how the ideas of participatory budgeting could be captured and distorted: see R Wilson, 'The Local Residents Given Control of Budgets' *The Guardian* (London, 27 October 2010).

[97] See Balakrishnan, Elson and Patel above n 58, 28–29.

[98] The current crisis has brought to the fore some stark realities about the status of socio-economic rights in even the most developed countries, and as Albo, Gindin and Panitch argue, what is needed in response to this crisis are 'not technical solutions to capitalist economic crises, but political ones that challenge property rights in the name of democratic and social rights': Albo, Gindin and Panitch above n 46, 10.

[99] These criteria for a democratic and egalitarian society are borrowed from Wright above n 8, 13–20.

[100] This phrase is taken from Jan Aart Scholte; see JA Scholte, *Globalisation: A Critical Introduction*, 2nd edn (London, Palgrave Macmillan, 2005) 213.

substantive realisation of socio-economic rights, and, indeed, all human rights. The present period, therefore, presents us with both challenges and opportunities, but also tough choices; for while the global human rights movement has, for the most part, heretofore remained agnostic about the type of social, economic and political system that could deliver on the promises of human rights,[101] the current conjuncture may mean that such neutrality is no longer feasible.[102] As Saiz rightly puts it:

> The economic crisis has exposed the bankruptcy of values by which we have chosen to order our societies. It has therefore opened the space for debate about principles: the principles which should underpin our economic order; the principles guiding the regulatory role of the state; and the principles on which institutions of international economic governance should be based.[103]

The contemporary economic crisis and concomitant age of austerity have caused the mask to slip, and to reveal that behind the formal commitments to socio-economic rights and protecting the needs of the 'most vulnerable', lies a set of economic and ideological presuppositions which invariably militate against such stated commitments. If the substantive protection of socio-economic rights is to stand any chance in the future, these presuppositions need to be challenged in each and every forum, in particular in the arenas in which the crucial decisions about national revenue and expenditure are made.

[101] Eg, the former UN Special Rapporteur on the Right to Health, Paul Hunt, has argued that, subject to certain caveats, 'International human rights law takes a position neither for nor against any particular trade rule or policy'. See P Hunt, 'Report of the Special Rapporteur on the right of everyone to the enjoyment of the highest attainable standard of physical and mental health—Mission to the World Trade Organisation' (UN Doc E/CN.4/2004/49/Add.1), para 11.

[102] See Balakrishnan, Elson and Patel above n 58, 28, who note that neoliberal orthodoxy firmly entrenches structural denials of socio-economic rights, and that seeking to meaningfully advance the cause of socio-economic rights will require breaking with this orthodoxy.

[103] Saiz above n 53, 280.

4

Resourcing Rights: Combating Tax Injustice from a Human Rights Perspective

IGNACIO SAIZ*

I. Introduction

Taxation is a rarely explored topic on the human rights agenda, yet it is one of the most important policy instruments governments can deploy to generate the resources needed to realise the full range of human rights. This chapter looks at tax as a human rights issue, and explores how inequitable tax policies can be assessed and challenged from the perspective of human rights principles and standards.

The chapter begins by highlighting three central functions of taxation from a human rights perspective: its role in generating the 'maximum available resources' to finance human rights-related expenditure; its potential role in redistributing resources in order to mitigate and redress social inequalities; and its role in cementing the bonds of accountability between state and citizen. The author argues that it is particularly critical to bring taxation under the lens of human rights scrutiny in the wake of the global financial and economic crises, and the international community's failure to meet many of the Millennium Development Goals (MDGs), contexts which have brought to the fore the need to bolster the resourcing, redistributive and accountability functions of taxation.

In doing so, the author highlights two recent examples of the application of human rights analysis to domestic tax policy, drawing on the experience of the Center for Economic and Social Rights (CESR) in tracing the link between inadequate revenue generation and poor human development outcomes in Guatemala, and assessing the human rights impact of fiscal austerity measures adopted in Europe in the aftermath of recession. The author concludes with some reflections on further opportunities for linking human rights and tax justice advocacy at the

* The author wishes to thank Gaby Oré Aguilar, Nicholas Lusiani and Emily Button Aguilar for their invaluable help in researching and editing this chapter.

international as well as national level, including the potential for human rights principles to strengthen the case for a global financial transactions tax and more effective action against international tax evasion.

II. Fiscal Policy and the Resourcing of Rights

The effective protection of all human rights—whether civil, political, economic, social or cultural—has resource implications. Training law enforcement officials in the prevention of torture, combating gender stereotypes in society or guaranteeing defendants a fair trial all involve the creation of state institutions and programmes which require a considerable investment of public funds. Yet, as argued elsewhere in this volume, the question of resources is particularly critical to the fulfilment of economic, social and cultural rights (ESC rights), since a country's ability to ensure the conditions in which these rights can be fully realised will be conditioned to a great extent by the resources it has at its disposal to fund the requisite public services and social policy interventions.[1]

Article 2(1) of the International Covenant on Economic, Social and Cultural Rights (ICESCR) places an obligation on each State Party to the Covenant

> to take steps, individually and through international assistance and co-operation, especially economic and technical, to the maximum of its available resources, with a view to achieving progressively the full realisation of the rights recognised in the present Covenant by all appropriate means, including particularly the adoption of legislative measures.[2]

Despite its ungainly phrasing, Article 2(1) articulates what should be seen as a fundamental tenet of economic and social policymaking: that advancing swiftly towards the fulfilment of these rights is an obligation of all states, regardless of their level of development, and that in order to do so they must deploy the maximum resources they can generate domestically and, where necessary, through international cooperation and assistance.[3] A lack of adequate resources cannot

[1] See Elson, Balakrishnan and Heintz, ch 1 in this volume.

[2] International Covenant on Economic, Social and Cultural Rights (ICESCR), adopted by UN General Assembly resolution 2200, 16 December 1966, Art 2(1).

[3] The normative scope and content of the principle of progressive realisation according to the maximum of available resources has been addressed in a number of General Comments issued by the United Nations treaty bodies. See in particular UN Committee on Economic, Social and Cultural Rights, ComESCR, General Comment No 3 on the nature of States parties' obligations (art 2 (1)), UN Doc E/1991/23 (1990). It has been further elucidated in the case law of several jurisdictions around the world. See International Network for Economic, Social and Cultural Rights, 'Database of Economic, Social and Cultural Rights Related Jurisprudence, Cases and Other Decisions': www.escr-net.org/caselaw. The content of Art 2(1) ICESCR has also been the subject of extensive legal scholarship. See eg, M Sepúlveda, *The Nature of the Obligations under the International Covenant on Economic, Social and Cultural Rights* (Antwerp, Intersentia, 2003) ch 7.

be invoked by any state as an excuse for inaction in the face of deprivations of economic and social rights (ESR).[4]

The principle of 'progressive realisation', with its apparent underlying premise of linear progress fuelled by increasing growth and ever expanding resources, may seem ill-suited to our current age of economic recession and fiscal retrenchment. Yet it is particularly important to ensure it is given effect to in times of economic downturn. As affirmed by the Committee on Economic, Social and Cultural Rights (the Committee)—the UN expert body which monitors compliance by States Parties with the provisions of the Covenant—even in times of resource constraints, all states have a duty to move as expeditiously and effectively as possible towards the goal of fully realising all rights.[5] Any deliberately retrogressive measures require strict justification and must be carefully considered with regard to the totality of rights set forth in the Covenant.[6] In straightened circumstances, states must demonstrate that every effort has been made to use all resources at their disposal to satisfy as a matter of priority their minimum core human rights obligations, to take deliberate and targeted measures to safeguard the rights of vulnerable members of the population and to ensure the widest possible enjoyment of rights in the prevailing circumstances.[7]

Much attention has rightly been paid to the essential role of international cooperation in helping resource-constrained states to fulfil their economic, social and cultural rights obligations. As the Committee has emphasised,

> in the absence of an active programme of international assistance and cooperation on the part of all those States that are in a position to undertake one, the full realisation

[4] ComESCR General Comment No 3, para 10.

[5] Ibid paras 9 and 11.

[6] Ibid para 9. The Committee has since elaborated on the concept of non-retrogression in other General Comments, including those on the rights to housing (ComESCR General Comment No 4 on the right to adequate housing, UN Doc E/1992/23) Annex iii, 114 (1991), para 11; health (ComESCR General Comment No 14 on the right to the highest attainable standard of health (art 12), UN Doc E/C.12/2000/4 (2000), para 32); and social security (ComESCR General Comment No 19 on the right to social security, UN Doc E/C.12/GC/19), para 42), as well as in a recent letter to States Parties to the ICESCR from the ComESCR Chairperson, AG Pillay following its 48th session in May 2012. Committee on Economic, Social and Cultural Rights, 'Letter from ComESCR Chairperson to States Parties in the context of the economic and financial crisis', CESCR/48th/SP/MAB/SW, 16 May 2012: www2.ohchr.org/english/bodies/cescr/docs/LetterCESCRtoSP16.05.12.pdf. For further analysis of the concept of non-retrogression in international human rights law, see C Courtis (ed), *Ni Un Paso Atrás, La Prohibición de Regresividad en Materia de Derechos Sociales* (Buenos Aires, Del Puerto, 2006) and Sepulveda above n 3.

[7] ComESCR General Comment No 3, paras 10–12. See also the Committee's 2007 statement, 'An Evaluation of the Obligation to Take Steps to the Maximum of Available Resources under an Optional Protocol to the Covenant', UN Doc E/C.12/2007/1 (2007), para 4. The duty to satisfy minimum core obligations irrespective of the level of resources is reaffirmed in the Maastricht Guidelines on Violations of Economic, Social and Cultural Rights drawn up by a group of international experts convened by the International Commission of Jurists and Maastricht University in January 1997, paras 9 and 10: www1.umn.edu/humanrts/instree/Maastrichtguidelines.html.

of economic, social and cultural rights will remain an unfulfilled aspiration in many countries.[8]

Nevertheless, this obligation in no way absolves states of their primary duty to organise and deploy the resources domestically available to them. Fiscal policy—referring to the use of government revenue collection and expenditure to influence the economy[9]—is one of the key policy instruments states have to shape the conditions in which all human rights, and particularly ESR, can be fulfilled.

III. Tax as a Human Rights Issue

Within the human rights community, there have been growing efforts over the last decade to analyse budgetary processes and assess the allocation of resources in light of human rights criteria.[10] Rights-based budget analysis has been part of a broader trend towards greater oversight of how public funds are spent, in order to bring about greater accountability and transparency in policymaking.[11] Although the wealth of experience from different parts of the world makes it difficult to generalise, budget analysis from a human rights perspective has tended to involve assessing the adequacy of public expenditure on specific sectors, such as health or education, as well as the equity or fairness of budgetary allocations in terms of their distributional impacts on disadvantaged population groups such as women or indigenous people.[12]

Less attention has traditionally been paid from a human rights perspective to the revenue side of the fiscal policy equation. For example, as highlighted in the chapter by Elson, Balakrishnan and Heintz in this volume, two key treaty body statements from 2007 analysing the meaning of 'maximum available resources' under Article 2(1) ICESCR and Article 4 of the UN Convention on the Rights of

[8] ComESCR General Comment No 3, para 14. The content of the obligation to provide international cooperation and assistance for the realisation of ESC rights has been further articulated in the Maastricht Principles on the Extra-Territorial Obligations of States in the area of Economic, Social and Cultural Rights, drafted by a group of 40 distinguished experts in international law and human rights from around the world convened by the International Commission of Jurists and Maastricht University in February 2012. See, in particular, Principles 28–35: www.maastrichtuniversity.nl/web/Institutes/MaastrichtCentreForHumanRights/MaastrichtETOPrinciples.htm.

[9] A O'Sullivan and SM Sheffrin, *Economics: Principles in Action* (New Jersey, Pearson, 2003) 387.

[10] For more on human rights-based budget work, see the contributions by Nolan, Rooney and Dutschke in this volume.

[11] See M Robinson (ed), *Budgeting for the Poor* (Basingstoke, Palgrave Macmillan, 2008) for an analytical overview of the field of civil society budget work.

[12] For a selective overview of budget work across the globe, including human rights-based analysis, see International Budget Partnership (IBP), 'Who Does Budget Work: Case Studies': internationalbudget.org/who-does-budget-work/case-studies. On budget analysis from a women's rights perspective, see D Elson, *Budgeting for Women's Rights: Monitoring Government Budgets for Compliance with CEDAW* (New York, UNIFEM, 2006).

the Child do not address the issue of taxation as a means of resource generation, focusing largely on budget allocations and international assistance.[13] International human rights standards grant governments a wide margin of discretion in matters of economic and social policy, acknowledging that they are often faced with invidious choices regarding the resources to be assigned to competing social policy priorities within their existing budgetary constraints.[14] This may in part account for the traditional reluctance of human rights adjudication and oversight mechanisms to weigh in on politically contentious aspects of fiscal policy such as taxation.

Increasingly, however, voices from within the international human rights system as well as from the broader human rights movement have begun to raise concerns that inadequate efforts to generate more resources for the public coffers can pose a serious obstacle to the realisation of human rights.[15] In particular, a number of UN Special Rapporteurs with mandates focused on economic, social and cultural rights have highlighted the role of taxation in creating conditions in which all can enjoy these rights.[16] Similarly, other UN human rights experts have warned that inadequate revenue generation can also jeopardise civil and political rights, where for example the effective administration of justice is undermined through under-resourcing of the judicial or law enforcement systems.[17]

Taxation can be seen as having several essential functions of great relevance to states' human rights obligations. First, and most obviously, as described above, taxation has a *resourcing* function, enabling investment in public services and programmes in areas such as health, education, housing, justice, security social protection, transport and communications.[18] For most states, taxation is the primary

[13] See ComESCR, 'An Evaluation of the Obligation to Take Steps to the "Maximum of Available Resources"' above n 7 and Committee on the Rights of the Child, 'Day of General Discussion—Resources for the Rights of the Child: Responsibility of States', 46th Session (2007).

[14] The Optional Protocol to the International Covenant on Economic, Social and Cultural Rights recognises that a 'State Party may adopt a range of possible policy measures for the implementation of the rights set forth in the Covenant': Optional Protocol to the International Covenant on Economic, Social and Cultural Rights, adopted by the UN General Assembly on 10 December 2008, art 8(4).

[15] See eg, ComESCR, 'Concluding Observations: Hong Kong', UN Doc E/C.12/1/Add. 58 (2001), para 14; ComRC, 'Concluding Observations: Georgia', UN Doc CRC/C/15/Add. 124 (2000), paras 18–19, followed up in CRC/C/15/ADD.222 (CRC, 2003); and on Guatemala, CRC/C/GTM/CO/3-4 (CRC, 2010), paras 25 and 26.

[16] See D Türk, 'Report of the Special Rapporteur on the Realisation of Economic, Social and Cultural Rights, (UN Doc E/CN.4/Sub.2/1992/16), para 83; M Sepúlveda Carmona, 'Report of the Independent Expert on the question of human rights and extreme poverty on the human rights based approach to recovery from the global economic and financial crises, with a focus on those living in poverty' (UN Doc A/HRC/17/34), paras 80–81 (on the obstacle posed by low levels of taxation to the protection of the human rights of those living in poverty in the context of the global economic crises); and A Grover 'Report of the Special Rapporteur on the right of everyone to the enjoyment of the highest attainable standard of physical and mental health' (UN Doc A/67/302), para 15 (on the role of progressive taxation in financing of the right to health).

[17] See eg, P Alston, 'Report of the UN Special Rapporteur on Extrajudicial, Summary or Arbitrary Executions, Mission to Guatemala' (A/HRC/4/20/Add.2), para 61.

[18] M Todaro, and S Smith, *Economic Development* (Harlow, Pearson, 2006) 762.

source of public resource generation.[19] It is therefore one of the critical areas of policy to interrogate when assessing whether states are drawing on the maximum of available resources,[20] and an indispensable policy instrument for mobilising additional public resources without necessarily sacrificing spending priorities, thereby expanding what economists refer to as 'fiscal space'.[21] In many countries, both north and south, it is not simply a question of assessing how the budgetary pie has been divided up, but of questioning the size of the pie.

Second, taxation has a potentially *redistributive* function, providing mechanisms for transferring and redistributing wealth from upper to lower income groups so as to reduce income inequalities and disparities in human rights enjoyment that flow from these.[22] Redistributive tax measures are thus part of the arsenal of measures that states should deploy to tackle and redress systemic discrimination, and to ensure universal access to ESR.[23] Taxation has been shown to be a key determinant of gender inequality in the enjoyment of ESR, as tax structures frequently discriminate against women directly or indirectly, whether in their formulation or impact.[24] While eliminating adverse discrimination in the economic and social sphere is a human rights imperative in its own right,[25] the existence of stark social inequalities is a factor fuelling societies' vulnerability to conflict and political instability, contexts in which an even broader range of rights are put at risk.[26]

[19] M Moore, 'How Does Taxation Affect The Quality of Governance?' (2007) Institute of Development Studies Working Paper 280, 14. The exceptions are the few states which obtain a larger proportion of their revenue from natural resource export surpluses or from international development assistance.

[20] See R Balakrishnan, D Elson, J Heintz and N Lusiani, *Maximum Available Resources and Human Rights: Analytical Report* (New Jersey, Center for Women's Global Leadership, Rutgers University, 2011). Balakrishnan et al identify taxation as one of five points in the 'Maximum Available Resources (MAR) Star', along with public spending, monetary and debt policy and international cooperation.

[21] I Ortiz, J Chai and M Cummins, 'Identifying Fiscal Space: Options for Social and Economic Development for Children and Poor Households in 184 Countries' (2011) Social and Economic Policy Working Paper (New York, UNICEF) 7–16. On the concept of 'fiscal space' and its relationship to the principle of progressive realisation according to maximum available resources under Art 2(1) ICESCR, see Elson, Balakrishnan and Heintz, ch 1 in this volume.

[22] Türk, 'Report of the Special Rapporteur' above n 16, para 83. On the role of progressive taxation policies in reducing inequalities, see I Ortiz and M Cummins, *Global Inequality: Beyond the Bottom Billion: A rapid review of income distribution in 141 countries* (UNICEF, New York, 2011) 38–45.

[23] On the links between progressive fiscal policy, the reduction of inequality and promoting universal access to social rights, see M Hopenhayn, *Desigualdades Sociales y Derechos Humanos: Hacia un Pacto de Protección Social* (Santiago, CEPAL, 2006).

[24] See Elson above n 12, 69–103.

[25] Art 2(2) ICESCR obliges each State Party to guarantee that all Covenant rights are exercised without discrimination of any kind. The General Comments of the Committee on Economic, Social and Cultural Rights analyse the application of this principle to specific Covenant rights. ComESCR General Comment 20 on non-discrimination provides further clarification of the Committee's understanding of the normative content and scope of Art 2(2). See ComESCR General Comment No 20 on Non-discrimination in economic, social and cultural rights, UN Doc E/C.12/GC/20 (2009).

[26] On the role of taxation in tackling inequalities and mitigating the risk of social conflicts, see F Stewart, G Brown and A Cobham, 'The Implications of Horizontal and Vertical Inequalities for Tax and Expenditure Policies' (2009) Crise Working Paper 65 (Centre for Research on Inequality, Human Security and Ethnicity).

Taxation also has an *accountability* function, helping to promote social citizenship and responsive government. Drawing on an extensive body of thought on the role played by taxation in the emergence of the modern state, recent development practice has increasingly focused on taxation as a manifestation of the social contract between state and citizen, and as a means of strengthening accountable governance.[27] Taxation incentivises those in power to promote citizen prosperity and to develop institutional capability, while motivating taxpayers to scrutinise how revenue is used and engage in public policy deliberation.[28] Its central role in state-building is thus seen as residing in two principal areas: the rise of a social contract based on bargaining around tax; and the institution-building stimulus provided by the revenue imperative, fostering accountability, capability and responsiveness of state institutions.[29] Research suggests that states which get their primary revenues from sources other than taxation of their citizens—for example from natural resource exploitation or heavy dependence on foreign aid donors—tend to be more corrupt, conflict-ridden, authoritarian, poorer, more unequal, and have lower long-term economic growth, whereas governments which are dependent to a greater extent on domestic taxes for their revenue have incentives to be more answerable to taxpayers.[30]

Human rights concerns are particularly likely to occur where a country's tax structures and policies undermine these resourcing, distributive and accountability functions. The need to bolster these functions of taxation has increasingly come to the fore in recent years, as the international community takes stock of the slow progress made in meeting the MDGs agreed at the turn of the century,[31] and as countries of the global north and south struggle to recover from the impact of the global financial and economic crises. One of the key lessons learnt from the current MDG process is that greater attention must be paid to the role of domestic resource mobilisation as a key determinant of poverty eradication efforts in developing countries.[32] This is all the more pertinent as economic recession in donor

[27] See eg, Moore, 'How Does Taxation Affect the Quality of Governance?' above n 19; and D Brautigam, OH Fjeldstad and M Moore (eds), *Taxation and State-Building in Developing Countries: Capacity and Consent* (Cambridge, Cambridge University Press, 2008).

[28] Moore, 'How Does Taxation Affect the Quality of Governance?' above n 19, 17.

[29] D Brautigam, 'Taxation and State Building in Developing Countries' above n 27, 1.

[30] Brautigam above n 29. See also ML Ross, 'Does Taxation Lead to Representation?' (2004) 34 *British Journal of Political Science* 229.

[31] On the progress made in meeting the Millennium Development Goals, see United Nations, *The Millennium Development Goals Report 2012* (New York, UN, 2012).

[32] In 2005 the Millennium Campaign projected that the increased investments needed to achieve the MDGs could be financed through domestic resource mobilisation in developing countries through a four per-cent increase in tax revenue as a percentage of GDP. See UN Millennium Campaign, 'Resources Required to Finance the Millennium Development Goals', in *Investing in Development: A Practical Plan to Achieve the MDGs* (UN Millennium Campaign, 2005). In the outcome document of the MDG Review Summit in September 2010, states resolved to enhance and strengthen domestic resource mobilisation and fiscal space through more efficient tax collection, broadening the tax base and effectively combating tax evasion and capital flight. See 'Keeping the Promise: United to Achieve the Millennium Development Goals', resolution adopted by the UN General Assembly at its 64th session, 17 September 2010, UN Doc. A/65/L.1, 30.

countries threatens to reduce levels of official development assistance (ODA), and as the incidence of poverty is increasingly to be found in middle-income developing countries less reliant on ODA.[33]

In many developing countries, the resourcing function has been undermined because weak and ineffective tax systems continue to yield a far smaller tax base than in industrialised countries, meaning that the amount of revenue generated for the public coffers is often insufficient to enable adequate investment in areas of public spending critical for the fulfilment of human development objectives.[34] More than 20 low-income countries still have tax ratios (tax revenue relative to Gross Domestic Product (GDP)) below 15 per cent, and in no region has there been a significant increase in the average tax ratio over the last three decades, other than in Latin America and the Caribbean.[35] Tax yields have also reduced in many industrialised as well as developing countries as a result of rising unemployment and declining consumption in the wake of the global economic crisis, exacerbating their fiscal deficits and prompting further reductions in areas of social spending essential to the realisation of ESR.[36]

The redistributive function of taxation has also been undermined where tax reforms implemented in the context of development or economic recovery strategies are regressive, falling disproportionately on lower-income quintiles and therefore aggravating social inequalities instead of reducing them.[37] Tax reforms promoted by the World Bank and International Monetary Fund (IMF) in developing countries since the 1980s have tended to favour the introduction or expansion of indirect taxation (in particular through value added taxes or VAT) and reductions in the rates of corporate and personal income taxation.[38] Taxation regimes which rely heavily on indirect taxes on consumption rather than direct income taxes are often regressive, ie, they place a greater burden on the poor and may be discriminatory in effect, particularly if proper exemptions and other safeguards are not in place and if tax is applied to items of mass consumption such as basic

[33] See A Sumner, 'Global Poverty and the New Bottom Billion: Three Quarters of the World's Poor Live in Middle-income Countries', Institute of Development Studies Working Paper 349, November 2010.

[34] See International Monetary Fund (IMF), *Revenue Mobilisation in Developing Countries*, March 2011; T Minh Le, B Moreno-Dodson and J Rajchaichanintham, *Expanding Taxable Capacity and Reaching Revenue Potential: Cross-country Analysis*, World Bank Working Paper (2008).

[35] IMF, *Revenue Mobilisation* above n 34, 7.

[36] See I Ortiz and M Cummins (eds), *A Recovery for All: Rethinking Socio-Economic Policies for Children and Poor Households* (New York, UNICEF, 2012). See also J Brondolo, 'Collecting Taxes during an Economic Crisis: Challenges and Policy Options', IMF Fiscal Affairs Dept, Staff Position Note July 2009: www.imf.org/external/pubs/ft/spn/2009/spn0917.pdf.

[37] D Itriago, *Owning Development: Taxation to Fight Poverty* (Oxfam International, Oxford, 2011).

[38] See M Ruiz, R Sharpe and MJ Romero, *Approaches and Impacts: IFI Tax Policy in Developing Countries* (Eurodad/ActionAid, 2011): www.actionaid.org.uk/doc_lib/ifi_tax_policy_developing_countries.pdf.

foods, clothing and household utensils.[39] For example, the UN Special Rapporteur on the Right to Food noted that tax rates in Brazil were comparatively high for goods and services and low for income and property, with the inequitable result that government social programmes 'are essentially funded by the very persons whom they seek to benefit, as the regressive system of taxation seriously limits the redistributive aspect of the programmes'.[40]

Direct taxation on income and property is generally considered more progressive, in that the amount deducted rises proportionate to income.[41] Yet personal income taxes still yield much less revenue as a proportion of GDP in developing countries than in OECD (Organisation for Economic Co-operation and Development) countries.[42] Indirect taxation such as value added taxes on sales and import, export and excise duties on commodities constitutes the primary source of fiscal revenue in least developed countries.[43] Data also suggest that the contribution of consumption taxes to overall revenue increased in middle-income countries from around 10 per cent of GDP in 2000 to 14 per cent in 2009, with a slightly lower increase for lower-income countries.[44] The comparative ease and efficiency of collecting indirect taxes on sales and commodities, as opposed to income, is often advanced as one of the reasons why these account for such a large proportion of public revenues in many developing countries, yet the evidence for this is conflicting.[45]

On the other hand, corporate tax benefits have tended to be ring-fenced and safeguarded in tax reforms promoted by international financial institutions, both in the context of development assistance to low income countries and in rescue packages to countries facing fiscal deficits.[46] Corporate tax incentives, concessions and exemptions offered to companies in a bid to attract and retain investment deprive many countries of potentially available resources for human rights realisation. Developing countries across all regions decreased commercial tax rates, on

[39] See OECD, 'Income Inequality and Growth: The Role of Taxes and Transfers', OECD Economics Department Policy Notes, No 9, January 2012. Ortiz and Cummins, *A Recovery for All* above n 36, 242. As Ortiz and Cummins point out, consumption taxes can be progressively designed by allowing exemptions for basic goods such as fuel or food staples, while setting higher rates for luxury goods that are consumed principally by wealthier sectors, such as certain types of car or alcoholic beverages, or goods with negative public health effects such as tobacco: ibid 246.

[40] O de Schutter, 'Report of the Special Rapporteur on the Right to Food—Mission to Brazil' (UN Doc A/HRC/13/33/Add.6, 2009), para 36.

[41] Ortiz and Cummins, *A Recovery for All* above n 36, 247.

[42] J Stiglitz, 'Development-oriented Tax Policy' (2008) Initiative for Policy Dialogue Working Paper Series, (Columbia University) 7: academiccommons.columbia.edu/catalog/ac:126733. See also, IMF above n 34, 31.

[43] Todaro and Smith above n 18, 760.

[44] Ortiz and Cummins, *A Recovery for All* above n 36, 245.

[45] Joseph Stiglitz, for example, argues that in many developing countries VAT is not an efficient tax and can undermine growth and fuel unemployment. See Stiglitz, 'Development-oriented Tax Policy' above n 42, 9. The IMF, on the other hand, finds VAT to be a 'relatively efficient' instrument and that its distributional impact is 'benign'. See IMF, *Revenue Mobilisation* above n 34, 25.

[46] Ortiz and Cummins, *A Recovery for All* above n 36, 248.

average, between 2005 and 2010.[47] The argument that lowering corporate taxes is a prerequisite for encouraging business investment and entrepreneurial activity is increasingly being questioned based on the experience of many countries which have dramatically cut corporate tax rates without seeing corresponding benefits in economic activity and ability to invest in human and social development.[48] Analysts increasingly converge on the conclusion that other factors play a more decisive role in determining investment decisions.[49] In the case of multinational foreign enterprises, the ability of developing countries to collect substantial taxes is frustrated where locally run enterprises are able to shift profits to affiliates in countries offering lower levels of taxation through transfer pricing (artificially inflating the price paid for intermediate products purchased from overseas affiliates so as to lower stated local profits). Estimates place the loss of revenue resulting from transfer pricing at scores of millions of dollars.[50]

Such imbalances and inequities in the tax structure often reflect broader deficits in democratic governance, which result in tax systems skewed in favour of wealthy economic elites or powerful business interests rather than accountable to the ordinary citizen. For example, in countries where the ownership of property is heavily concentrated and therefore represents a major determinant of inequality, property taxes can be an efficient and administratively simple mechanism, both for generating public revenues and correcting gross inequalities in income distribution.[51] Nevertheless, the share of property taxes has not increased in the majority of developing countries in recent decades, a fact attributable to the political influence of large landowning elites in many regions.[52]

Entrenched cultures of 'elite capture' not only permit the lawful avoidance of taxes by those able to influence fiscal policy decisions. They encourage large-scale tax evasion by the wealthiest sectors of the population.[53] Estimates by the Tax Justice Network based on World Bank data indicate that US$3.1 trillion is lost annually to tax evasion globally; Africa is estimated to lose tax revenues amounting to approximately US$79 billion annually, representing 98 per cent of total health care expenditures for that continent, while in Bolivia, tax losses due to evasion were estimated at over four times the annual health care budget.[54]

[47] Ibid.

[48] Ibid. On challenges to orthodox economic assumptions regarding the benefits of low tax rates, see generally JE Stiglitz, *The Price of Inequality, How Today's Divided Society Endangers Our Future* (New York, Norton, 2012) and J Quiggin, *Zombie Economics: How Dead Ideas Still Walk Among Us* (Princeton, Princeton University Press, 2010).

[49] IMF, *Revenue Mobilisation* above n 34, 35.

[50] See Christian Aid, *False Profits: Robbing the Poor to Keep the Rich Tax-free*, (March 2009).

[51] Todaro and Smith above n 18, 762.

[52] Ibid.

[53] See J Henry, *The Price of Offshore Revisited* (Tax Justice Network, 2012): www.taxjustice.net/cms/upload/pdf/Price_of_Offshore_Revisited_120722.pdf.

[54] See Tax Justice Network, *The Cost of Tax Abuse: A Briefing Paper on the Cost of Tax Evasion Worldwide* (Tax Justice Network, 2011): www.tackletaxhavens.com/Cost_of_Tax_Abuse_TJN%20Research_23rd_Nov_2011.pdf. See also D Kar and S Freitas, *Illicit Financial Flows from Developing Countries 2001–2010* (Global Financial Integrity, 2012) 27 which estimates that US$859 billion in

The weakness of tax administration systems, particularly in developing countries, undermines their effectiveness in dealing with large-scale tax evasion and thus expanding the tax base. The perception of tax administration systems as corrupt, unfair and inefficient fosters greater tax secrecy on the part of the citizen and lack of transparency on the part of the state, undermining faith in taxation as an expression of the social contract linking both in a bond of mutual accountability.[55]

The following sections highlight how human rights analysis can be brought to bear in specific contexts to address the failure of taxation policy to fulfil its resourcing, redistributive and accountability functions, as described above. Drawing on research and advocacy carried out by the Center for Economic and Social Rights, they look at the application of human rights analysis to taxation in two different contexts: the impact of inadequate tax mobilisation in Guatemala, a low-to-middle income country, on the country's human development objectives and on its population's basic ESR; and the failure to put in place equitable tax policies in response to the fiscal deficits created by the economic crises in Ireland and Spain.

IV. Tax and Stunted Human Development: The 'Rights or Privileges' Project in Guatemala

In the project, *Rights or Privileges? Fiscal Commitment to the Rights to Health, Education and Food in Guatemala*, CESR and the Instituto Centroamericano de Estudios Fiscales (ICEFI) developed and applied a rights-based framework for holding the Guatemalan State accountable for the role that its tax and budget policies played in stunting the fulfilment of ESR in the country.[56] A collaboration between an international human rights organisation and a Central American civil society organisation specialising in monitoring fiscal policies, the project aimed to assess Guatemala's development efforts through the lens of its human rights obligations. Taking as its starting point the country's astonishingly high rates of maternal death, child stunting (an indicator of chronic malnutrition) and primary school incompletion, the project sought in particular to interrogate the State's efforts

revenues is lost annually due to illicit financial flows, including tax avoidance, tax evasion and other forms of financial crime and corruption.

[55] See Brautigam above n 29; Moore, 'How Does Taxation Affect the Quality of Governance?' above n 19.

[56] See Center for Economic and Social Rights and Instituto Centroamericano de Estudios Fiscales (CESR/ICEFI), *Rights or Privileges? Fiscal Commitment to the Rights to Health, Education and Food in Guatemala*, Executive Summary (Guatemala City/Madrid, CESR/ICEFI, 2009). The full study is available in Spanish as *Derechos o Privilegios? El Compromiso Fiscal con La Salud, La Educación y La Alimentación en Guatemala*. Both are available at: www.cesr.org/guatemala. The footnote references below refer to the English version.

to generate the maximum of its potentially available resources to progressively fulfil the rights to reproductive health, food and education. Tax analysis was an integral part of a more holistic assessment of Guatemala's compliance with its obligations under Article 2(1) ICESCR.

Despite being a middle-income country with the largest economy in Central America, Guatemala's human development indicators are alarming, with more than half the population living below the national poverty line and one in seven Guatemalans living in extreme poverty.[57] The country has among the highest rates of child malnutrition, maternal mortality and child primary incompletion in Latin America, despite these issues having been declared a national priority for many years by successive governments in Guatemala, and the renewed commitments made in the context of the MDGs.[58] The persistence of systemic inequality and discrimination could be partially explained by the legacy of almost 40 years of armed conflict. Nevertheless, the study was motivated by the conviction that the dismal state of ESC rights in Guatemala could not be attributed solely to limited state resources, but to inadequate and inequitable fiscal policies which constrain how resources are generated and distributed.

In consultation with development economists and public health experts, CESR and ICEFI devised a methodological framework for assessing the compliance of Guatemala's tax and budget policies with the range of principles applicable to the obligation to fulfil ESR, and in particular the rights to health, education and food.[59] These principles included the duty of states to prioritise minimum core obligations, to use maximum available resources to progressively realise rights, to ensure equality and non-discrimination, to promote the availability, accessibility, acceptability and good quality of relevant social services and to ensure participation, transparency and accountability in the process of policy implementation.[60]

The methodological framework which sought to operationalise these principles consisted of four basic steps, encapsulated in the acronym OPERA. First, Guatemala's maternal health, child nutrition and education outcomes were analysed through the lens of the above principles. Second, the State's policy efforts including legal and policy commitments relating to these rights, were examined, as well as efforts in practice to ensure access to essential social services and programmes. Third, the project analysed the resources assigned to relevant areas of social spending from a human rights perspective, examining tax policies to determine the use of maximum available resources in line with human rights principles. Finally, an overall assessment was made of the State's compliance with

[57] CESR/ICEFI, *Rights or Privileges?* above n 56, 7.

[58] Ibid 11–13.

[59] For a detailed explanation of the methodological framework employed in the study, see Center for Economic and Social Rights, *Assessing Fiscal Policies from a Human Rights Perspective: Methodological Case Study on the Use of Available Resources to Realise Economic, Social and Cultural Rights in Guatemala* (Madrid, CESR, 2012): www.cesr.org/downloads/assessing.fiscal.policies.from.a.human.rights.perspective.pdf.

[60] Ibid 5.

the obligation to fulfil ESC rights, based on a triangulation of the above elements, and taking into account contextual factors and the political constraints faced by the government.[61]

A range of quantitative and qualitative assessment tools was used at each step. For the first step, selected quantitative indicators were identified relating to health/education/nutritional outcomes. Comparisons with other countries in the region, particularly those with similar levels of GDP, were used as benchmarks for assessing whether Guatemala's outcomes could be considered reasonable given its level of resources. A comparative analysis of outcome indicators highlighted how far Guatemala's ESR outcomes at the aggregate level fell below what could be considered 'minimum essential levels' of the rights to health, food and education. By plotting rates of maternal mortality, chronic malnutrition and primary school completion for all countries in the region taking into account their levels of GDP per capita (as a proxy for the country's available resources), the resulting standard deviation line provided a benchmark for quantifying Guatemala's shortfall in respect of regional standards of achievement at comparable levels of resources (see Figure 1).

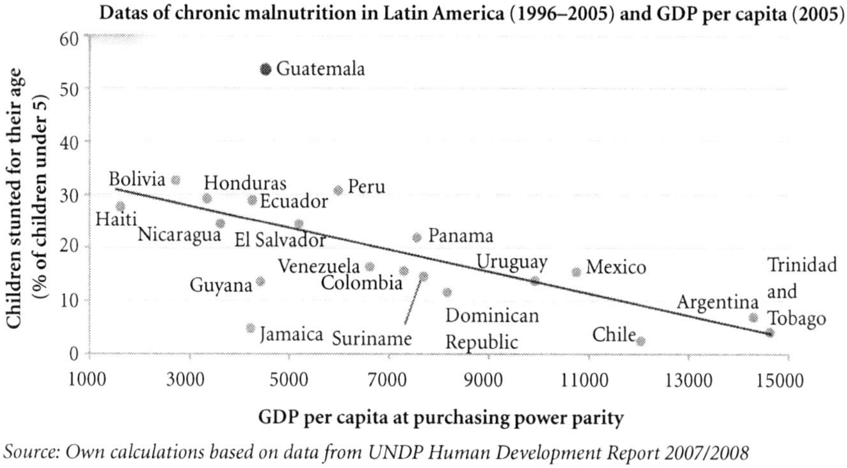

Figure 1: Comparing Right to Food Outcomes in Latin America in Light of Resources

Source: CESR/ICEFI 2009

Indicators were disaggregated where possible to identify disparities along lines of gender, ethnicity, region and socio-economic status, and were tracked over time to

[61] Ibid. For a comprehensive explanation of the OPERA framework and methodology for assessing ESR fulfillment, see Center for Economic and Social Rights, *The OPERA Framework: Assessing Compliance with the Obligation to Fulfill Economic, Social and Cultural Rights* (Madrid, CESR, 2012): www.cesr.org/downloads/the.opera.framework.pdf.

assess their progress.[62] This revealed striking disparities that raised questions about what the State was doing to ensure substantive equality and non-discrimination in access to relevant services. For example, while Guatemala was found to have one of the highest estimated maternal mortality rates in Latin America, indigenous women were three times more likely to die in pregnancy or childbirth.[63] Those who died tended to be poor, rural and uneducated women. Moreover, such disparities had not reduced over time. Progress over time in reducing Guatemala's maternal mortality rate had been much slower than that of poorer countries in the region, flagging a concern regarding efforts to progressively realise the right to maternal health.[64]

In step two, qualitative as well as quantitative methods were also used to analyse the adequacy of policy efforts to combat maternal mortality, school desertion and child malnutrition. This part of the analysis looked first at legal and policy commitments on paper, and the extent to which these reflected relevant international human rights standards. This was done through a combination of desk and field based research.[65] The assessment of policy efforts found a striking contrast between the state's legal and policy commitments, which by and large embodied its international commitments to the rights to health, education and food, and its policies in practice. Across all three areas studied, the scope and coverage of policy interventions was found to be woefully inadequate, failing to meet any reasonable standard of availability, accessibility, cultural acceptability and quality. For example, Guatemala had the same proportion of births attended by skilled personnel as Sierra Leone, one of the world's poorest countries.[66] Disparities in outcomes (for example, variations in maternal mortality rates across regions) were found to correlate with disparities of policy effort. For example, a mapping of obstetric services by region revealed that services were least available in regions with the highest maternal mortality rates.[67]

For the third step of the analysis, in order to understand the resources Guatemala had 'available' to it—and how it had used those resources—it was necessary to examine the system of raising revenue (especially through tax collection) and determining expenditures (including income redistribution and financing of public social services). A range of assessment methods was used to interrogate fiscal policies through the lens of human rights principles (see Figure 2). Budget analysis was used to assess the reasonableness of resource allocations, using international comparisons as a benchmark, longitudinal data to assess changes over

[62] See CESR, *Assessing Fiscal Policies* above n 59, 5–10.

[63] CESR/ICEFI, *Rights or Privileges?* above n 56, 11.

[64] Ibid 12.

[65] Policy efforts were examined by conducting a review of the literature on effective public policy interventions and carrying out interviews with professionals in the health, education and child nutrition sectors, as well as with policymakers in these fields. Case research and interviews were then carried out with individuals and families affected by maternal death, child malnutrition and school desertion in the predominantly indigenous community of Senahú, Alta Verapaz. Group interviews also assessed community members' perceptions of the availability, accessibility, acceptability and quality of social services. For more on the methods used to analyse Guatemala's policy efforts, see CESR, *Assessing Fiscal Policies* above n 59, 12–17.

[66] CESR/ICEFI, *Rights or Privileges?* above n 56, 14–16.

[67] Ibid 12–16.

Element	Human Rights Principles	Types of Assessment Techniques
Evaluate planned and actual resource expenditures	*Core obligations* *Non-discrimination* *Progressive realization according to maximum available resources* *Transparency and accountability*	Calculate the percentage of the state's budget allocated to social spending relevant to specific right, comparing to relevant benchmarks. Identify which population groups are benefitting from spending; contrasting spending disparities with disparities in human rights outcomes. Compare allocations to previous budgets to see how spending has evolved overtime, taking into account economic growth over the period. Track public expenditure (e.g. using PETS, QSDS, or social audits).
Evaluate resource generation	*Progressive realization according to maximum available resources* *Non-discrimination*	Calculate the state budget as a percentage of the overall economy and compare to similar countries. Identify and assess the adequacy and equity of the state's main revenue sources (e.g. taxation, borrowing, international assistance). Evaluate the state's fiscal and/or monetary policies governing the raising of revenue (e.g. identify tax base as % of GDP and track its evolution over time, taking into account economic growth over the period).
Analyze relevant policy processes	*Participation, accountability, transparency*	Collect feedback on public participation in the design, implementation and evaluation of fiscal and monetary policies (e.g. through interviews or other qualitative methods and quantitative data, if available). Analyze indicators related to transparency and accountability of economic policy process

Figure 2: Assessing available resources through a human rights lens (breakdown of step 3 of the OPERA framework)

Source: CESR, Assessing Fiscal Policies, 2012 (see n 59)

time and benefit incidence analysis to assess distributional impacts across social groups and income quintiles. Again, disparities in the allocation of resources were correlated with disparities of outcome. Analysis of the tax structure examined whether available resources were being marshalled in line with principles of non-discrimination and progressive realisation. In order to identify deficiencies in the raising of revenue, the project compared the size of the state's budget to the overall size of the economy and analysed how taxation affected different groups of the population (for example, whether taxes attach to income or to goods; whether they are fixed or proportionate to means etc).[68]

[68] For more on the methods used to analyse Guatemala's resource mobilisation efforts, see CESR, *Assessing Fiscal Policy* above n 59, 18–22.

The assessment of resources found that Guatemala's social spending as a proportion of GDP was among the lowest in Latin America, despite being a low-middle income country.[69] Allocations to health had not exceeded 1 per cent of GDP since the end of the war in 1996 (compared, for example, with the 5 per cent devoted by Costa Rica).[70] Distribution of spending was found to be highly inequitable, with per capita health spending three times higher in the capital than in Quiché, the poorest region.[71] Resource allocations on health had not evolved over time, despite targets set under the 1996 Peace Accords, and were in fact lower in 2008 than in 2001.[72] Budgetary spending on maternal health was opaque, making it next to impossible for policymakers and civil society organisations to track amounts of spending and their impact in reducing maternal death among the most vulnerable populations.[73]

Low social spending was directly linked to the small size of the public budget. Despite 10 years of economic growth, the national budget remained one of lowest in the region (15 per cent of GDP, while the regional average was almost 27 per cent).[74] One of the main reasons for this was the country's low tax base—still one of the lowest in Latin America, despite commitments under the Peace Accords to increase it.[75] Unlike other countries with low tax burdens, however, tax revenue constituted the main source of revenue for the Guatemalan State.[76] In terms of its resourcing function, therefore, the tax system did not generate the sufficient resources needed for the State to comply with its obligation to progressively realise ESC rights and universalise certain minimum levels of rights enjoyment.

With regard to its redistributive function, the tax system was also found to be highly inequitable, with more than 75 per cent of income generated through generally regressive indirect taxes rather than direct taxation on income and assets.[77] This disproportionately affected the poorest sectors of the population, who instead of benefiting from redistributive transfers of resources, were effectively shouldering the main burden of funding the state's social programmes. In contrast, the country's most profitable business sectors (for example, coffee and sugar producers, textile 'maquilas' and the tourism, mining, energy and telecommunications sectors) enjoyed unparalleled tax privileges and incentives. In 2008, the total amount of these tax breaks, deductions and exemptions was twice the amount the State expected to collect in income tax. For each quetzal collected in

[69] CESR/ICEFI, *Rights or Privileges*? above n 56, 16. For a more detailed analysis of the findings, in Spanish, see CESR/ICEFI, *Derechos o Privilegios*? above n 56, ch 5 'La Política Fiscal y la Inversión en los Derechos Económicos y Sociales'.

[70] Ibid 16–17.

[71] Ibid.

[72] Ibid.

[73] Ibid.

[74] Ibid.

[75] Ibid.

[76] Ibid.

[77] Ibid 18.

income tax, the State effectively 'gave back' over 2.5 quetzals in exemptions and deductions.[78]

The tax system was also found to be deficient with regard to its accountability function. Analysis of the political economy of fiscal reform revealed that the lack of adequate investment in the realisation of ESR resulted not simply from the State's incapacity or inefficiency in gathering and reassigning public resources, but from a historical co-option of the State by economic elites that had blocked all attempts at fiscal reform and ensured that public policymaking protected their privileges at the expense of the rights of the whole population.[79] Following the Peace Accords, a fiscal pact had been agreed in broad consultation with civil society, aimed at creating a more just and equitable tax system that was progressive, universal and obligatory. However, the pact did not win approval in Congress and attempts to introduce the fiscal reforms contemplated in the Pact were systematically thwarted by the politically powerful business sector, continuing a decades-long practice of using a series of tactics to block any attempt at reform.[80] The exceptional degree of influence that economic elites traditionally had over Guatemalan political life enabled them to maintain tax privileges on a scale surpassing those in other countries in the region. Furthermore, while the system for tax oversight and the legal regime against tax evasion had been strengthened since 1998, evasion continued to have a devastating impact.[81]

Overall, a compelling picture emerged from the three-stepped analysis of outcomes, policy efforts and resources, which pointed to a failure of the State to comply with its obligation to draw on the maximum of available resources to progressively realise ESR without discrimination. That Guatemala's democratic transition had not resulted in significant progress in the fulfilment of ESR was due, in large part, to the vision of the state that had dominated fiscal policymaking in recent decades. Guatemala had become a 'minimal' state that had increasingly ceded more space to private markets, treating its people as consumers rather than rights-holding citizens. The result had been to transform education, health and food into privileges for those who can afford them, rather than universal rights the state has a duty to uphold.[82]

The findings—backed by quantitative and qualitative evidence—enabled CESR and ICEFI to make detailed recommendations to the Government on the need for more equitable approaches to taxation and expenditure that would be aimed at the fulfilment of basic human rights. The report's recommendations included an approximate estimation of the resources and spending increases necessary to enable universal coverage of essential health, education and food programmes

[78] Ibid.

[79] Ibid 18–19.

[80] Ibid 20. For a more detailed discussion of the political economy of fiscal reform in Guatemala, see CESR/ICEFI, *Derechos y Privilegios*? above n 56, 5.4 'El Bloqueo a la Reforma Fiscal' 91–94.

[81] Ibid 18–19.

[82] Ibid 20.

in line with the state's core obligations and its commitments under the MDGs. It also recommended specific tax reforms that could make this increase in funding possible, as well as enhancing citizen participation in the decision-making process.[83]

Launched in the context of parliamentary discussions on the 2010 budget, the project report was intended to support the efforts of civil society groups and progressive policymakers to push for more equitable tax reforms. By framing issues such as maternal mortality, child malnutrition and education incompletion as human rights issues, and tracing the link between these poor human rights outcomes and inequitable tax policies, the report sought to shift the public debate from the speculative and highly ideological discussions on taxation that had dominated public discourse for decades, towards a more evidence-based and rights-grounded consideration of the need for tax reform as part of a fairer fiscal policy.

At the launch of the report in November 2009, CESR and ICEFI secured a public commitment from the Minister of Finance to significantly increase social spending and to push through progressive tax reforms, taking into account the report's findings and recommendations.[84] However, powerful lobbying by the country's business sector confederation led to the stalling of these promised fiscal initiatives and eventually to the minister's resignation.[85] Once again, powerful economic elites in the country were able to thwart attempts at progressive reforms thanks to their inordinate influence on the political process, the revolving door between high-level business and government positions and the co-option of influential media outlets, academic institutions and think tanks propagating traditional neo-classical arguments against 'enlarging the state' through increasing social spending and broadening the tax base.[86]

Nevertheless, the approach taken in the project was embraced and taken forward by other relevant official bodies, including the Reproductive Health Observatory (Observatorio en Salud Reproductiva or OSAR), a supervisory body set up by the Guatemalan Congress in association with civil society organisations to monitor maternal health policies and the resources allocated to them.[87] Internationally, the project succeeded in drawing the links between fiscal

[83] Recommended measures included increasing the rate of income and property taxes; eliminating or reducing certain tax exemptions shown to have inequitable impacts; strengthening programs against tax evasion and non-compliance; and improving the transparency and accountability of the tax administration system: ibid 20–22.

[84] Ministerio de Finanzas Públicas, 'Ministro de Finanzas recibe estudio sobre compromiso fiscal', Nota Informativa No 43, dcs-pr-no-43 (5 November 5, 2009): www.minfin.gob.gt/archivos/prensa/notas_informativas/notinfo43_051109.pdf.

[85] 'La renuncia del Ministro de Finanzas guatemalteco', Central American Data.com: www.centralamericadata.com/es/article/home/La_renuncia_del_Ministro_de_Finanzas_guatemalteco.

[86] On the historical co-option of the state by the economic elite in Guatemala, see CESR and ICEFI, *Derechos y Privilegios* above n 56, 91–94.

[87] The project's methodology enabled OSAR to incorporate a human rights framework more systematically in its monitoring of maternal health policy and in its proposals for reform. Members of Congress linked to OSAR subsequently presented a new maternal health law to Congress, the *Ley*

policy and preventable maternal death in Guatemala to the attention of UN treaty bodies, including the Committee on the Elimination of Discrimination against Women (CEDAW), the Committee on the Rights of the Child and the Human Rights Committee, all of which raised concerns regarding reproductive health with the state.[88] In the context of maternal mortality, the monitoring framework developed in Guatemala was also welcomed by donor agencies and UN specialised agencies in the context of efforts to operationalise a human rights perspective in monitoring progress on Goal 5 of the MDGs.[89]

Indeed, the *Rights or Privileges* project provides invaluable lessons for current efforts to set and monitor future human development goals to replace the MDGs in 2015. It illustrates how rights-based tax policy analysis can be integrated into an assessment of whether states are taking all reasonable efforts to meet their development objectives, and are doing so in light of their human rights obligations to progressively realise ESR according to the maximum of available resources. As patterns of poverty evolve, becoming more prevalent in middle-income countries less dependent on international development assistance, and as inequalities persist or widen in emerging economies experiencing sustained levels of economic growth, domestic resource mobilisation is taking on additional significance as a sustainable source of financing for development in low and middle-income countries.[90] Future progress in meeting human development goals will depend on such countries increasing their tax self-sufficiency and decreasing their dependence on international assistance.[91] It will become all the more relevant for human rights advocates in such contexts to scrutinise the role of domestic resource mobilisation in realising rights and redressing social inequalities.

de Maternidad Saludable, which was adopted in September 2010. The law aims to guarantee safe motherhood by ensuring the right of all women to universal, timely and free access to reproductive health information and services, which should be accessible to all, culturally appropriate and of good quality (Arts 1 and 13). The law prioritises efforts to reduce maternal mortality among rural, indigenous women and mandates that the necessary resources be provided, including through earmarked funding generated from specific direct taxes (Arts 2 and 25–27). See Congreso de Guatemala, Ley para la Maternidad Saludable, Decreto No 32-2010. For more information on the Observatorio en Salud Reproductiva, see: www.osarguatemala.org.

[88] See Committee on the Elimination of Discrimination against Women (CEDAW), 'Concluding Observations: Guatemala', UN Doc C/GUA/CO/7 (2009); Committee on the Rights of the Child, 'Concluding Observations: Guatemala', UN Doc CRC/C/GTM/CO/3-4 (2010): Human Rights Committee, 'Concluding Observations: Guatemala' (2012).

[89] See eg, Netherlands Ministry of Foreign Affairs, *Report of the Seminar on Human Rights and the Millennium Development Goals Report*, (The Hague, 2009): waterwiki.net/images/e/e5/HRandMDGSSeminarReportDec2009.pdf, where the Rights or Privileges project was used as a case study on how the Goals could be more effectively framed and monitored from a human rights perspective.

[90] See *Keeping the Promise: United to Achieve the Millennium Development Goals*, resolution adopted by the UN General Assembly at its 64th session, 17 September 2010 (N Doc A/65/L.1) 30.

[91] See UN Millennium Campaign, 'Resources Required to Finance the Millennium Development Goals' in *Investing in Development: A Practical Plan to Achieve the MDGs* (UN Millennium Campaign, 2005).

V. Tax and Rights-Based Alternatives to Austerity in the Context of Economic Crisis: A Focus on Ireland and Spain

Fiscal policy has moved to the centre of the political debate in recent years in the context of fiscal austerity measures implemented in the wake of the global financial and economic crises. Whereas in 2008 and 2009, many governments initially launched fiscal stimulus plans and policies that resulted in increased spending on public infrastructure and social protection programmes to mitigate the effects of the economic downturn, 2010 saw a sharp shift from fiscal stimulus to fiscal austerity. This was characterised primarily by a severe reduction in public spending. While this trend was observed in many parts of the world, with more than 90 developing countries expected to reduce budgetary expenditures in 2012, it was particularly pronounced in several European Union Member States facing large budget deficits as a consequence of the crisis. These came under pressure from international and regional financial institutions to reduce their deficits as a condition of international loans and rescue packages, and in order to maintain the confidence of investors and the financial markets.[92] Fiscal tightening has also taken hold in many developing countries and emerging economies where the impacts of the economic downturn in Europe and North America have been more indirect.[93]

Fiscal austerity measures in both developing and industrialised countries have tended to focus on cuts in public expenditure, rather than on increasing revenue through progressive tax reforms or other potentially more equitable forms of expanding 'fiscal space'.[94] Yet, drastic social expenditure cuts are not inevitable during periods of economic adjustment if all available fiscal alternatives are explored. Increasing tax compliance and/or raising tax rates are alternative strategies for mobilising additional public resources without necessarily sacrificing spending priorities or increasing debt, and they can potentially also support equity objectives, especially where progressive taxation from the richest income groups is increased to finance social and pro-poor investments.[95]

Nevertheless, where tax reforms have been introduced in the aftermath of the economic crisis, these have typically consisted of potentially regressive increases in sales and consumption taxes, rather than changes to personal income, property or corporation taxes.[96] An estimated 71 governments worldwide were reported to have increased or expanded consumption taxes in recent years.[97] Unless the

[92] Ortiz and Cummins, *A Recovery for All* above n 36, 18–20.
[93] Ibid 18–23.
[94] See Ortiz, Chai and Cummins above n 21.
[95] Ibid 7.
[96] Ortiz and Cummins, *A Recovery for All* above n 36, 241–53.
[97] Ibid 246.

distributional impacts of such reforms are properly addressed, they risk shifting the tax burden to already vulnerable low-income households, further exacerbating existing inequalities. Moreover, 12 countries were reported in 2009 as having cut higher rates of income tax for the wealthiest in comparison to pre-crisis years.[98] Although it is often argued that tax cuts for the wealthy will stimulate increased spending and investment, thereby prompting economic recovery, evidence calls into question this correlation and indicates that such tax cuts are less effective in stimulating the economy in times of recession than investments in social protection programmes.[99] As income taxes are the principal redistribution tool available to policymakers, such measures are also highly problematic from an equity perspective.[100] Corporate tax rates in developing countries are reported to have decreased on average across all regions between 2005 and 2010, in some cases being reduced by more than 25 per cent.[101] While some governments have sought to increase fiscal space post-crisis by introducing or increasing taxes on property, land and natural resource extraction, such examples are the exception.[102]

This skewed approach to fiscal policy—privileging austere social spending cuts over the creation of a progressive and broad based tax regime—has risked depriving the public coffers in many countries of the resources needed to maintain essential public services, deepening social inequalities already exacerbated by the crisis and undermining democratic accountability by fuelling distrust in the capacity of elected governments to safeguard the inherent human rights of ordinary citizens against the implacable demands of the financial markets.[103]

The Center for Economic and Social Rights has documented the threat to human rights posed by some of the fiscal austerity measures imposed in Ireland and Spain in the context of the economic crisis. In both countries, the failure to implement or even consider alternative taxation policy options to narrow the budget deficit led CESR to conclude that drastic social spending cuts in successive government budgets may have been retrogressive and in breach of ICESCR, to which both Ireland and Spain are party.

In its 2012 report on Ireland, CESR found that a poorly managed recession, followed by a series of austerity budgets characterised by significant cuts to social spending, had markedly undermined the rights to education, health, housing, work and an adequate standard of living.[104] The National Recovery

[98] Ibid 247.

[99] See Institute on Taxation and Economic Policy, '"High Rate" Income Tax States are Outperforming No-Tax States' (2012): www.itepnet.org/pdf/junkeconomics.pdf. See also AWID, CESR, COC, CWGL and ESCR-Net, *Bringing Human Rights to Bear in Times of Crisis: A Human Rights Analysis of Government Responses to the Economic Crisis*, Submission to the High level Segment of the 13th Session of the UN Human Rights Council on the global economic and financial crises (March 2010) 9.

[100] Ortiz and Cummins, above n 36, 248.

[101] Ibid.

[102] Ibid 250–53.

[103] AWID et al above n 99, 13.

[104] See Center for Economic and Social Rights (CESR), *Mauled by the Celtic Tiger: Human Rights in Ireland's Economic Meltdown*, (New York, CESR, 2012) 4.

Plan 2011–14 prioritises drastic cuts in social expenditures over progressive tax reforms in a country ranking among the lowest in Europe in terms of overall tax levels (only Romania and Latvia source less revenue from taxation).[105] While increases to Value Added Tax (VAT) have hit poorer households most severely, Ireland has maintained a generous regime of tax incentives and exemptions for corporations and high-income earners, long part of its strategy to compete with other jurisdictions for investment inflows.[106]

Ireland's tax structure continues to be characterised by very low effective income tax rates for high earners, and generous tax breaks which, if reduced in line with EU norms, could raise €5 billion for the public coffers, according to estimates.[107] Corporate tax rates are exceptionally low (at just 12.5 per cent, one of the lowest in the EU). The ability of many companies to route profits through Ireland on the way to paying little if any tax in any jurisdiction has pushed Ireland into the realm of a tax haven.[108] An estimated €7.64 billion are lost to illegal tax evasion in Ireland. This figure is several times the €1.24 billion removed from the social protection budget between 2011 and 2012.[109] VAT accounts for over 40 per cent of all tax income, far higher than the EU average, and is markedly regressive (representing 15 per cent of income for the lowest decile and only 6.8 per cent for the highest). Nevertheless, VAT rates have been increased in recent years as a response to the fiscal deficit.[110]

In its recommendations, CESR called on the Government to increase incrementally the remarkably low overall tax base in order to mobilise the maximum available resources for ESR and redistribute more equitably the social costs of the crisis.[111] It also recommended reviewing the incidence of VAT increases and tax breaks and eliminating those found to be regressive or discriminatory. It urged the Government to support the establishment of an EU-wide minimum rate of corporation tax, as well as to take meaningful steps against tax evasion.[112]

Similarly, Spain's fiscal austerity measures have come under scrutiny from CESR and other non-governmental organisations based in the country, which have increasingly questioned the preference for social spending cuts over progressive tax reforms in response to the fiscal deficit.[113] As in the examples of

[105] Ibid 11.
[106] Ibid 14.
[107] Ibid 14–15.
[108] Ibid 15.
[109] Ibid 15.
[110] Ibid 15.
[111] Ibid 25.
[112] Ibid 25.
[113] See Center for Economic and Social Rights, *Factsheet No 12: Spain* (2012). For an analysis of the retrogressive nature of Spanish fiscal policy in recent years, see N Lusiani, 'Rationalizing the Right to Health: Is Spain's Austere Response to the Economic Crisis Impermissible under International Human Rights Law?' in A Nolan (ed), *Economic and Social Rights after the Global Financial Crisis* (Cambridge, Cambridge University Press, forthcoming 2014).

Guatemala and Ireland, Spanish tax policy is criticised not only for failing to generate sufficient resources for the fulfilment of ESR, but for exacerbating social inequalities. Indeed, it is striking to note that both Spain and Ireland are among the EU countries which collect the lowest levels of government revenue as a percentage of GDP, while also having the highest levels of income inequality as indicated by the Gini coefficient (see Figure 3). Spain also has one of the fastest rising levels of income inequality in the EU since 2007, pointing to the inequitable nature of resource generation and distribution in the aftermath of the economic downturn.[114]

A coalition of 20 Spanish civil society groups, coordinated by CESR, presented concerns regarding the human rights impact of austerity measures to the Committee on Economic, Social and Cultural Rights, on the occasion of Spain's review in May 2012.[115] They argued that social spending cuts had been retrogressive as the state had not taken into consideration tax policy alternatives that could have served to increase the state's available resources in a more equitable manner, including taking serious steps against tax evasion, which according to the National

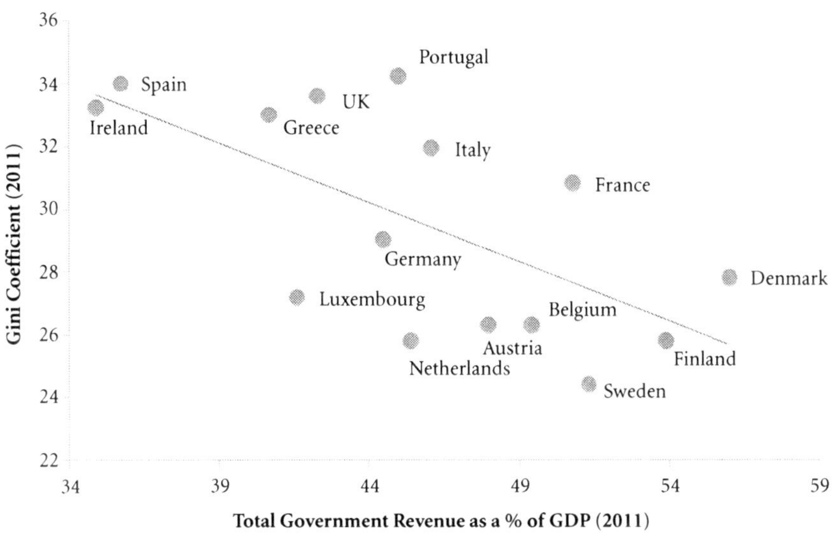

Source: Eurostat 2012. Codes:

Figure 3: Government Revenue and Income Inequality in Europe (2011)

[114] CESR, *Factsheet No 12: Spain* ibid, Figure 13.

[115] Center for Economic and Social Rights, Observatori DESC et al, 'Joint Submission to the Committee on Economic, Social and Cultural Rights, on the occasion of the review of Spain's fifth periodic report at the 48th Session, May 2012': www.cesr.org/section.php?id=161.

Union of Tax Inspectors (GESTHA) resulted in a tax loss of some €88 billion in 2010.[116] The Tax Justice Network ranks Spain among the ten countries in the world with the greatest losses due to tax evasion in absolute terms. GESTHA further estimates that 72 per cent of tax fraud is committed by large companies and wealthy individuals.[117]

As well as echoing many of the concerns raised by human rights groups regarding Spain's fiscal austerity measures in its Concluding Observations,[118] the Committee took the unusual step of issuing a letter to all States Party to the ICESCR. The letter reminded them that, before embarking on austerity measures such as social spending cutbacks which could have a retrogressive impact on human rights, international human rights law mandates governments to ensure that an exhaustive examination of all other options has been undertaken. This includes progressive tax increases, in order to ensure that such measures are justified as strictly necessary, proportionate and temporary.[119]

As the examples of Ireland and Spain illustrate, states' leeway to determine their domestic tax policies is increasingly constrained by the policy prescriptions of international and supranational bodies. The measures undertaken in both Ireland and Spain have been carried out in the context of the Fiscal Compact adopted by 25 EU states in February 2012, which effectively obliges all signatory states to enshrine a permanently balanced budget, or face exclusion from future crisis financing. The ceiling can only be raised in a severe economic downturn or other 'exceptional circumstances' which only the European Court of Justice in Luxembourg can define.[120]

The Fiscal Compact's new enforcement capabilities and the constitutional status of the deficit caps may in practice exacerbate austerity-driven human rights setbacks by constraining even moderate deficit financing, limiting the fiscal tools available for current and future governments to mitigate the human rights impacts of further financial or economic crises and to sustainably invest in ESR programmes which are at the heart of a just and sustainable recovery. In the words of Amartya Sen, entrenching austerity measures in economic downturns risks triggering a 'spiraling catastrophe'[121] for the economy and for human rights.

[116] Ibid 2.

[117] CESR, *Factsheet No 12: Spain* above n 113, 7.

[118] See ComESCR, 'Concluding Observations: Spain', UN Doc E/C.12/ESP/CO/5 (2012).

[119] Letter from ComESCR Chairperson to States Parties above n 6.

[120] See Treaty on Stability, Coordination and Governance in the Economic and Monetary Union (Fiscal Compact), adopted by the Council of the European Union, 2 March 2012.

[121] 'Nobel Economist Blasts Europe's Austerity Plans' (Financial Times, 14 December 2011): www.ft.com/home/europe.

VI. Opportunities for Linking Human Rights and Tax Justice Advocacy in the Current Context

The examples described above illustrate how human rights analysis can be fruitfully brought to bear to advocate for tax policy reforms at the domestic level in the post-crisis and post-MDG contexts. However, as highlighted already, national-level policies are shaped and constrained by trends in the international tax policy framework.[122] In taking stock of the factors that led to the global economic downturn and to inadequate progress in achieving the MDGs, intergovernmental institutions have increasingly recognised the need to revisit some of the fiscal policy orthodoxies that have undermined the role of taxation in promoting human development and economic recovery for all.[123] This has created space and momentum for previously unheeded tax reform proposals to make headway on the international agenda. Two key international issues which offer broad scope for collaboration between human rights and tax justice advocates in the current context are described here.

The global economic crisis, with its roots in the loose and biased regulation of the financial system, has brought the issue of financial sector accountability and reform to the centre of public attention. A focus of much civil society advocacy in this regard has been the push for a global financial transaction tax (FTT).[124] The FTT currently under debate has two basic policy objectives. First, it would raise significant revenue. By introducing a tiny tax rate on the trading of bonds, shares

[122] See A Christians, 'Global Trends and Constraints on Tax Policy in the Least Developed Countries' (2009) 40 *University of British Columbia Law Review* 1: www.law.ubc.ca/files/pdf/ncbl/papers/Christians.pdf.

[123] Eg, the Commission of Experts established by the UN General Assembly in 2009 to propose international policy responses to the global economic crisis, referred to growing income inequality and the reduced progressivity of tax regimes as factors which contributed to the crisis. Its recommendations included an 'International Tax Compact' to strengthen progressive means of domestic resource mobilisation, and to promote international cooperation in tackling tax evasion and avoidance, including via offshore financial centres. *Report of the Commission of Experts of the President of the UN General Assembly on Reforms of the International Monetary and Financial System* ('Stiglitz Commission') (September 2009) 219. Similarly, the outcome document of the MDG Review Summit in September 2010 affirmed a new resolve to strengthen domestic resource generation systems through fairer and more efficient tax collection, and effectively combating tax evasion and capital flight. See *Keeping the Promise: United to Achieve the Millennium Development Goals*, 17 September 2010 (UN Doc. A/65/L.1) 30. More recently, even the IMF appears to be questioning its traditional fiscal policy prescriptions to countries undergoing fiscal adjustment. A working paper by IMF Chief Economist Olivier Blanchard acknowledges that IMF forecasters seriously underestimated the negative impact of austerity measures, both budget and tax-related, on growth and economic recovery. See O Blanchard and D Leigh, 'Growth Forecast Errors and Fiscal Multipliers' (2013) IMF Working Paper WP/13/1.

[124] See D Beitler, *Raising Revenue A Review of Financial Transaction Taxes Throughout the World* (Just Economics, 2010); United Nations High Commissioner for Human Rights (UNHCR), 'G-8/ EU: A Global Financial Transaction Tax, A Human Rights Imperative Mow More than Ever' (May 2012): www.ohchr.org/en/NewsEvents/Pages/DisplayNews.aspx?NewsID=12150&LangID=E (reporting the call by several United Nations independent experts urging the EU to adopt a global financial transaction tax).

and derivative products, such as futures contracts, the FTT would yield about US$48 billion at its lowest rate across the G20 countries, with higher rates offering up to US$250 billion per year—significant amounts to offset the widespread austerity measures in countries north and south. Second, the FTT aims to stabilise financial markets by discouraging speculation (especially in high-frequency trades) and mitigating price volatility.[125] Financial transaction taxes can thus serve to generate additional resources, to introduce greater progressivity into the tax system and to exact accountability from the sector whose excessive risk taking and speculative activity led to the near collapse of the financial system.[126]

Although moves to approve a eurozone-wide FTT were adopted at the European Finance Ministers' Meeting in June 2012, such taxes continue to meet strong opposition from powerful states and the financial sector itself.[127] To date, few human rights voices have joined the call for an FTT.[128] Yet framing the demand for the FTT from the perspective of states' domestic and extraterritorial human rights obligations could serve to underscore the moral force of existing campaigns by development agencies. Human rights principles can also inform the debate on how the proceeds from such a tax should be used as a priority.

Similarly, the role of 'tax havens' (or offshore banking in secrecy jurisdictions) has also been the focus of development and social justice advocacy in the context of responses to the crisis and debates on future financing for development, though it has yet to figure prominently on the human rights agenda. On a conservative estimate, tax revenue lost through offshore banking totals some US$250 billion, more than three times the total development assistance of all OECD countries.[129] Tax havens have a corrupting effect on national tax regimes, undermine financial regulation and deprive governments of significant revenue that should be used to realise human rights. The use of tax havens and offshore banking may also contravene the extraterritorial obligations of states to respect, protect and fulfil ESR.[130] Growing advocacy by groups such as the Tax Justice Network has prompted stronger international commitments to clamp down on tax havens and secrecy jurisdictions, to foster progressive and transparent tax systems and to ensure greater international cooperation on tax, regulation and crime.[131]

[125] See Center of Concern, CESR and others, *Financial Transaction Tax: A Human Rights Imperative*, Righting Financial Regulation series, No 3 (2012).

[126] Ibid.

[127] See CESR, 'Europe Moves Forward on Robin Hood Tax While US Balks' (10 October 2012): www.cesr.org/article.php?id=1370.

[128] See, however, Office of the High Commissioner for Human Rights (OHCHR), 'A Global Financial Transactions Tax, A Human Rights Imperative Now More than Ever', joint statement by five UN Special Rapporteurs (14 May 2012); and Center of Concern, CESR and others above n 125.

[129] See Tax Justice Network, *The Price of Offshore* (Tax Justice Network, 2005).

[130] See N Lusiani, 'Only the Little People Pay Taxes: Tax Evasion and Switzerland's Extraterritorial Obligations to Economic, Social and Cultural Rights in Zambia' in W Vandenhole et al (eds), *Extraterritorial Human Rights Obligations: Hypothetical Case Studies* (forthcoming, 2013).

[131] See eg, the commitments made by G20 leaders at the June 2012 G20 Summit in Los Cabos, Mexico, to tackle illicit financial flows by moving towards the automatic exchange of tax information and calling on other countries to do the same. See 'G20 Leaders' Declaration, Los Cabos, 18–19 June

Given these and other potential areas of common interest between the human rights and tax justice movements, there is strong potential for advocacy agendas to converge. Indeed, at the national, regional and global levels, inspiring examples of increasingly broad based and collaborative advocacy on tax and human rights can already be found.[132] As Allison Christians argues, human rights principles can help to shift the dominant tax policy discourse and provide a powerful vocabulary for advocating for taxation systems which fairly distribute the benefits and burdens among society's members.[133] Of particular relevance to today's context, the duty to devote the 'maximum of available resources' to the full realisation of human rights gives legal force to the imperative to tax, as well as articulating the ultimate goal of tax policy. The principles of 'equality' and 'non-discrimination' can act as a much needed corrective to the long-standing tendency in traditional tax discourse to privilege the pursuit of 'efficiency' over that of 'equity' or 'fairness'.[134] Human rights can enrich understandings of the accountability relationship between decision-makers and taxpayers by recasting it in terms of the rights and corresponding obligations of each. And the duties of states to cooperate in the realisation of human rights beyond their borders can provide a useful counterpoint to the notion of 'tax sovereignty' which has hampered effective action against the transnational impacts of tax evasion and harmful tax competition.[135]

VII. Conclusion

As this chapter has argued, tax policy is critical in determining a state's ability to generate and assign resources in ways that fulfil ESR. Taxation is also a key vehicle for redressing social inequalities, and goes to the heart of the accountability bond between state and citizen. Yet, despite the grave human rights impact of manifestly inequitable fiscal policies in many countries, including the regressive fiscal austerity measures being pursued in many countries in the wake of the economic crisis, and the role of tax evasion and avoidance in undermining progress in human

2012', 48: www.gfintegrity.org/content/view/553/70/. The Tax Justice Network is an independent organisation which carries out research, analysis and advocacy in the field of tax and regulation. It works to map, analyse and explain the role of taxation and the harmful impacts of tax evasion, tax avoidance, tax competition and tax havens, and to encourage reform at the global and national levels. For more on the work of the Tax Justice Network, see: www.taxjustice.net/cms/front_content.php?idcatart=2&lang=1.

[132] See CESR, *Tax Policy and Human Rights: Opportunities for Collaboration By Human Rights and Tax Justice Advocates* (forthcoming, 2013).

[133] A Christians, 'Fair Taxation as a Basic Human Right' *International Review of Constitutionalism 2009* University of Wisconsin Legal Studies Research Paper No 1066, 3 and 4: ssrn.com/abstract=1272446.

[134] See DJ Ventry, 'Equity vs Efficiency and the US Tax System in Historical Perspective' in JJ Thorndike and DJ Ventry (eds), *Tax Justice: The Ongoing Debate* (Washington DC, The Urban Institute Press, 2002) available at: ssrn.com/abstract=1345349.

[135] Christians, above n 133, 6–9.

rights and development, a coherent approach to addressing tax injustice from a human rights perspective has yet to emerge. An agenda around the three rights-related functions of taxation—resourcing, redistribution and accountability—could be devised in alliance between human rights and tax justice advocates, and mutually enriched through increased interdisciplinary collaboration and exchange. The global discussions underway on the content and goals of the post-2015 development agenda to succeed the MDGs, and growing awareness of the fallacies underpinning conventional fiscal policy responses to the global economic crisis,[136] provide opportunities to forge and advance such an agenda and to bring the voice of human rights to the worldwide struggle for tax justice.

[136] See Center for Economic and Social Rights: *Fiscal Fallacies: Eight Myths About the Age of Austerity, and Human Rights Responses* (Madrid, CESR, 2012).

II

Governance

5

Recovering the History of Human Rights: Public Finances and Human Rights

RORY O'CONNELL

I. Introduction

The focus of this collection, as with most work on budget analysis, is with contemporary legal and political norms: the 1966 International Covenant on Economic, Social and Cultural Rights (ICESCR); the 1979 Convention on the Elimination of all Forms of Discrimination against Women (CEDAW) and gender budgeting; and the 1989 Convention on the Rights of the Child (CRC) and budgeting for children are all examples. The aim of this chapter is to look back at the history and even prehistory of human rights law and examine the role of public finance in the early understanding of human rights (or natural rights or—forgive the term—the 'rights of man').

The chapter will consider a number of themes. First, it will highlight that questions about revenue and expenditure were often not far removed from the early debates about rights. Second, as might be expected, the concerns of these early rights advocates were dissimilar to the aims of modern mainstream human rights law, frequently being bound up with the protection of private property. This does not mean that early concerns about rights and public finances are irrelevant today. Third, some rights advocates (Paine and Kant) highlighted more progressive arguments about finance and rights that are still especially relevant today. Fourth, that the early debates treat rights as more a political than a juridical notion and this more political notion needs to be reasserted for modern rights advocacy.

This chapter first examines the English tradition of limited government before exploring what the American and French revolutionaries had to say about public finances. The contributions of Kant and Paine are then discussed before considering the lessons learned from this foray into the history of human rights.

II. The English Tradition of Limited Government

One of the precursors to our modern human rights law was the European[1] medieval concept of limited government. Probably the most famous example of this tradition is the English one. This tradition is by no means exclusive to England and later Britain, though many of the English examples tend to be emphasised given their influence on American and French writers and politicians in the eighteenth century.[2]

In England, the principle that the monarch required the approval of Parliament for the raising of taxes is alluded to in thirteenth and fourteenth century statutes.[3] This was not understood as an absolute rule and the principle was at issue in many of the seventeenth century struggles between the monarch and Parliament. While debt ridden monarchs required extra revenues, parliaments refused taxation unless grievances were addressed.[4] Monarchs in the late sixteenth and seventeenth centuries sought to raise monies by exploiting privileges not covered by this principle of parliamentary consent.[5] Monarchs could not entirely ignore Parliament though, and had to return to it for financial support. In 1628, Parliament granted Charles I financial support but the Commons also insisted on his support for the 1628 Petition of Right. The 1628 Petition of Right urged that no one be compelled to pay loans, taxes or charges to the Crown 'without common consent by Act of Parliament'.[6] The Petition did not end royal efforts to raise money without parliamentary consent. Continuing disagreement between the monarch and Parliament led to Charles I trying to rule without Parliament from 1629–40. During this period of 'personal rule' the monarch sought to exploit other sources of revenue.[7] When Parliament was eventually re-summoned in 1640 in order to address the monarch's financial needs, it insisted on a range of reforms, including the regular summoning of parliaments, the abolition of the Star Chamber and financial reforms.

[1] This chapter specifically focuses on European debates. This is not meant to deny the importance of indigenous rights philosophies and struggles in other parts of the globe.

[2] 'Perhaps never before and surely never since has any single nation's constitution so dominated Western man's theorizing about politics': GS Wood, *The Creation of the American Republic* (WW Norton, 1969) 11.

[3] See Acts passed during the reign of Edward I in 1297 and Edward III in 1362 and 1371, as translated in DJ Medley, *Original Illustrations of English Constitutional History* (London, Methuen, 1910) 255, 178–80. Maitland traces origins of this in Magna Carta 1215 and in pre-Norman practices: FW Maitland, *The Constitutional History of England* (Cambridge, Cambridge University Press, 1913) 60–64.

[4] GE Aylmer, *The Struggle for the Constitution* (London, Blandford, 1965) 63.

[5] JP Kenyon, *The Stuart Constitution* (Cambridge, Cambridge University Press, 1966) 53.

[6] Art VIII of the Petition, ibid 84.

[7] Aylmer above n 4, 80.

During this constitutional dispute in early seventeenth century England, the judges played an important role in these disputes about revenue.[8] Kenyon portrays the judiciary of this period as largely subservient to the Crown and unwilling to uphold individual rights to property or liberty as against the Crown.[9] The period marked a 'crisis' in the common law, as the legal process proved unable to restrain governmental abuses.[10] Judges were not in a position to resist the king effectively as they only held office during the king's pleasure as witnessed by the dismissal of Coke in 1616.[11] Shortly before the English Civil War, several judges who had ruled in favour of the king were subject to parliamentary impeachment.[12]

The disputes over royal power and the prerogative (including, though certainly not limited to, money raising powers) precipitated the mid-century civil wars,[13] the ill-fated proposals of Levellers for greater democracy and liberty,[14] the execution of Charles I (1649) and the temporary creation of a republic (1649–60). The post-Republican Restoration of the monarchy saw a refutation of early monarchical practices of trying to raise taxes without parliamentary consent.[15] Indeed, the Restoration Parliament introduced the idea of voting 'appropriations' for specific expenditures.[16] However, the Restoration did not signal the end of the dispute between the monarchy and Parliament over prerogative powers more generally, but only established a temporary lull.

The matter was not settled until the so-called Glorious Revolution of 1688. The principle of no taxation without parliamentary consent is enshrined in the constitutional texts adopted during the climax of this struggle: the 1689 Bill of Rights (England) and its sister document, the 1689 Claim of Right (Scotland). The Bill of Rights covers much more than just individual rights; indeed, despite its name it is not really about individual rights; for example, it regulates the succession to the throne. On taxation it is trenchant—the levying of money by the Crown without the 'consent of Parliament' is 'illegal'.[17]

[8] Kenyon above n 5, 103–05. These cases include the famous ones of the *Five Knights* and the *Ship-Money case (R v Hampden)*, both excerpted in Kenyon, 106–16. The King's Bench rejected a plea to release the Knights, who had been imprisoned for failing to pay a forced loan. In *Hampden*, the Exchequer Chamber ruled by seven judges to five that the king could raise monies in an emergency and crucially it was for the king to determine when there was an emergency. See C Russell, *The Crisis of Parliaments: English History 1509–1660* (Oxford, Oxford University Press, 1971) 322.

[9] For this reason, Kenyon notes that there were repeated calls to reform the common law during this period. See Kenyon above n 5, 105 and 333, 337, 420. These reforms included proposals on codification and to abolish the use of law French.

[10] G Burgess, *The Politics of the Ancient Constitution* (Basingstoke, MacMillan, 1992) 213.

[11] Aylmer above n 4, 51.

[12] Burgess above n 10, 217–19.

[13] The period commenced with wars in Scotland (1639) and rebellion in Ireland (1641) as preludes to the more famous English Civil War 1642–51.

[14] Aylmer above n 4, 133.

[15] Ibid 171.

[16] Ibid 176.

[17] Medley above n 3, 293. This part of the Bill of Rights is still on the statute book in the UK. The Claim of Right provision similarly prohibits 'giving gifts or grants for raising of money without the Consent of Parliament of Convention of Estates' and is still in force.

Thus it was that in England, the control of taxation was intimately linked to the idea of political liberty. Locke would summarise that there must be no taxation 'without the consent of the People, or their Deputies'.[18] The English experience also is testimony to the importance of the more representative chamber in financial measures; questions of taxation and finance were of especial concern to the House of Commons which in principle, at least, was more representative than the noble House of Lords.

It is not with the English Bill of Rights (or the Scottish Claim of Rights) that we find the first declarations of rights in our modern sense as proclamations of individual rights as against government. They do, however, form the background to the late eighteenth century innovation of Bills or declarations of rights that emerge during the 'Atlantic revolution'[19] of the late eighteenth century.

III. American Revolutionaries

The American War of Independence was precipitated by disputes over the governance of the North American colonies, and in particular disputes about public finances. Most notably this involved the power to tax; the British authorities claimed this right for the sovereign Parliament in London, while the revolutionaries insisted it vested only in the local assemblies.[20]

The Declaration of Independence, echoing John Locke,[21] affirms the right and duty of a people to rebel when faced with the threat of 'despotism'. Among the long list of complaints against the UK Government[22] was that it had imposed taxation without the consent of the persons affected (ie, the consent of their representatives).[23] In making this claim, the revolutionaries could point not merely to the historic claims of the Bill of Rights or Locke, but also to the contemporary arguments of some such as Edmund Burke: 'in all monarchies, the people must in effect themselves mediately or immediately possess the power of granting their own money, or no shadow of liberty could subsist'.[24] As Burke put it, the Americans made the taxing power the very 'pulse' of liberty.[25] A few weeks

[18] J Locke, *Two Treatises of Government* (Cambridge, Cambridge University Press, 1967) Second Treatise, s 142.

[19] Revolution was a feature from 'the Urals to the Alleghenies'. See J Godechot, *France and the Atlantic Revolution of the Eighteenth Century, 1770–1799* (New York, Free Press, 1965) 3.

[20] JP Reid, *Constitutional History of the American Revolution: The Authority to Tax* (Madison WI, University of Wisconsin Press, 1987) 282.

[21] Locke above n 18, cc 18–19.

[22] The 1706–07 Acts of Union created a new United Kingdom of Great Britain.

[23] Transcript available at: www.archives.gov/exhibits/charters/declaration_transcript.html.

[24] E Burke, 'Conciliation with America' in E Burke and I Harris, *Pre-Revolutionary Writings* (Cambridge, Cambridge University Press, 1993) 222.

[25] Ibid 223. That the claim of liberty was being invoked by slave holders in North America did not escape the sarcastic attention of British politicians.

before the American War of Independence, Burke argued in Parliament that Parliament should pursue conciliation with the Americans by recognising that their local assembles should be relied upon to vote monies for the Crown, rather than have taxation imposed on them by a Parliament in London wherein they had no representation.[26] The failure to make this concession on principle cost Britain its North American colonies.[27]

The War of Independence resulted in the Articles of Confederation, a system of government which was rapidly shown to be deficient. One key problem with the Confederation was that the central government had no settled way of raising income.[28] The subsequent 1787 Constitution created a federal congress which could raise monies, though with restrictions as to the proportionate apportionment of direct taxes among the states according to population, and the requirement that any 'duties, imposts and excises' should be uniform throughout the union.[29]

The American revolutionaries were animated by a belief that government was a permanent threat to the liberty of the people.[30] The perception of the relationship between liberty and taxation is indicated by the word chosen by Justice Field a century later to describe the danger of excessive taxation—'oppression'.

In later years, some parts of these constitutional provisions would become troublesome. This was most notably the case in 1895 when a federal tax on income from land was struck down by the Federal Supreme Court on the grounds it was not apportioned among the states in proportion to population, as all federal direct taxes needed to be.[31] Since an income tax would also be a direct tax, and thus subject to apportionment among the states according to numbers, rather than across the states in proportion to the income, the implication was that any federal income tax would be constitutionally suspect. That some members of the Supreme Court were worried about the power of the federal government to tax, and the consequent implications for liberty, are indicated in a concurring speech in the Supreme Court judgment:

> If the provisions of the Constitution can be set aside by an act of Congress, where is the course of usurpation to end? The present assault upon capital is but the beginning. It will be but the stepping stone to others, larger and more sweeping, till our political contests will become a war of the poor against the rich; a war constantly growing in intensity and bitterness.[32]

The Sixteenth Amendment, passed by Congress in 1909 and becoming effective in 1913, authorises Congress to levy an income tax on the inhabitants of the

26 Burke above n 24, 253.
27 Reid above n 20, 284.
28 As explained by Field J in *Pollock v Farmers Loan and Trust Company* 157 US 429 (1895).
29 Art I, ss 2 and 8. Text available at: www.archives.gov/exhibits/charters/constitution_transcript.html.
30 Wood above n 2, 18.
31 *Pollock v Farmers Loan and Trust Company* above n 28.
32 Ibid.

states without having to be based on the numbers in each state. This episode is a salutary reminder that judges may wield powers so as to strike down revenue raising laws.

It is noteworthy that in 1787 the United States drafters inserted these rules on taxation, understandably, in the provisions dealing with the structure and powers of government, rather than treating them as an issue of rights. The federal Bill of Rights—the first ten Amendments to the 1787 US Constitution, adopted in 1791—do not explicitly address issues of taxation or public finance, except through the recognition of the right to property in the Fifth Amendment.[33] Otherwise the 1791 Bill of Rights is silent on matters of taxation and finance. By 1791, the French had already adopted a different approach in their Declaration of Rights.

IV. French Revolutionaries

Financial questions of revenue and expenditure were central to the French Revolution.[34] It was a budgetary crisis which precipitated the events of 1789.[35] The French state was facing bankruptcy thanks to its expenditure during the American War of Independence.[36] This crisis led to repeated initiatives including a public 'budget',[37] and more importantly a need to increase revenues. This crisis fundamentally put in question the system of taxation in France. The problem facing the finance ministers was that taxation was deeply and rigidly inegalitarian, indeed, 'decrepit, incoherent, complicated, unequal and unjust',[38] being based on the three 'estates' of nobles, clergy and commoners. The first two of the three estates benefited from immunities and privileges with respect to taxation, thanks largely to their bargaining power with the monarchy;[39] this meant that the richer one was, the less one paid in taxes.[40] These privileges and immunities hindered any response to the financial crisis; meanwhile the situation was aggravated by an economic crisis marked by bad harvests, fluctuating food prices and rising unemployment.

[33] Text of the Bill of Rights available at: www.archives.gov/exhibits/charters/bill_of_rights_transcript.

[34] JM Roberts, *The French Revolution* (Oxford, Oxford University Press, 1997) 4; Godechot above n 19, 69–73.

[35] K Norberg, 'The French Fiscal Crisis of 1788 and the Financial Origins of the Revolution of 1789' in P Hoffmann and K Norberg (eds) *Fiscal Crises, Liberty and Representative Government 1450–1789* (Stancford, Stanford University Press, 1994) 254.

[36] G Lefebvre, *The Coming of the French Revolution* (New Jersey, Princeton University Press, 1976) 21.

[37] This was important for making more transparent the actual costs of the royal court. Godechot above n 19, 70–71.

[38] Godechot above n 19, 69.

[39] Lefebvre above n 36, 7–9.

[40] Ibid 23.

The financial crisis could not be tackled without interfering with these privileges. Efforts to introduce some reforms were stymied by the Parisian and regional *parlements* which, despite their name, were primarily courts and not representative assemblies. Members of these courts were frequently granted noble status and this gave rise to the 'nobility of the robe'.[41] However, these courts were not solely judicial bodies; they had a role to play in 'registering' official measures and had refused to register a number of fiscal reforms.[42] At the time the *parlements* were able to argue they were defending fundamental principles in insisting on a recall of the Estates General, a body representing all three estates which had not met since 1614. While incommoding the king, and apparently siding with the commons, the *parlements* were defending sectional interests and unleashing a crisis of legitimacy that would undermine both the monarchy and nobility. In response to this impasse, Louis XVI eventually summoned the Estates General to meet; its character as representative of all three estates was essential to give legitimacy to financial reform. A key prelude to the meeting of the Estates General was the collection throughout the country of complaints, compiled in *cahiers de doléances*. Among the many demands, 'fiscal equality' featured prominently.[43]

The Estates General convened, but a dispute about the relationship between the three estates erupted and the Third Estate declared itself to be a National Assembly,[44] entitled to draft a constitution. It quickly set about abolishing the remnants of feudalism,[45] and debating and announcing the 1789 Declaration of the Rights of Man and of the Citizen (1789 Declaration), intended as a preamble to a new constitution. The drafting of this Declaration was accomplished in less than four weeks,[46] though the Assembly did not finish its work on a constitution until 1791. During the Revolution several Declarations and constitutions were to be debated and adopted. However, the 1789 Declaration remains the most significant, still being part of French constitutional law today.

Given the specific catalyst of the Revolution, it is unsurprising that budgetary matters figure prominently in the 1789 Declaration. The Declaration is brief—only 17 Articles—but pithily covers not only a list of fundamental rights but also fundamental constitutional principles. The rights listed are mainly civil and political in nature, with the right to property being described as 'inviolable and sacred' (Article 17). The fundamental principles are national sovereignty (Article 2), popular sovereignty

[41] Ibid 12.

[42] Ibid 28; Godechot above n 19, 80.

[43] Roberts above n 34, 14.

[44] In doing so they repudiated the view of the *Parlement* of Paris that the Estates should be organised as they had been in 1614, ie, equal numbers in each estate and voting by order, not by head. See Roberts above n 34, 11–12.

[45] Roberts above n 34, 24–29.

[46] The French Constitutional Council provides an English translation of the 1789 Declaration, calling it the 'Declaration of Human and Civic Rights': www.conseil-constitutionnel.fr/conseil-constitutionnel/root/bank_mm/anglais/cst2.pdf.

(Article 6)[47] and the separation of powers (Article 16). The invocation of the Rousseauian general will in Article 6 also had the effect of sanctifying statute law at the expense of any judicial law-making role, while the revolutionaries set themselves the task of 'subjugating the judiciary'.[48]

No fewer than four of the seventeen Articles deal with financial matters (Articles 12–15). These four Articles identify important principles still relevant in the twenty-first century. First, the protection of fundamental rights requires state action and agencies, including coercive action. That is to say a 'public force' is necessary. Given the principles of national and popular sovereignty, this public force must serve the interests of everyone.[49] This recognises that state action is a public good (not merely a necessary evil) and that it must serve the common good rather than the personal interests of those who are entrusted with its exercise. Being established for the benefit of all, the public force should not serve any sectional interest.

Second, the costs of this public force must be met by a general tax, which should be 'equally distributed among all citizens, in proportion to their ability to pay'.[50] This highlights the ideas of equality but also progressivity. While everyone is equally subject to the duty of taxation, this equality is based on ability to pay. Requiring the same amount of taxation from everyone, or even perhaps the same percentage of income, would presumably violate the last clause.

Third, there must be public participation in the process of collecting revenue.[51] This is a right of all citizens, either in their own right or through their representatives. This right requires that there be public consent to the existence and scope of any taxation. This echoes the representation principle of the English and American constitutionalists. Fourth, there must be accountability in how public funds are spent; citizens have a right to 'watch over' the use of public funds (Article 14) and demand an 'accounting of its administration'.[52]

These four principles: necessity of a public force; equality and progressivity; public participation; and accountability—are principles that still seem relevant to questions of public finance and human rights today. Indeed, several of these principles, even if not mentioned explicitly in the text of international human rights treaties, are frequently mentioned in accompanying general comments or state reports.

[47] Art 6 does not use the exact term 'popular sovereignty' but its references to the people and the Rousseauian idea of the 'general will' convey the principle that the people are sovereign.

[48] JP Dawson, *The Oracles of the Law*, (University of Michigan, 1968) 375.

[49] Art 12: To guarantee the Rights of Man and of the Citizen a public force is necessary; this force is therefore established for the benefit of all, and not for the particular use of those to whom it is entrusted.

[50] Art 13: For the maintenance of the public force, and for administrative expenses, a general tax is indispensable; it must be equally distributed among all citizens, in proportion to their ability to pay.

[51] Art 14: All citizens have the right to ascertain, by themselves, or through their representatives, the need for a public tax, to consent to it freely, to watch over its use, and to determine its proportion, basis, collection and duration.

[52] Art 15: Society has the right to ask a public official for an accounting of his administration.

We should not, of course, get too caught up in the ideals of the French revolutionaries.[53] Their inconsistent even hypocritical views are well known.[54] The 1789 Declaration focuses mainly on civil and political rights and so largely ignores the economic and social rights (ESR) that are the main concern of this work. This is despite the existence of some early proposals which included social and economic rights.[55] Further, the Declaration includes very strong protection for the right to property in Article 17, the unrestricted enjoyment of which would likely undermine the protection of many human rights and other important public interests.

The 1789 Declaration was not the only declaration of rights in France during the revolutionary era. The constitutional instability of the Revolution meant that constitutional texts were adopted again in 1793 and 1795, both of which were preceded by a declaration of rights. The 1793 Declaration recognises rights relating to occupation and work (slavery is prohibited)[56] and to education.[57] Even stronger than this, public assistance is described as a sacred debt, and society owes 'subsistence' to the unfortunate.[58] The provisions on public finances are not quite as elaborate as in 1789, but the essential principles remain[59] and the aim of taxation is broadened to include the general good (*l'utilité générale*).[60] The later 1795 Declaration does not contain such elaborate provisions on what we now call social and economic rights, though it does retain some provisions on work (and freedom from slavery) and public finances.[61] Intriguingly, the 1795 Declaration is a Declaration of the Rights *and Duties* of Man (italics added) and so it also includes a list of duties. These duties do not include matters like paying taxes, though this is presumably implicit in the earlier recognition of a contribution to serve the public good.[62]

[53] SM Singham, 'Betwixt Cattle and Men: Jews, Blacks, and Women, and the Declaration of Rights and Man' in D Van Kley (ed), *The French Idea of Freedom: The Old Regime and the Declaration of Rights of 1789* (Palo Alto CA, Stanford University Press, 1996).

[54] SM Singham 'Betwixt Cattle and Men: Jews, Blacks, and Women, and the Declaration of the Rights of Man' in D Van Kley (ed), *The French Idea of Freedom: The Old Regime and the Declaration of Rights of 1789* (Stanford University Press, 1994).

[55] For instance, Sieyes speaks of rights of economic freedom and of the right of everyone who is unable to provide for his needs, to assistance (*secours*) from his co-citizens; the Sieyes text is found in S Rials, *La Declaration des Droits de l'Homme et du Citoyen* (Paris, Hachette, 1989) 601–05.

[56] Arts 17–18. Text in French available at: www.conseil-constitutionnel.fr/conseil-constitutionnel/francais/la-constitution/les-constitutions-de-la-france/constitution-du-24-juin-1793.5084.html.

[57] Art 22.

[58] Art 21.

[59] Art 20: Nulle contribution ne peut être établie que pour l'utilité générale. Tous les citoyens ont le droit de concourir à l'établissement des contributions, d'en surveiller l'emploi, et de s'en faire rendre compte.

[60] Rials above n 55, 348.

[61] Arts 15 and 16. Text available at: www.conseil-constitutionnel.fr/conseil-constitutionnel/francais/la-constitution/les-constitutions-de-la-france/constitution-du-5-fructidor-an-iii.5086.html.

[62] Art 16.

V. Radical Visions

The English, American and French examples discussed so far reflect largely a concern with the protection of private property. Such, indeed, is the kernel of much criticism of the early rights declarations from Marx,[63] to MacPherson,[64] to Brown.[65] The merits of these criticisms notwithstanding, this does not detract from the importance placed by these early rights declarations on representation (today though we may stress the wider notion of participation as well as a more inclusionary conception of representation). Nevertheless, some of the eighteenth century contributions to rights discourse started to identify some important progressive aspects of financial matters and rights. Two critical contributions come from Kant and Paine.

The German philosopher Kant made numerous contributions to legal and political theory; these do not attract as much attention as his contributions to theories of epistemology, morals or judgement.[66] However, for the purposes of this chapter, three key observations stand out.

First, Kant did not ground rights in empirical nature; rather rights are determined through the exercise of reason. This means that rights are not something grounded in nature and so something that have to be taken for granted. Admittedly, Kant's faith in the power of reason may well recreate some of the problems associated with the idea of nature but it at least moves the debate on to less philosophically shaky ground.

Second, and even more strikingly, Kant cleanly and precisely nails the ideological myth that is frequently invoked to stymie progressive change. Against the argument that one has some sort of inalienable right to one's property and that any taxation is at best a necessary evil, Kant makes it explicit that property is an institution created by law and upheld by the force of the state. It is only possible to make a claim about property rights under the condition that there are laws created by civil government.[67] There is then, no pre-political or pre-legal entitlement to any particular property, but only an entitlement to what the just laws of the state permit.

Third, to be just, the laws of the state must provide for the less fortunate. Kant explains that a people unite into a civil constitution for self-preservation; part of this is that the state must preserve those who cannot do so by their own efforts. For this purpose the state may demand resources from the wealthy:

[63] K Marx, 'On the Jewish Question' in E Easton and K Guddat (eds), *Writings of the Young Marx on Philosophy and Society* (Garden City NY, Doubleday Books, 1967).

[64] CB MacPherson, *The Theory of Possessive Individualism* (Oxford, Oxford University Press, 1962).

[65] W Brown, 'Suffering the Paradoxes of Rights' in W Brown and J Halley (eds), *Left Legalism/Left Critique* (Durham NC, Duke University Press, 2002).

[66] H Arendt, *Lectures on Kant's Political Philosophy* (Brighton, Harvester Press, 1982).

[67] I Kant, *The Metaphysics of Morals* (Cambridge, Cambridge University Press, 1991) 255–56 (Prussian Academy pagination).

> The wealthy have acquired an obligation to the commonwealth, since they owe their existence to an act of submitting to its protection and care, which they need in order to live; on this obligation the state now bases its right to contribute what is theirs to maintaining their fellow citizens.[68]

There is therefore no injustice (not even a necessary evil) in taxation for this purpose. To be explicit: the wealth of the more fortunate in society exists only because of the care and protection of the state. These theoretical points of Kant's seem to be equally relevant to late twentieth and early twenty-first century arguments about property and taxation. There is still a tendency to portray property and wealth as being deserved, earned and merited by those who possess them. There are good arguments for recognising some right to property; however, these cannot justify claims that one's wealth is somehow entirely of one's own creation. The Kantian objection that property depended on the laws and force of the state is just as valid or perhaps more so today.

Writing in less abstract language, though certainly no less forceful for that, is the work of English pamphleteer, citizen of America and France, Thomas Paine. Paine's *Rights of Man* is a defence of the principles of the French Revolution and in particular the Declaration of the Rights of Man and of the Citizen, against the criticisms made by Edmund Burke. *The Rights of Man* includes a significant section engaging in what might be called human rights budget analysis; this is found in a chapter entitled 'Of Ways and Means'. This follows his discussion of the 'new' system of government which is a defence of representative democracy as against government founded on the hereditary principle. There are links between the rights of man (or 'human rights' as Paine at one points translates from the French), representative government and the budgetary questions he addresses. For Paine, one of the key aspects of representative government is that things must be done publicly; this gives the opportunity for everyone to supervise public business. People will naturally, Paine feels, conduct this supervision, because public business affects their interests in their property.[69] Perhaps very significantly, he highlights how political power must not be controlled by any vested interests for fear the latter will obstruct financial measures in the cause of self-interest. In this matter he has in mind the House of Lords' opposition to taxation on its source of wealth (ie, land),[70] though he also criticises the franchise system in England.[71]

His discussion of ways and means addresses numerous questions, from the financing of the military to a scheme to pay off the national debt. It starts by identifying ways of reducing expenditure, most notably imagining that the expenditure on the armed forces could be reduced thanks to a hypothetical alliance with France (and America).[72] This would generate substantial savings.

[68] Ibid 326.
[69] T Paine, *Rights of Man* (London, Penguin, 1984, first published in 1791) 184.
[70] Ibid 224–25.
[71] Paine above n 69, 223.
[72] Ibid 234.

His proposals for dealing with these savings are the most interesting, for they include the idea of directing these resources to the neediest in society. Specifically he proposes major schemes to provide grants to the elderly poor, and also to families on condition they educate their children.[73] Paine shows a need to tackle both poverty and ignorance, and appreciates that educating the young is the key to reducing poverty in the long term. He also proposes several other welfare measures (for childbirth, marrying and certain funeral expenses) and a scheme to provide shelter and occupation for the casual poor migrating to London. With regard to this last proposal, Paine again shows an understanding of the interlinked social nature of social problems; failing to attend to the needs of this group would likely lead to other social costs, notably in the form of crime.[74] As well as these provisions, he also proposes some tax relief (carefully chosen so as not to disturb trade). He finally proposes a new *progressive* tax on land bequests which would discourage the practice of primogeniture.[75]

These suggestions of Paine are noteworthy in their prescience. First, Paine makes a link between the financial proposals and the political system. He considers that it is necessary to have a political system in which no one privileged elite or vested interest has a stranglehold or veto power on the decisions made. Second, he shows an awareness of the need for prioritisation and efficiency. Economies, or cuts, should be sought by looking at the payment of the military and the public service (indeed, he regularly rails against court expenditure). Third, resources should be directed at the most vulnerable. Fourth, taxation should aim to be progressive. Fifth, there is a need to appreciate the interconnectedness of social problems—a failure to educate the young may lead to poverty later; a failure to provide for shelter and employment may lead to petty crime. Sixth, this is all a matter of politics, even economics; Paine does not look to judges to decide these matters. Seventh, the welfare payments that Paine has in mind are not acts of 'charity, but of a right'; Paine outlines how the recipients of the payments for the elderly have earned this support through their life time of paying taxes.[76] Finally, it should be noted that Paine is also concerned with the protection of trade in any reform; indeed, he links commerce to the idea of civilisation.[77]

VI. Post-Revolutionary Era

The late eighteenth century discussions of human rights and public finances, especially those around the French Declaration and Paine's novel ideas, show a

[73] Ibid 240–41.
[74] Ibid 246.
[75] Ibid 250–58.
[76] Ibid 243.
[77] Ibid 212.

sense of awareness of the interrelationship of human rights with matters of public money. Undoubtedly this is due to the particular social and economic context. However, the awareness of this interrelationship becomes much more muted, at least when one turns to formal texts of human rights, after the revolutionary era.

This absence of express concern with public finance matters in declarations of rights is most obvious with the foundational document of the modern international human rights law system. The 1948 Universal Declaration of Human Rights (UDHR) is the product of many political, social and philosophical influences. It is famously agnostic in terms of foundational values so that it might appeal to people of all nations and traditions, notwithstanding their religious beliefs (or lack thereof).[78]

The genuine multiplicity of influences on the Universal Declaration should not lead us to overlook the similarities with the 1789 Declaration.[79] This is evident in its title as a declaration, the pedagogic nature of its preamble and the brevity of its language. The Universal Declaration's Article 1 reference to all being born free and equal in rights is an echo of Article 1 of the 1789 Declaration. Many of the rights in the 1789 Declaration make their way into the UDHR. On the other hand, there are several that do not. Many of the 1789 provisions that do not make the translation to the twentieth century Declaration are those most concerned with political principles rather than individual rights. There is no reference to national sovereignty for example (or the concept of self-determination), while the 1789 right of 'resistance to oppression' is downgraded from a 'natural and imprescriptible' right to an empirical consequence, a negative side effect of the disrespect of rights (UDHR Preamble). The French provisions on financial matters, although included in an early draft put forward by René Cassin,[80] get lost entirely.

VII. Conclusion

As we have seen, issues of public financing have been historically important to the emerging language of human rights in the late eighteenth century revolutions. Many of the contributions are still relevant today. Kant's admonition that those with property only possess it because of the laws and power of the state is a healthy antidote to excessive clams about the sacredness of property rights.

[78] J Morsink, *The Universal Declaration of Human Rights: Origins, Drafting and Intent* (Philadelphia, University of Pennsylvania Press, 2000) 283.

[79] See S Marks, 'From the "Single Confused Page" to the "Decalogue for Six Billion Persons": The Roots of the Universal Declaration in the French Revolution' (1998) 20 *Human Rights Quarterly* 459; LA Hunt, *Inventing Human Rights: A History* (New York, WW Norton & Co, 2007).

[80] Draft Art 26: 'Everyone has the right to take an equal part, directly or through his representatives, in the formation of law, the institution of taxes for public expense and the government of the State of which he is a citizen or of depending territories. Each citizen shall take his part of public expenses according to his means' (E/CN.4/AC.1/W.2/REV.2) 20 June 1947.

Paine's schemes for economic reform find their modern form in arguments for progressive human rights oriented theories of economics,[81] while his insistence on protecting the most vulnerable finds echoes both in General Comments of the Committee on Economic Social and Cultural Rights and in the example of group-specific budget work.[82] The French Declaration of 1789 offers a useful set of human rights principles that need to apply to questions of taxation and public finances: taxation is justified to provide a public force, taxation should be based on ideas of equality and progressivity; there must be participation (directly or through representatives) and accountability.

The most striking feature of some of these early debates about the rights of man and public affairs is their deeply political nature. For the most part, the discussion is not about what judicial authorities make of rights, but as to how practical persons understand them and implement them. The French Revolution itself was partly a revolution against judicial power, against the *noblesse de la robe*. The American Bill of Rights was adopted before the striking affirmation of judicial review in *Marbury v Madison*.[83] When American judges get involved in these debates, their decisions are by no means happy ones.

Yet the debates are political in another sense, beyond merely going further than a consideration of the judicial role; they are bound up in wider questions of the legitimacy of the political system. This is so with Kant and even more so with Paine. Paine believes that a representative democratic system, where public business is conducted publicly and for the common good, is the only system where the rights of man are realised. That entails promoting commerce, curtailing unnecessary expenditure but also directing resources to the most vulnerable. This emphasis on the legitimacy of the wider political system is important. Sadly today we need to be more cautious, indeed sceptical, than was Paine of the merits of the representative democracy. It is not so obvious today that existing representative democracies conduct their business publicly, for the common good, without care for special interests.

This deeply political nature of the rights of man was somewhat sidelined in many of the human rights law debates of the later twentieth century. The Universal Declaration lost the pre-eminently political rights of self-determination, resistance to oppression and public finances. Whilst the right to take part in public affairs was included, for most of the Cold War this right was downplayed. It is therefore welcome that as we come back to the idea of looking at budgets and public finance through the prism of human rights that we attend to the more political understanding of the role of rights.

This reflects a key aspect of human rights work in the area of public finances and budgets. It is directed more explicitly at the political rather than the judicial

[81] See the contribution by Elson, Balakrishnan and Heintz to this volume.
[82] See the contributions by Quinn and Ganguly Thukral to this volume.
[83] *Marbury v Madison* (1803) 5 US 137 Cranch.

arena. This does not mean that judges are irrelevant—far from it.[84] However, the focus is put where it properly belongs, on those entrusted by the public with the management of public affairs. Human rights work in this area pays tribute therefore to the promise in the Preamble of the UDHR, that 'every individual and organ of society' should aim to secure 'universal and effective recognition and observance' of all human rights. This requires educating (or re-educating) politicians in the importance of human rights. In doing this, the work is perhaps made easier by the creation of specialist human rights committees within parliaments, which can help generate a distinctive parliamentary voice in human rights debates.[85]

It is not just a question of politicians *speaking* the language of human rights however.[86] With that we also need to attend to questions of the wider political system. Paine was right to see representative government as practised in America as an improvement, indeed a revolutionary improvement, over the systems of hereditary government as practised in Europe. However, representative democracy has probably not lived up to his ideals of openness, public scrutiny and pursuit of the common good rather than vested interests. The level of meaningful participation or even scrutiny in representative democracies has been troublesome. This has become even more of a problem as political parties in mass democracies have become election winning machines. Such competitions between political parties may devalue politics by putting an emphasis on the techniques of political marketing rather than political discussion. Election winning machines also require considerable financial support. At a deeper, structural level, politicians are dependent on economic actors to generate the wealth that keeps the political system going.[87] There are challenges here about the nature of the political system.

To some extent, that is to be met by enhancing opportunities for participation perhaps through mainstreaming processes or participatory budgeting. Such participatory processes should allow for persons affected by public decisions and organisations representing such people, to make their views known and so influence the decision-making process. This means reinserting in modern political practice the Athenian model that Paine thought was lost. Such participatory practices may take the form of statutory duties to consult. In the UK, there is already

[84] See the cases discussed in A Nolan and M Dutschke, 'Article 2(1) ICESCR and States Parties' Obligations: Whither the Budget?' (2010) 3 *European Human Rights Law Review* 280, 280–89.

[85] M Hunt, 'The Impact of the Human Rights Act on the Legislature: A Diminution of Democracy or a New Voice for Parliament?' (2010) 6 *European Human Rights Law Review* 601, 601–608; M Hunt, 'Enhancing Parliament's Role in Relation to Economic and Social Rights' (2010) 3 *European Human Rights Law Review* 242. Keith Ewing though is more wary of the merits of such parliamentary committees: K Ewing, 'The Parliamentary Protection of Human Rights' (2007) 3 *Studies—Oxford Institute of European and Comparative Law* 253.

[86] Harvey and Rooney warn of the danger of human rights language being misappropriated: C Harvey and E Rooney, 'Integrating Human Rights? Socio-economic Rights and Budget Analysis' (2010) 3 *European Human Rights Law Review* 266, 266–79.

[87] See the discussion of Claus Offe's *Contradictions of the Welfare State* (London, Hutchinson, 1984) in D Held, *Models of Democracy* (Cambridge, Polity, 2006) 176–79.

an example of a local authority being told to reconsider its plans to implement budget cuts because of a failure to consider properly the impact of the cuts on people with disabilities and a failure to consult properly on the proposals.[88]

Whilst introducing participatory elements where possible is welcome, it can only be part of the response. In modern large-scale societies, Paine's basic insight still seems right, that we require representative institutions. The key here is how might representative institutions be designed so that they live up to their promises; we need to reconsider how the mechanisms of representative democracy can be made more transparent and open, and less susceptible to dominance by elites. There is considerable work being done on how to improve the mechanisms of democracy, including representative democracy, from the Power Inquiry in the UK,[89] the Democratic audit in several countries[90] and also in the work of the United Nations Development Programme (UNDP).[91] What all this highlights is that the protection of social and economic rights is interdependent with the protection of political rights.

[88] *R (W) v Birmingham City Council* [2011] EWHC 1147 (Admin) 19 May 2011.

[89] Power Inquiry, *Power to the People* (London, Power Inquiry, 2006).

[90] See eg, D Beetham, I Byrne, P Ngan and S Weir, *Democracy under Blair* (London, Politico, 2002), I Hughes, P Clancy, C Harris and D Beetham, *Power to the People? Assessing Democracy in Ireland* (Dublin, TASC, 2007).

[91] UN Development Programme (UNDP), *Human Development Report 2002: Deepening Democracy in a Fragmented World* (Oxford, Oxford University Press, 2002).

6

Better on the Margins? A Critique of Mainstreaming Economic and Social Rights

EOIN ROONEY AND COLIN HARVEY

I. Introduction

The development of a rights-based approach to budgets requires input from a number of disciplines. Legal expertise is used to establish the meaning of legal norms and what constitutes compliance with economic and social rights (ESR) obligations, while economic techniques are applied to budgets in order to measure compliance with those obligations. The question of how to *promote* compliance with ESR raises the need for analysis of a more political nature.

In recent years the human rights movement has turned its attention to mainstreaming in a sustained attempt to extend ownership and responsibility for the promotion and protection of rights beyond the confines of the legal system, and into the heart of public administration. This was to be expected given that many justifications of rights, across the political spectrum, often accord a central role to government for their realisation and delivery—with the concept of the constitutional state arising precisely for this purpose. The idea of the liberal state emerged from the desire to advance collective forms of governance that would offer security and protection to individuals.

The aim of this chapter is to provide a critical appraisal of mainstreaming theory in relation to ESR. It discusses the theory of change underpinning the concept—the transformation of government via the absorption of rights-based discourse into state policies and practices primarily through procedural mechanisms—in the context of the pervasive influence of 'neoliberal' thought. We conclude that if the contestation brought by human rights discourse (with its intrinsic resistance to all notions of closure) is to remain productive, strategies to promote human rights may benefit from a more circumspect relationship with the state than that envisaged by mainstreaming.

II. Human Rights Law and Mainstreaming in Perspective

As human rights attained a more prominent role in discussions of democratic governance, ESR have become a reasonably secure aspect of the global discursive landscape—anti-poverty and social justice work is now often expressed through rights-based language and approaches.[1] Yet some remain discomfited by the deployment of rights to socio-economic justice issues, with most anxiety directed towards the judicial role and the dangers of processes of constitutionalisation.[2] An 'argument from democracy' emerges, voicing concern with the prospect of the judiciary assuming responsibility for setting priorities, allocating scarce resources and generally shaping the approach. The debates are frequently hampered by underexplored assumptions about ESR. Human rights scholarship has, in fact, worked to detach rights-based approaches from narrow versions of court-centred legalism, an excessive focus on judges and lawyers and sought to challenge default assumptions about rights and individualism.

Mainstreaming can be viewed as one part of this wider challenge to more conventional accounts. The concept emerged in the mid-1970s from a feminist critique of UN aid programmes.[3] The argument was that 'special' development initiatives for women were inadequate to deliver gender equality because they allowed the gender bias of the core programmes to go unchallenged. This developed into a broader analysis that rather than being a separate add-on, gender equality should be considered at *all* levels of government, at *all* stages of decision-making and on *all* policies—including budgetary policies. The main tools for incorporating a gender analysis were gender impact assessments[4] and consultations with women.

The idea has since extended to other group-based inequalities,[5] and it is entirely conceivable that mainstreaming could further expand to human rights through the application of Human Rights Impact Assessments and more extensive

[1] See eg, the Vienna Declaration and Programme of Action, adopted by the World Conference on Human Rights in 1993 (UN Doc A/CONF.157/23); UN Office of the High Commissioner for Human Rights, *Human Rights and Poverty Reduction: A Conceptual Framework* (New York and Geneva, UN, 2004); UN Office of the High Commissioner for Human Rights, *Principles and Guidelines for a Human Rights Based Approach to Poverty Reduction Strategies* (Geneva, UN, 2006).

[2] See the chapters collected in M Langford (ed), *Social Rights Jurisprudence: Emerging Trends in International and Comparative Law* (New York, Cambridge University Press, 2009).

[3] See H Charlesworth, 'Not Waving but Drowning: Gender Mainstreaming and Human Rights in the United Nations' (2005) 18 *Harvard Human Rights Journal* 1.

[4] Specific techniques were fashioned for assessing the gender impact of budgets. See D Elson, 'Integrating Gender Issues into National Budgetary Policies and Procedures: Some Policy Options' (1998) 10 *Journal of International Development* 929.

[5] For instance the mainstreaming duty in Northern Ireland (s 75 Northern Ireland Act 1998) specifies nine equality grounds. See C McCrudden, 'Mainstreaming Equality in the Governance of Northern Ireland' (1998) 22(4) *Fordham International Law Journal* 1694.

participation of disadvantaged groups in decision-making.[6] For example, in order to decide how to allocate its budget between various projects, a public body could first screen the options (conduct a brief assessment) to establish a shortlist. Human Rights Impact Assessments of each shortlisted project could then be conducted in order to more thoroughly appraise their respective merits.[7] The public body could then fund the projects that are most beneficial to human rights, until its budget is exhausted. Each stage of this process could be carried out in consultation with vulnerable and affected groups.

This is not to erode or deny the judicial role in forging interpretative clarity; in our view if 'mainstreaming' is to have meaning this must also involve a critical appraisal of the judicial role—and more work should be undertaken to map this into and onto both the public and private sectors. Why should legal cultures and the institutions of law be exempted from the rigours of a mainstreaming analysis?[8] Rather, a process of 'bottom up' and 'top down' constitutionalisation of governance arrangements is envisaged.

From this perspective, the appeal of mainstreaming to advocates of socio-economic rights is easy to understand. By requiring states to consider human rights on every issue and across all its spheres of operation, mainstreaming seeks to embed the *comprehensive* promotion of rights within administrative systems and logics. It anticipates that with the repeated application of impact assessments and regular dialogue with disadvantaged groups, mainstreaming will move beyond a technical exercise, and rights will gradually become ingrained in the very *culture* and ecology of government. On this basis mainstreaming is often described as having 'transformative' potential.[9]

If this potential is to be realised, the state must fulfil four main conditions. In the first instance, the state must adopt a procedural requirement to conduct screening exercises and impact assessments, and to solicit the views of affected groups as part of its decision-making processes. Second, these exercises must actually be carried out. Both of these requirements are amenable to formal enactment through legislation, with mainstreaming typically given a statutory status, although enforcement is often left to the political domain.[10] Third, it is essential that impact assessments and consultations are administered in good faith, as opposed to in a tokenistic manner. Finally, the government must use the information gathered to select options that maximise the enjoyment of

[6] See the chapters by Quinn and Harrison and Stephenson in this collection.

[7] For a discussion of how economic techniques might be used as part of such a process see C Harvey and E Rooney, 'Integrating Human Rights? Socio-economic Rights and Budget Analysis' (2010) 3 *European Human Rights Law Review* 266.

[8] See the chapters in C Harvey (ed), *Human Rights in the Community: Rights as Agents of Change* (Oxford, Hart Publishing, 2005) which examine legal mainstreaming approaches.

[9] Indeed, mainstreaming has been described as a 'potentially revolutionary concept' in E Hafner-Burton and MA Pollack, 'Gender Mainstreaming and Global Governance' (2002) 10 *Feminist Legal Studies* 285, 288.

[10] For example, s 75 Northern Ireland Act 1998 puts equality mainstreaming on a statutory footing but it is the Secretary of State who enforces compliance.

ESR—the idea being that the knowledge gained will be used to achieve practical changes. Legal mechanisms are of little direct relevance to these last two requirements—what might be called compliance with the 'spirit' of mainstreaming. This is why mainstreaming is typically characterised as a form of 'soft law'[11] that carries a particularised version of normativity with it—there may well be associated operational norms capable of direct enforcement through the courts, but mainstreaming also requires the good will and commitment of the state. The normative commitments should ideally be absorbed into the very 'being' of governance—constituting the new 'common sense' of public administration.

What interests us here is the prospect of these requirements being satisfied in the contemporary social and economic environment. Our approach flows from an appreciation of the counter-hegemonic and emancipatory opportunities that are still carried forward within rights discourse, the value of social movements in promoting rights (globally and locally) and the danger of human rights being reduced to corrosive versions of narrow legalism that are all too easily absorbed and tamed by institutional cultures of domination and control.[12] We thus seek to view *human rights law in perspective.*[13] In our view, the influence of neoliberalism is an important part of that context.

III. Neoliberalism and Human Rights

In order to assess whether the necessary commitment to mainstreaming is likely to be present, it is useful to consider the compatibility of the intellectual basis of ESR with the mindset that underpins contemporary approaches to governing. Of course, governments are characterised by considerable complexity, variation and specificity—and we are mindful not to endorse any reductionist approaches.

[11] S Mazey, 'Gender Mainstreaming Strategies in the EU: Delivering on an Agenda?' (2002) 10 *Feminist Legal Studies* 228, 232.

[12] See eg, A Hunt, 'Rights and Social Movements: Counter-Hegemonic Strategies' (1990) 17 *Journal of Law and Society* 309; SE Merry et al, 'Law from Below: Women's Human Rights and Social Movements in New York City' (2010) 44 *Law and Society Review* 101, 'human rights offer a variety of discursive, political, and strategic benefits to social movements even when they do not mobilise them as law' 101–02; they also note that 'the human rights system is surprisingly open to relatively powerless groups' 101; B de Sousa Santos and CA Rodriguez-Gavravito, 'Law, Politics, and the Subaltern in Counter-Hegemonic Globalisation' in B de Sousa Santos and CA Rodriguez-Gavravito (eds), *Law and Globalisation from Below: Towards a Cosmopolitan Legality* (Cambridge, Cambridge University Press, 2005); C Douzinas, *The End of Human Rights* (Oxford, Hart Publishing, 2000). For a critical assessment of the role of rights-based litigation, see M Pieterse, 'Health, Social Movements and Rights-based Litigation in South Africa' (2008) 35 *Journal of Law and Society* 364; cp J Dugard and M Langford, 'Art or Science? Synthesising Lessons from Public Interest Litigation and the Dangers of Legal Determinism' (2011) 27 *South African Journal of Human Rights* 39. See also, A Estévez, 'Human Rights in Contemporary Political Sociology: The Primacy of Social Subjects' (2011) 33 *Human Rights Quarterly* 1142 where she usefully explores 'the way social subjects use power in the construction of human rights discourse' 1144.

[13] C Harvey, 'A Conversation without End?' (2011) 80 *Fordham Law Review—Res Gestae* 1.

However, with the spread of neoliberalism since circa 1979—part of modern processes of globalisation—a relatively coherent discourse on how socio-economic life should be governed has attained widespread acceptance.

At its core, neoliberalism extols the virtue of markets, which are regarded as the basis of freedom and prosperity. What this faith in markets means for the role of the state causes considerable confusion. Does it signal a return to the 'minimal state' of classical liberalism? Some neoliberal theorists advocate such a position. Robert Nozick, for example, argues:

> [A] minimal state, limited to the narrow functions of protection against force, theft, fraud, enforcement of contracts, and so on, is justified ... the state may not use its coercive apparatus for the purpose of getting some citizens to aid others, or in order to prohibit activities to people for their *own* good or protection.[14]

In addition, opposition to government 'interference'—the 'nanny state'—has characterised much of the political rhetoric associated with neoliberalism. This interpretation also has a strong basis in practice; many forms of government intervention that characterised 'social liberalism' such as regulatory frameworks, state ownership of assets, public services and currency and price controls, have been dismantled. Accepting this interpretation, some conceive the active state demanded by mainstreaming as a countervailing force to the passive state advocated by neoliberalism.[15]

Others point out that governments in the neoliberal 'era' are in fact typically highly interventionist,[16] and attribute the inconsistency between theory and practice to political artifice. Harvey argues that the rhetoric of free markets and non-intervention is employed when it accords with the interests of 'economic elites'[17] and 'abandoned'[18] when it does not. Chomsky characterises 'really existing' neoliberalism as 'market discipline is good for you but not for me'[19] while Stiglitz also discerns duplicity: 'The critics of globalisation accuse Western countries of hypocrisy, and the critics are right. The Western countries have pushed poor countries to eliminate trade barriers, but kept up their own barriers'.[20]

Without denying the influence of vested interests or the presence of opportunism, it is important to acknowledge that there is a body of neoliberal theory which is more

[14] R Nozick, *Anarchy, State, and Utopia* (Oxford, Basic Books, 1974) ix.

[15] In reference to the equality mainstreaming duty in Northern Ireland, Campbell argues that: 'At a time when the global political ascendancy of neo-liberalism was promoting the withdrawal of the state, the new Northern Ireland state was expected to be interventionist, redistributive, and disciplined by a generous dialogue with the civil society': B Campell, *Agreement! The State, Conflict and Change in Northern Ireland* (London, Lawrence & Wishart, 2008) 11. See also C Bacchi and J Eveline, 'Mainstreaming and Neoliberalism: A Contested Relationship' (2003) 22 *Policy and Society* 102.

[16] As indeed was the state in the era of classical liberalism, from which neoliberal thought draws much inspiration. See H Chang, *Kicking Away the Ladder* (London, Anthem Press, 2003) and P Bairoch, *Economics and World History* (Chicago, University of Chicago, 1995).

[17] D Harvey, *A Brief History of Neoliberalism* (Oxford, Open University, 2007) 19.

[18] Ibid.

[19] N Chomsky, *Profit Over People: Neoliberalism and Global Order* (London, Turnaround, 1999) 34.

[20] J Stiglitz, *Globalisation and its Discontents* (London, Penguin, 2002) 6.

consistent with the practice: which accepts that markets will not spontaneously flourish as the state withdraws; that a society modelled on market principles must be *created*; and that the state has a vital role to play in its construction.[21] The neoliberal state is 'active, vigilant and intervening'[22] creating markets where they are absent, restoring them when they break down and managing their socially and politically hazardous consequences.[23] The shift from social liberalism to neoliberalism has not involved a reduction of state intervention as much as a change in the nature of its activity. Government intervenes in order to 'make markets work'.[24] In human rights terms the state is recast primarily as an 'enabler' rather than a direct 'provider' or 'regulator'. Its role is to 'empower' people to participate effectively in social, economic and political life.[25] This could even be viewed as a resurgence of social liberalism, part of a newly revived and revised social democratic project—aligned to developments in social scientific research agendas—that diagnoses the obstacles to social inclusion, social mobility and participation.[26]

Whichever way the 'neoliberal turn' is expressed, under human rights law the role of the state is not to encourage the domination of the public and private spheres by markets; what matters is the protection and promotion of human rights, whatever political or economic system happens to be in place. This subordination of markets to rights provokes criticism from Petersmann who, in articulating a market-based approach to socio-economic rights, complains that the International Covenant on Economic, Social and Cultural Rights (ICESCR) 'neglect for economic liberty rights and property rights … reflects an anti-market bias'.[27] However, ICESCR (like human rights law in general) is not *anti*-market; it is a pragmatic tool that recognises that rights can be promoted through a range of mechanisms.[28] The optimum approach, whether market, non-market or some hybrid, is that which best advances ESR in particular circumstances. The market is viewed as a means, not as an end in itself. This sits uncomfortably with the tendency within neoliberalism to promote markets as *inherently* virtuous, due in

[21] See M Foucault, *The Birth of Biopolitics: Lecturers at the College de France 1978–1979* (Basingstoke, Palgrave Macmillan, 2008) 132–33.

[22] Ibid 133.

[23] Eg, the threat to 'the social' posed by the liberation of selfish individualism—as expressed in concerns around social exclusion, social cohesion, social capital etc.

[24] J Lovering, 'The Relationship between Urban Regeneration and Neoliberalism: Two Presumptuous Theories and a Research Agenda' (2007) 4 *International Planning Studies* 354.

[25] See eg, A Giddens, *The Third Way* (Cambridge, Polity Press, 1998); Special Issue 'Social Democracy' (2004) XVII *Canadian Journal of Law and Jurisprudence*.

[26] Cp Giddens ibid. For a critique of the notion that the New Labour project harnesses markets towards a social democratic agenda see S Hall, 'New Labour's Double-shuffle' (2005) 27 *Review of Education, Pedagogy, and Cultural Studies* 319.

[27] E Petersmann, 'Time for a United Nations "Global Compact" for Integrating Human Rights into the Law of Worldwide Organisations: Lessons from European Integration' (2002) 13 *European Journal of International Law* 621.

[28] See ComESCR General Comment No 3 on the nature of States parties' obligations (art 2 (1)), UN Doc E/1991/23 (1990), para 8 which confirms the neutrality of the Covenant with respect to political and economic systems.

part to their equation with freedom. As put starkly by Hayek: 'to be free may mean freedom to starve'.[29]

Nevertheless, it could be argued that markets maximise economic growth, providing the optimal basis for the enjoyment of ESR[30]—therefore states committed to ICESCR will invariably privilege market solutions. However, growth has not been particularly strong in the neoliberal era.[31] Comparing the 1950 to 1973 period of 'managed capitalism' with the 'market capitalism' of 1980 to 2009, Lansley concludes that on a range of indicators,

> [o]n only one count—curbing inflation—can the post-1980 era be judged a clear success ... On all other counts the economic record of market capitalism has been inferior to that of managed capitalism. Growth and productivity rates have been slower, unemployment levels higher ... Financial crises have become more frequent and more damaging in their consequences.[32]

In addition, the benefits of growth have primarily accrued to the wealthiest social groups, widening economic inequality.[33] Such inequality is associated with disparities in a range of indicators of social welfare including health and education[34] (key ESR) and undermines social mobility,[35] meaning that these inequalities are likely to be reproduced in subsequent generations. This is difficult to reconcile with ESR obligations, which place a duty on the state to work towards equal enjoyment and to give priority to disadvantaged groups. Indeed, Special Rapporteurs have noted with concern the differential impact of neoliberal policies. For example, the Special Rapporteur on the Right to Adequate Housing comments that the marketisation[36] of housing had 'good results for a part of the population'[37] but undermined housing availability and affordability for many,

[29] F Hayek, *The Constitution of Liberty* (London, Routledge, 2009) 17.

[30] This is presumably what Petersmann means when he argues that the 'global division of labour' creates 'additional economic resources' in turn presenting 'new opportunities for the worldwide enjoyment of human rights': 'Time for a United Nations "Global Compact"' above n 27, 624. On this contested relationship, see also D Beetham, *Democracy and Human Rights* (Cambridge, Polity, 1999).

[31] A Glynn, *Capitalism Unleashed: Finance, Globalisation, and Welfare* (Oxford, Oxford University Press, 2007) 131; JN Cohen and MA Centeno, 'Neoliberalism and Patterns of Economic Performance, 1980–2000' (2006) 606 *Annals of the American Academy of Political and Social Science* 32, 53–55.

[32] S Lansley, *The Cost of Inequality: Why Equality is Essential to Recovery* (London, Gibson Square, 2012) 126.

[33] Eg, in the US from 1979 to 2003 real wages stagnated for those in the bottom decile of the income scale and increased by 27.2% for those in the top decile: Glynn above n 31, 116–19, 167–70. See also Cohen and Centeno above n 31, 55–57; AB Atkinson, 'The Distribution of Earnings in OECDt Countries' (2007) 146 *International Labour Review* 41, 53; Lansley above n 32.

[34] R Wilkinson and K Pickett, *The Spirit Level: Why More Equal Societies Almost Always Do Better* (London, Penguin, 2009).

[35] Ibid; K Busby, 'Social Mobility' (2012) 4 *The Equality Trust: Research Digest.*

[36] The decline of public/social housing, the promotion of homeownership and the deregulation of mortgage financing.

[37] R Rolnik, 'Report of the Special Rapporteur on the Right to Adequate Housing as a Component of the Right to an Adequate Standard of Living, and the Right to Non-discrimination in this Context: Promotion and Protection of all Human Rights, Civil, Political, Economic, Social and Cultural Rights, including the Right to Development' (UN Doc A/HRC/10/7 2009) 13.

particularly lower-income households.[38] Whatever normative view is taken, it seems that rigid adherence to neoliberal ideology will not necessarily ensure the full protection of ESR.

The above discussion in no way attempts to provide a comprehensive comparison of ESR and neoliberalism. Our purpose is merely to highlight the *potential* for conflict between the two and consequently to raise the possibility that the political commitment required for successful mainstreaming of ESR may not be present in the current environment. We now turn to the implications of this contention.

IV. Power, Discourse and the Interpretative Struggle over Rights

It could be argued that notwithstanding the challenges, human rights advocates should pursue mainstreaming as far as is possible. The allure of 'immanent critique'[39] for societal change remains strong given that a range of human rights standards are widely endorsed and that interpretative tools offer 'real world' normative footholds for practical advancement. Some state officials may carry out tokenistic impact assessments and consultations, but others will embrace it. Even in a difficult intellectual environment, mainstreaming surely has the potential to produce *some* change?

In pursuing this line of thinking it is useful to reflect more thoroughly on the theory of change—and therefore of power—upon which mainstreaming is premised. In many respects it is grounded in a very credible analysis. Mainstreaming targets the state, a key site of societal power. It calls for the participation of the disadvantaged, in acknowledgment that notwithstanding universal suffrage, different social groups have unequal influence over government decision-making. Moreover, mainstreaming moves beyond a narrow coercive understanding of the state and recognises the productive power of *discourse*. Drawing on Foucault, Hall describes discourse in the following manner:

> Discourse … governs the way that a topic can be meaningfully talked about and reasoned about. It also influences how ideas are put into practice and used to regulate the conduct of others. Just as a discourse 'rules in' certain ways of talking about a topic, defining an acceptable and intelligible way to talk, write, or conduct oneself, so also, by

[38] See also Rooney and Dutschke's chapter in this volume.

[39] The idea being that social criticism should be based on concrete, existing and accepted politico-legal standards (rather than simply contested and abstract moral or ethical criteria). This is particularly appealing in the realm of human rights because of the sheer volume of voluntarily assumed standards and the regularity with which human rights are endorsed in political rhetoric.

> definition, it 'rules out', limits and restricts other ways of talking, of conducting ourselves in relation to the topic or constructing knowledge about it.[40]

Mainstreaming then, attempts to promote not just a set of goals or procedures, but more fundamentally a vocabulary and a *mentality* for thinking about governance. Appreciating the key role of knowledge in this endeavour, it also provides techniques with which to systematically apply a human rights approach. Mainstreaming recognises that the state is a negotiable site (as opposed to a monolithic institution imposing its will on society from 'on high') and that the discourses circulating within it are contestable. On this basis it attempts to ensure that human rights dominate the discussion, or that they are at least part of the conversation.

However, in recognising the negotiable nature of the state it is important to also acknowledge the malleability of human rights.[41] In other words, the meaning of ESR is itself a matter of interpretation and the points at which it complements, differs from and is antagonistic to other discourses depends on how they are articulated. The Petersmann–Alston debate provides a pertinent example. In response to Petersmann's argument for a market-based interpretation of socio-economic rights,[42] Alston contends:

> In a form of epistemological misappropriation he [ie Petersmann] takes the discourse of international human rights law and uses it to describe something which is in between a Hayekian and an ordoliberal agenda. It is one which has a fundamentally different ideological underpinning from human rights law.[43]

Whatever the merits of each author's arguments,[44] the exchange underlines the capacity of ESR to be framed and understood in accordance with a broadly neoliberal perspective. Given this flexibility, the question is: would mainstreaming bring state discourses into alignment with ESR or would the rights-based approach be brought into conformity with the neoliberal agenda of the state? The experience of gender mainstreaming may offer some answers.

[40] S Hall (ed), *Representation: Cultural Representations and Signifying Practices* (London, SAGE, 1997) 44.

[41] See GCN Webber, *The Negotiable Constitution: On the Limitation of Rights* (Cambridge, Cambridge University Press, 2009).

[42] What Petersmann understands by ESR is not entirely clear, but it appears as though they are confined to the correction of 'market failures' and a minimal safety net for vulnerable groups; or in human rights terms, they are limited to the duty to 'protect' and the minimum core. See particularly Petersmann, 'Time for a United Nations "Global Compact"' above n 27, 640–41.

[43] P Alston, 'Resisting the Merger and Acquisition of Human Rights by Trade Law: A Reply to Petersmann' (2002) 13 *European Journal of International Law* 815, 842.

[44] See E Petersmann, 'Taking Human Dignity, Poverty and Empowerment of Individuals More Seriously: Rejoinder to Alston' (2002) 13 *European Journal of International Law*; R Howse, 'Human Rights in the WTO: Whose Rights, What Humanity? Comment on Petersmann' (2002) 13 *European Journal of International Law* 651.

V. Integration or Transformation?

Jahan distinguishes between 'agenda-setting' and 'integrationist' approaches to mainstreaming gender equality.[45] The former attempts to transform dominant state discourses in accordance with the goal of gender equality and the latter seeks to accommodate gender equality within existing paradigms. Whatever the intention of its proponents, a number of studies suggest that gender mainstreaming has tended to result in integration, yielding some benefits but not leading to transformative change.[46] In our view, a key part of the explanation is that, as highlighted above, mainstreaming operates on the basis of consent. The onus is on the advocates of mainstreaming to 'seduce'[47] state actors. As cooperation is unlikely to result from antagonistic approaches which emphasise challenge, conflict and transformation, a more unthreatening position tends to be adopted, with mainstreaming marketed to appeal to discourses that *already* have purchase within government. Thus gender equality is reframed in terms of—and discursively subordinated to—economic concepts such as efficiency, productivity, growth and profitability.[48]

The alternative tactic of giving the government flexibility to interpret and operationalise its meaning invariably leads to the same outcome—that is of gender equality being viewed from the perspective of *existing* frameworks. Thus the transformative goal is conceded as the price of admittance into state structures. Indeed, it is the 'mainstreamed' discourse which becomes transformed. We therefore question the extent to which interpretative ground may be ceded in attempts to secure consent and acceptance *within* other governing discursive formations. *In these circumstances myth-busting around rights discourse can become a subtle form of interpretative retreat in which transformative ambitions are eroded.* Is the meaning of rights modified in attempts to secure institutional and cultural acceptance? What might be lost in translation? Is there a temptation to offer more palatable meanings when the occasion demands? Or is this precisely the sort of challenge that human rights movements themselves need to confront, maturely and reflectively?

In essence what is at stake here is a transfer of *ownership* of ESR discourse from human rights movements to the state. This concern is expressed by McCrudden who ponders whether mainstreaming would give government

[45] R Jahan, 'The Elusive Agenda: Mainstreaming Women in Development' (1995) *Seeds 2: Supporting Women's Work around the World* 216.

[46] Hafner-Burton and Pollack above n 9; J Squires, 'Is Mainstreaming Transformative? Theorizing Mainstreaming in the Context of Diversity and Deliberation' (2005) 12 *Social Politics: International Studies in Gender, State & Society* 366, 374; M Verloo, 'Mainstreaming Gender Equality in Europe. A Critical Frame Analysis Approach' (2005) *The Greek Review of Social Research* 117.

[47] M Verloo, 'Another Velvet Revolution? Gender Mainstreaming and the Politics of Implementation' (2001) IWM Working Paper No 5, 9.

[48] Hafner-Burton and Pollack above n 9; Squires above n 46, 374; Verloo, above n 46, 117.

officials with a 'non-human rights orientation ... a dominant position of interpretation'.[49] Government decision-makers would assume greater responsibility for interpreting what ESR mean, what weight they should be given in relation to other priorities and how they should be pursued. This would create the *impression* that rights have been given due consideration, disarming ESR as a discourse of potential challenge. The de-energising impact of this on social movements should not be downplayed, as a 'totalising administration' drains the emancipatory life from rights and equality. Indeed, Petersmann urges international organisations to conduct impact assessments precisely in order 'to clarify the claims by anti-globalisation activists that "human rights offer a principle on which to base opposition to the challenges posed by economic globalisation"'.[50] It is, after all, through such processes of assimilation—the formation of 'chains of equivalence'[51] with other discourses—that neoliberalism has assumed such dominance.[52]

It could be argued that this represents a reductionist way of viewing the discursive space created by human rights, and that mainstreaming has continuing traction because it keeps the tension with dominant interpreting frameworks alive and operational. What should not be in doubt is that mainstreaming should be seen by its advocates as *one strand only* of a wider strategy for the advancement of human rights.[53] This brings the focus back to a mature politics of mobilisation around rights and equality—something that can be downplayed in legalistic accounts—and one which is all too aware of the productive potential of existing tensions.

VI. Conclusion

The promotion of compliance with ESR raises difficult questions about the nature and operation of power in contemporary societies. We recognise both the interpretative battles within rights discourse, and the complexity of societal power relations. Conventional accounts of the existing interactions can underplay the sheer scale and extent of contestation. However, we believe some tentative conclusions can be advanced.

[49] C McCrudden, 'Mainstreaming Human Rights' in C Harvey (ed), *Human Rights in the Community: Rights as Agents of Change* (Oxford, Hart Publishing, 2005) 16.

[50] Petersmann, 'Time for a United Nations "Global Compact"', above n 27, 642.

[51] E Laclau and C Mouffe, *Hegemony and Socialist Strategy: Towards a Radical Democratic Politics*, 2nd edn (London, Verso, 2001) 170.

[52] For a classic account of this process in the UK see S Hall, *The Hard Road to Renewal: Thatcherism and the Crisis of the Left* (London, Verso, 1988).

[53] Note, for example, that in their study of social movements in New York City Merry et al express the concern that 'emphasizing human rights as good governance can derail attention from human rights values': Merry et al above n 12, 109. This is worrying precisely because the values side of the rights-based approach 'is more open to mobilisation by grassroots social movements than the law side' (ibid).

In some respects, mainstreaming is grounded in a plausible and appealing analysis of how to affect change. It targets the state—a major site of societal governance—points to existing normative commitments derived from the liberal state's self-understanding as a collective guarantor of rights and seeks to ensure that a rights-based culture emerges throughout public administration. Mainstreaming thus reminds the liberal state—and its administrative and regulatory institutions—of their own original systemic logics, as well as normative commitments subsequently assumed.

Importantly, mainstreaming operates by consent. It calls on institutions to take responsibility for realising rights as an integral part of the normative framework of governance—and then expects them to hold themselves to account on that basis. It attempts to equip the state with tools capable of gathering particular information, trusting that armed with this knowledge public decision-makers and administrators will then do the 'right' thing. In this respect it is a project that seeks to enable the 'enabling state' to protect and promote rights.

This notion of the benevolent state (albeit one that needs a bit of a push) leaves mainstreaming open to the charge of paying insufficient attention to the harsh realities of discursive struggle (though we do not, of course, endorse any reductionist or simplistic juristic or top-down notion of societal power relations). It is for good reason that theories of politics and power often use military analogies.[54] The progressive ideal of rights envisages ESR transforming the mainstream but needs to be mindful of how the mainstream can transform and co-opt rights-based discourses. Given current structural realities and power relations, the latter is often more likely. Such co-option undermines the capacity of ESR to provide a vehicle through which orthodox approaches to governing can be scrutinised and challenged—functions vital to a healthy democracy.

Strategies for change must manage the considerable intellectual and practical challenges of retaining independence from, while exercising influence over, the state—a task further complicated by the diffuse, indistinct and complex nature of modern day 'power without a centre'.[55] Despite its allure, it is not clear that mainstreaming theory adequately overcomes or even grasps these challenges.

Rather than finding a convivial accommodation with the state, perhaps a more promising strategy lies with encouraging rights movements that are internally self-reflective and sufficiently autonomous to challenge and unsettle dominant discursive formations that contradict human rights. In order to realise the continuing emancipatory potential of rights discourse, such an approach would benefit from a more sophisticated understanding of global and local power relations, and a greater appreciation of both the dangers of engagement with the state and the value of social movement mobilisation on rights and equality. Impact assessments

[54] Eg, Foucault commented: 'The history that bears and determines us has the form of a war rather than that of a language': M Foucault, 'Truth and Power' in J D Faubion (ed), *Essential Works of Foucault 1954–1984 volume 3* (London, Penguin, 2000) 116.

[55] P Miller and N Rose, *Governing the Present* (Cambridge, Polity, 2008) 9.

and participatory mechanisms could provide useful tools within a broader strategy but on a more selective and focused basis than currently envisaged by mainstreaming. Rights-based approaches to budget analysis would be developed and applied by human rights activists rather than state officials.

Everyone talking about human rights might look like success, but if the diffusion is accompanied by dilution might the counter-hegemonic ambitions of human rights be better preserved on the margins?

III

Group-Specific Work

7

Budget for Children

ENAKSHI GANGULY THUKRAL

'There can be no keener revelation of a society's soul than the way in which it treats its children'.

Nelson Mandela

I. Introduction

The budget showcases the government's true priorities vis-a-vis planned expenditure. Therefore, analysing government budgets helps human rights activists, civil society organisations and voluntary groups to understand what is planned and where the gaps and the greatest need exist. It serves to ensure that budgets are transparent and accessible for the public and can also be used to challenge corruption and imbalances in resource allocation.[1] The actual allocation and spending of adequate financial resources, although not the only indicator, is definitely an important reflection of any government's commitment to the overall economic and social development of the nation and its citizens. It is the most solid and articulate expression of its priorities, performances, decisions and intentions.

Over the years, it has been widely recognised that regular analysis and monitoring of the budget provides critical evidence for advocacy strategies to ensure government accountability and to impel duty-bearers to make the necessary changes to ensure that the rights of their citizens are protected.[2]

[1] E Ganguly Thukral, 'Children and Governance' in E Ganguly Thukral (ed), *Every Right for Every Child: Governance and Accountability* (London, Routledge, 2011) 15. For more information read World Bank, *Social Accountability Sourcebook* (World Bank, 2012) ch 3 'Methods And Tools': www.worldbank.org/socialaccountability_sourcebook/Tools/toolsindex.html; www.worldbank.org/socialaccountability_sourcebook/PrintVersions/Methods%20and%20Tools%2006.22.07.pdf; V Ramkumar, *Our Money, Our Responsibility: A Citizen's Guide to Monitoring Government Expenditures* (Washington, The International Budget Project, 2008); E Vasquez, 'A Story of Neglect: Children in Peru's Public Budgets' in E Ganguly Thukral (ed), *Every Right for Every Child Governance and Accountability* (London, Routledge, 2011) 90; The International Budget Project; 'A Guide to Budget Work for NGOs' December 2001: www.internationalbudget.org/wp-content/uploads/guide_to_budget_work1.pdf.

[2] Ganguly Thukral, 'Children and Governance' ibid 15.

In the last decade and a half, several groups and organisations in India have been using budgets to monitor state performance and to hold government accountable. In the mid-1990s, a growing need for an independent scrutiny of government budget was recognised by several groups. Therefore, groups like DISHA in Ahmedabad and the Centre for Budget Studies in Mumbai began to analyse the budget to highlight the synchrony between government policies and government spending.[3] These included groups who worked on poverty and human rights, *dalits* and tribals, among others.[4] This was also the time when gender budgeting began to gain popularity among civil society groups and stakeholders; it has since found a place in the Government's budget.[5]

In 2000, the HAQ: Centre for Child Rights,[6] embarked on its Budget for Children (BfC) journey.[7] As discussed further below, BfC involves the disaggregation of budgetary allocations made specifically for programmes that benefit children from overall budgetary allocations. BfC has since found credence among policymakers, civil society organisations and other stakeholders within the country. This chapter will focus on the importance of using budget analysis as a tool for monitoring the realisation of child rights and holding the state accountable. Using examples of the work undertaken by HAQ: Centre for Child Rights in India, and drawing upon similar work in other countries, the chapter reflects upon how budget for children can be used to influence government policymaking, planning and budgets for children.

II. Budgets and Children—Making the Link

When we begin any discussion on children and budgets we need to ask why it is necessary to focus on children specifically. After all, are they not part of families

[3] A Shankar and M Robinson, *Budget Analysis and Policy Advocacy: Report from a National Workshop on Budget Analysis and Policy Advocacy in India* (The Ford Foundation/Times of India): internationalbudget.org/wp-content/uploads/Report-from-a-National-Workshop-on-Budget-Analysis-and-Policy-Advocacy-in-India.pdf.

[4] See eg, 'From Analysis to Impact: Partnership Initiative Case Study' 1 Series: internationalbudget.org/wp-content/uploads/LP-case-study-NCDHR-summary.pdf.

[5] For more on gender budgeting, see the chapter by Quinn in this volume.

[6] HAQ: Centre for Child Rights works towards the recognition, promotion and protection of rights of all children. It aims to look at the child in an integrated manner within the framework of the Constitution of India and the UN Convention of the Rights of the Child. HAQ aims at building a holistic understanding of child rights and exploring areas of concern that affect children and their rights. See: www.haqcrc.org/.

[7] Child rights-based budgeting does not differ from BfC as such, since the former refers to the process of preparation of a budget which exclusively lays down financial provisions for safeguarding the interests and rights of children. The analysis of said budget in terms of the extent to which its allocations result in the implementation of children's rights is known as child rights-based budget analysis.

or the larger society that benefits from allocations and expenditures? Do they not walk the same roads, drink the same water or breathe the same air for which government has invested resources? How can we disaggregate investments in children from the larger budget? Indeed, for a long time it was assumed that investing in families and empowering them would automatically benefit children.

The historic lack of a separate focus on children in budgetary processes is, according to Urban Johnson, because children are one of the best examples of 'invisibility' in the field of economics.[8] While most economists see children as consumers, producers/labourers and users of public services such as health and education, they seldom fully appreciate that children provide a great investment opportunity for high future returns and that their role in development ought to be recognised.[9]

As Sheridan Bartlett has pointed out, both (seemingly) 'progressive governments' as well as 'committed development professionals' who are fully aware of the benefits of taking gender into account and hence refer carefully in their policies to women and men, may express 'an unwitting bias against children' and 'it is not uncommon for their interest to fade if the topic of children comes up'.[10] She adds:

> the unspoken message is that bringing children into the discussion is a not-quite-relevant tangent—that surely their needs are met if their parents' needs are met. To some degree, this is true. But it is also true that boys and girls of different ages experience the world in particular ways, and may be affected in particular ways (sometimes profound and long-lasting) by a range of decisions and actions.[11]

The state often responds to lobbying and advocacy work around human rights with excuses such as a lack of available funds or budgetary constraints. This is especially true in the case of children who have no political voice – and even more so for children who are disadvantaged on account of their gender, caste, class, ethnicity, ability and location.[12] As Enrique Vasquez notes, many poor countries are unable to spend and invest what is necessary to guarantee that children develop in an integral way, facing as they do major fiscal obstacles to raising social expenditure. (For example, in Latin American countries, payments of wages, pensions

[8] U Johnson, 'The Economic Significance of Investing in Children', paper presented at the African Child Policy Forum (Addis Ababa, 2010): www.africanchildforum.org/site/index.php/resource-centre/the-economic-significance-of-investing-in-children.html.

[9] Ibid.

[10] S Bartlett, 'Good Governance: Making Age a Part of the Equation—An Introduction' (2005) 15 *Children Youth and Environments* 1, 8.

[11] Ibid.

[12] ComRC General Comment No 12 on the right of the child to be heard, UN Doc CRC/C/GC/12 (2009), paras 4 and 135; A Nolan, *Children's Socio-economic Rights, Democracy and the Courts* (Oxford, Hart Publishing, 2011) ch 2.

and debt servicing represent a regional fiscal burden of over 40 per cent of the budget.)[13]

The linkage between resources, budgets and the realisation of children's rights has been made strongly by the Committee on the Rights of the Child, the body with primary responsibility for monitoring the UN Convention on the Rights of the Child (CRC). This has been particularly notable with regard to the Committee's construal of Article 4 of the Convention, which states that:

> States Parties shall undertake all appropriate legislative, administrative, and other measures for the implementation of the rights recognised in the present Convention. With regard to economic, social and cultural rights, States Parties shall undertake such measures to the maximum extent of their available resources and, where needed, within the framework of international co-operation.

In its General Comment No 5, the Committee on the Rights of the Child stated:

> Implementation of the human rights of children must not be seen as a charitable process, bestowing favours on children ... In its reporting guidelines and in the consideration of States parties' reports, the Committee has paid much attention to the identification and analysis of resources for children in national and other budgets. No State can tell whether it is fulfilling children's economic, social and cultural rights 'to the maximum extent of ... available resources', as it is required to do under Article 4 [of the Convention], unless it can identify the proportion of national and other budgets allocated to the social sector and, within that, to children, both directly and indirectly ... Emphasizing that economic policies are never neutral in their effect on children's rights, the Committee has been deeply concerned by the often negative effects on children of structural adjustment programmes and transition to a market economy. The implementation duties of Article 4 and other provisions of the Convention demand rigorous monitoring of the effects of such changes and adjustment of policies to protect children's economic, social and cultural rights.[14]

Clearly, there is a case for making the connection between budgets and the human rights of children. Hence, even while we recognise that children are part of societies and families, there is a need to focus special attention on them, and what we may be missing out on for them.

[13] E Vasquez, *Global Handbook for Childhood: How to Measure Socio-Economic Indicators and Child Targeted Public Spending in Developing Countries* (Sweden, Save the Children, 2006) 119.

[14] Committee On The Rights Of The Child. Thirty-fourth session. 19 September–3 October 2003 General Comment No 5 (2003). General Measures Of Implementation Of The Convention On The Rights Of The Child (Arts. 4, 42 And 44, Para. 6). CRC/GC/2003/5. 27 November 2003.

III. Children and Governance—Role of Budget Analysis

Budgets are linked to recognition of citizenship and inclusion of children in governance.[15] Children and governance is about the recognition of children as citizens in their own right. Thus they are rights holders,[16] entitled to legal empowerment and justice, political participation and decision-making, social engagement, economic rights and access to resources leading to the realisation of their civil, political, social, cultural and economic rights.[17] The UN Committee on the Rights of the Child has noted that one of the satisfying results of the almost universal ratification of the CRC has been the development of a variety of child-focused and child-sensitive bodies, structures and activities: children's rights units at the heart of government; ministers for children; inter-ministerial committees on children; parliamentary committees; child impact analysis; children's budgets; 'state of children's rights' reports; NGO coalitions on children's rights; children's ombudspersons and children's rights commissioners etc. On a pragmatic note the Committee also states:

> While some of these developments may seem largely cosmetic, their emergence at the least indicates a change in the perception of the child's place in society, a willingness to give higher political priority to children and an increasing sensitivity to the impact of governance on children and their human rights.[18]

Fundamental to the recognition of citizenship is state action through formulation of legislation, policies and programmes and also through the systems it sets up to implement them—the Executive, Legislature and Judiciary. It has been recognised across the world that improved or 'good' governance is a precondition for sustained poverty reduction and a peaceful and stable society.[19] The term 'governance' refers to the way that the state exercises its political, economic and

[15] See Ganguly Thukral, 'Children and Governance' above n 1.

[16] The definition of citizenship that recognises foreigners and stateless persons, who are in the country on legal grounds, as being able to enjoy the same rights and freedoms and also bear the same duties as citizens, becomes important. This is because if access to rights is restricted to children who only have name and nationality, many children across the world who are fleeing their countries with their parents due to conflicts or economic distress etc, or who are born of parents who have migrated, will be denied protection: www.workingchild.org/International%20Colloquium%20on%20Children%20and%20Governance_HAQ%20Report%20.pdf; B Duncan, *Constitutional Reforms in Favor of Children* (New York, UNICEF, 2008) 27: www.unicef.org/policyanalysis/files/Constitutional_Reforms_in_Favour_of_Children.doc.

[17] Inter-Agency Working Group on Children's Participation (IAWGCP). Children as Active Citizens—Commitments and Obligations for Children's Civil Rights and Civic Engagement in East Asia and the Pacific (Bangkok, IAWGCP, 2008) 3.

[18] Ibid para 10.

[19] HAQ: Centre for Child Rights, 'Proceedings of International Colloquium on Children and Governance: Holding the State Accountable' 2: www.workingchild.org/International%20Colloquium%20on%20Children%20and%20Governance_HAQ%20Report%20.pdf.

administrative power.[20] Key attributes of good governance are that institutions and processes should build on the rule of law, be accountable, open, effective and responsive, and give space for equal and meaningful participation by all sections of the society irrespective of caste, creed, religion, class, culture and age group.[21] It is strongly arguable that this kind of governance would necessarily be based on a rights-based approach to all citizens, including children, by ensuring that their needs and rights are addressed and children themselves find a voice.

According to Save the Children,

> governance involves structures and systems. It is concerned with power and resources and opportunities to influence matters that affect individuals and their communities. For children and young people, governance relates to several contexts such as family, school governance and national and international governance.[22]

The participation of children vis-a-vis governance is envisaged in the UN Convention on the Rights of the Child. Article 12 recognises the right of children to be heard in matters that concern them.[23] This wide-ranging provision has been identified as one of the four General Principles of the Convention. Thus Article 12 establishes not only a right in and of itself, but should also be considered in the interpretation and implementation of all other rights.[24]

IV. State Accountability

This brings us to the need to hold the state accountable. Accountability is a distinctive, complex and central feature of human rights, and is concerned with the requirement of the state to fully comply with its obligations, whether national, regional or international.[25]

[20] European Association for American Studies, International Conference, 'Who Governs in the Americas and Europe': www.eaas.eu/conferences/other-conferences/qwho-governs-in-the-americas-and-in-europeq.

[21] According to the United Nations Economic and Social Commission for Asia and the Pacific (UNSCAP), 'Good governance has 8 major characteristics. It is participatory, consensus oriented, accountable, transparent, responsive, effective and efficient, equitable and inclusive and follows the rule of law. It assures that corruption is minimised, the views of minorities are taken into account and that the voices of the most vulnerable in society are heard in decision-making. It is also responsive to the present and future needs of society'. See: www.unescap.org/pdd/prs/ProjectActivities/Ongoing/gg/governance.asp.

[22] Save the Children, *Children and Young People as Citizens, Partners for Social Change Overview: Promoting Children and Young People Participation and Citizenship Rights in South and Central Asia* (Kathmandu, Nepal, International Save the Children Alliance, 2004) 5.

[23] Art 12(1) provides that, 'States Parties shall assure to the child who is capable of forming his or her own views the right to express those views freely in *all matters affecting the child*, the views of the child being given due weight in accordance with the age and maturity of the child' (italics added). For more on Art 12, see ComRC General Comment No 12.

[24] See eg, ComRC General Comment No 5, para 12.

[25] H Potts, *Accountability and the Right to the Highest Attainable Standard of Health* (University of Essex, Human Rights Centre, 2008) 7: www.essex.ac.uk/human_rights_centre/research/rth/docs/HRC_Accountability_Mar08.pdf.

However, accountability is not simply to rules and procedures for those are merely the means to ensuring accountability to the rights-holders. Ensuring accountability requires continuous monitoring by government and civil society. Concrete examples of individuals and groups seeking accountability show that the real challenge is to convert legal commitment into specific measures of implementation.[26] As Louise Arbour, United Nations High Commissioner for Human Rights has stated:

> Ensuring accountability on the road towards universal access involves a number of things. It means monitoring Governments' steps aimed at progressive realisation of these rights and highlighting any failure to do so. It means holding Governments accountable for obligations of immediate effect, for example where scaling up access discriminates a certain group such as *children* … it involves providing the framework, mechanisms and environment for holding officials accountable, including ensuring freedom of speech, accessible justice, transparent government (including transparent budget processes), the ability of civil society to organise and safety of activists to hold Governments to account.[27]

This is where budget analysis plays a critical role. The starting point, according to Vasquez, is access to good quality information and data. Only then can people be made fully aware and be persuaded that it is not speeches about laws, norms and plans of action that change things, but resources distributed efficiently, effectively and equitably.[28]

The keys to measuring good governance are monitoring the state's performance and holding the state accountable for its actions. This includes *financial accountability*, which is about allocation, disbursement and utilisation of funds; *performance accountability*, which is about demonstrating and accounting for performance through implementation of initiatives in the light of agreed indicators—the focus being service, output and outcome or result; and *political or democratic accountability*, which involves policymaking, political process and elections.[29] HAQ has focused on all three of the above.

HAQ came into existence in 1998 (formally as a registered organisation in 1999).[30] HAQ found that although almost one-third of India's population was children, and despite laws and policies and as many as 122 programmes and schemes directed at children in 2000, there was very little change visible in their status.[31] Time and again HAQ was told, 'the situation is grave, but the resources are limited'. That was indeed the crux. What were the resources being invested

[26] Ibid.

[27] Louise Arbour, Statement on the Occasion of World AIDS Day, 1 December 2006 cited in ibid 5.

[28] Vasquez, *Global Handbook for Childhood* above n 13, 119.

[29] See D Brinkerhoff, *Accountability and Health Systems: Overview, Framework, and Strategies* (Bethesda MD, The Partners for Health Reform *plus*, 2003): www.who.int/management/partnerships/accountability/AccountabilityHealthSystemsOverview.pdf.

[30] HAQ: Centre for Child Rights was registered under the Societies Registration Act XXI 1860; vide registration number: 35083 (28 June 1999).

[31] HAQ: Centre for Child Rights, *India's Children and the Union Budget: Budget for Children 1990–2000* (New Delhi, HAQ, 2001): www.haqcrc.org/publications/budget-children-1990–2000.

in children by the Government? Was the budget allocation and expenditure adequate? How did it match the outcomes in terms of indicators for children? In the wider context of poverty, disease, malnutrition, high mortality and the increase in the number of children coming into conflict with the law, could the neglect in financial terms of children's health, development and protection requirements be justified? As a consequence, HAQ began its foray into budget analysis.

For HAQ, budget analysis fitted perfectly into its work of watching over and monitoring state performance in all matters pertaining to the realisation of child rights. To understand better how serious the state is about realising the rights of children in any country, it is important for us to be able to empirically monitor and measure performance, and be able to hold states accountable.[32]

At the core of HAQ's work is developing tools for monitoring state response and holding it accountable for its omissions and commissions in the realisation of child rights, chief among which is its child budget analysis.[33] HAQ works on financial accountability through its Budget for Children in the context of the obligation of the state to fulfil rights through provision of adequate and appropriate financial resources as required by Article 4 CRC. It undertakes performance accountability through its status of children reports,[34] political and democratic accountability through its monitoring and analysis of parliamentary questions[35] and judicial accountability through its legal work. HAQ's work on monitoring state performance and accountability on child rights has become a model which can be used, not just for advocating child rights, but for pushing the framework for state accountability in general.

It has been found that, in general, civil and political rights law reform has fewer budgetary implications than reform directed at fulfilling ESR.[36] Not surprisingly, therefore, most groups who undertake budget monitoring concentrate on budgets for realisation of economic social and cultural rights (ESC rights). However, HAQ believes that both ESC rights and civil and political rights must be monitored; unless children are recognised as citizens, have a right to participate in decisions that concern them and have a right to fair justice, they cannot access or exercise their ESC rights. That is why monitoring resourcing of the justice delivery mechanism, particularly the implementation of juvenile justice, is a critical part of HAQ's work.

[32] ComRC General Comment No 5, paras 1, 2 and 65.

[33] See, HAQ: Centre for Child Rights, 'Children and Governance': www.haqcrc.org/children-and-governance.

[34] HAQ: Centre for Child Rights, *Children in Globalising India: Challenging Our Conscience* (New Delhi, HAQ, 2002); HAQ: Centre for Child Rights, *Status of Children in India Inc* (New Delhi, HAQ, 2005); HAQ: Centre for Child Rights, *Still out of Focus—Status of Children in India* (New Delhi, HAQ, 2008).

[35] HAQ: Centre for Child Rights, *Says a Child—Who Speaks for my Rights?* (New Delhi, HAQ, 2005).

[36] A Skelton, *Reforming Child Law in South Africa: Budgeting and Implementation Planning* (Florence, UNICEF Innocenti Research Centre, 2007) 6: www.unicef.de/fileadmin/content_media/mediathek/AR_034_reformingchildlaw.pdf.

V. Exploring Budget for Children

Budget for Children is not a separate budget. It is merely an attempt to disaggregate from the overall allocations made, those made specifically for programmes that benefit children. This enables us to assess how far the policy and programme commitments are translated into financial commitments. This would also indicate the extent of the political commitment of the government towards its young citizens.

Until 2000, the term in use—both nationally and internationally—for such analysis was Child Budget,[37] or Children's Budget.[38] HAQ, however, chose to use the more appropriate term 'Budget for Children'[39] or Budgeting for Child Rights.[40] This is because the meaning of the earlier description could be taken to suggest the participation of children—which is not the case at all. The term thus chosen attempted to do away with this unintended suggestion. HAQ's experience has shown that BfC is one of the most effective tools to track the situation of children in any economy.

According to child rights expert, Thomas Hammarberg, 'the maximum extent of their available resources' does not imply that poorer countries can avoid their responsibilities.[41] It should, instead, be understood as a call for prioritisation of children within the state budget so as to ensure appropriate levels of service delivery.[42] BfC represents an important policy analysis tool that can help India take stock of its development investments for children and identify glaring gaps in resource investment and utilisation. Sufficient resourcing of the country's policy framework is the first step to making real the constitutional and other national policy commitments to children that exist in India. Budgetary analysis also helps us to map those areas that are relatively neglected.

There are some important factors that must be kept in mind when undertaking BfC. First, it is important to study both allocation and expenditure, as the differences between what has been budgeted, and what is finally utilised or spent, point to the priorities of the government and help analyse the initial commitment versus the implementation.

Second, children are not a homogeneous group. Their programme needs and the resources set out to implement them must be determined by their age, gender, socio-economic status, physical and mental well-being and where they

[37] See Department of Women and Child Development, *National Plan of Action for Children* (Government of India, 2005) 47.

[38] See eg, ChildrensBudget.Org: www.childrensbudget.org/.

[39] HAQ: Centre for Child Rights, *Budget for Children in India 2007* (New Delhi, HAQ, 2007) 12.

[40] Skelton above n 36, 9; *The African Report on Child Well Being-Budgeting for Children* (Addis Ababa, African Child Policy Forum, 2011).

[41] T Hammarberg, 'Children' in A Eide, C Krause and A Rosas (eds), *Economic, Social and Cultural Rights* (The Hague, Kluwer, 2001) 366.

[42] Skelton above n 36, 9.

live.[43] For example, nutrition and health inputs in the early childhood years are critical for the child's growth.[44] Therefore, inputs and interventions on these aspects in the early years are critical. In the later years, enrolment and retention in schools becomes crucial, as does the issue of prevention of entry into the labour market. Programme interventions in the adolescent years need to target their educational, health and sexual needs as well as their transition into adulthood.[45] Similarly, children from disadvantaged communities such as tribal and indigenous groups, scheduled castes, children at risk such as street and working children, those who are being trafficked, children of prostitutes and children living with physical or mental disabilities, would require special attention.[46]

Interventions for children, and the resourcing of such, need to keep pace and be responsive to the changing needs of children. Oudenhoven and Wazir recommend that policymakers must be sensitive, flexible and increasingly prepared for new and as yet unfamiliar situations that we are constantly confronted with in a fast changing world.[47] They warn against a 'cookie cutter' approach to developing interventions. Due to changes brought about by a number of reasons, there are children's needs today that were not as evident two decades ago; these include the impact of HIV/AIDS, tsunami, increasing forced evictions, more cases of juvenile diabetes and even obesity.[48] Any BfC exercise must take into account these changes.

VI. Budget for Children—Analysis Across the World

Starting in the 1990s, several countries across the world have undertaken child budgeting. While some, like HAQ, have undertaken budget for children analysis and shared the results, there are others that have also engaged children themselves in the process by training them. We will look at two such examples: South Africa and Brazil.

[43] HAQ: Centre for Child Rights, 'India's Children and the Union Budget: Budget for Children 1990–2000' above n 31, 8.

[44] See eg, ComRC General Comment No 4 on adolescent health and development in the context of the Convention on the Rights of the Child, UN Doc CRC/GC/2003/4 (2003).

[45] See eg, ComRC General Comment No 7, on implementing child rights in early childhood, UN Doc CRC/C/GC/7/Rev.1 (2005).

[46] See eg, the Committee on the Rights of the Child's observation that addressing discrimination against indigenous children may 'require changes in legislation, administration and resource allocation, as well as educational measures to change attitudes'. (General Comment No 11 on indigenous children and their rights under the Convention, UN Doc CRC/C/GC/11 (2009), para 24.

[47] N van Oudenhoven and Rekha Wazir, *Newly Emerging Needs of Children, An Exploration*, (Antwerp, Garant, 2006) s 23, 26 and 31.

[48] Ibid ss 23, 26 and 31.

A. South Africa

One of the earliest experiences of undertaking budgeting for children was in South Africa which began with the establishment of the Children's Budget Unit (CBU) in 1995 by the Institute for Democracy in South Africa (IDASA) in Cape Town to conduct research and disseminate information on the Government's budgeting for children in South Africa.[49] The CBU began by framing national and provincial government budgets as mechanisms to advance child-specific economic and social rights. It 'built capacity within government and civil society bodies in developing countries to advocate for the generation and use of resources for the realisation of children's rights'.[50] In its first phase, the CBU teamed up with other stakeholders in the children's sector to produce the report, *First Call: The South African Children's Budget*,[51] which tracked government expenditure on children in areas such as health, education, welfare, justice and policing. The report also raised the question of whether the Government was directing its spending in the best way to deliver on its policy commitments to children, and recommended ways in which social spending could be more efficiently directed in these areas. The CBU's second study, *Where Poverty Hits Hardest*,[52] focused on the health, education, welfare and criminal justice sectors in all nine provinces of the country from 1995 to 1998, and examined the link between government spending on social services aimed at children, children's ability to access these services and the impact of social services delivery on the lives of children. In 2000, the CBU examined the national budget to monitor the Government's performance in delivering on its promises to poor children and reducing child poverty.[53] In 2001, a critical decision was taken to try and base the monitoring method more on government's obligations to deliver child *rights* and thereby adopt an approach that holds government accountable for its legal obligations to deliver child rights. This was evidenced in the report, *Budgeting for Socio Economic Rights: Government Obligations and Child's Rights to Social Security and Education*.[54]

Over the years CBU–IDASA developed a methodology to track budget allocations and programmes intended to reach children to highlight challenges in the delivery of services, and to analyse the legal framework that ensures social

[49] C Nomdo, *Reflections from the Children's Participating in Governance Project: Budget monitoring within a Rights Based Framework* (Cape Town, IDASA, 2007): resourcecentre.savethechildren.se/content/library/documents/reflections-children%E2%80%99s-participating-governance-project-budget-monitoring-; E Coetzee and J Streak, *Monitoring Child Socio-Economic Rights in South Asia: Achievements and Challenges* (Cape Town, IDASA, 2004) 4.

[50] Coetzee and Streak, ibid 4.

[51] L Biersteker and S Robinson, *First Call: The South African Children's Budget* (Cape Town, IDASA, 1997).

[52] S Robinson and M Sadan, *Where Poverty Hits Hardest* (Cape Town, IDASA, 1999).

[53] S Casseim, *Are Children Being Put First? Child Poverty and the Budget 2000* (Cape Town, IDASA, 2000).

[54] S Casseim and J Streak, *Socio Economic Rights: Government Obligations and Child's Rights to Social Security and Education* (Cape Town, IDASA, 2001).

and economic child rights in South Africa. This has been drawn upon by other researchers, including HAQ. Based on their experiences, the CBU developed a training manual in 2002.[55] It also produced a report, *Using Government Budgets as a Monitoring Tool* which was published in 2004.[56]

B. Brazil

The Centre for the Defence of Children and Adolescents (CEDECA-CEARÁ) in Brazil,[57] initiated its programme of monitoring the Fortaleza city budget in 1999 after Brazilian society had managed, through a process of broad social mobilisation, to have written into the 1988 Federal Constitution that children and young people have rights and that these need to be fully protected as a matter of absolute priority.[58] Further, the Children and Adolescents Act (ECA) stipulates that meeting this priority envisages children having first call on public resources.[59]

Using this legal basis, between 1999 and 2002, CEDECA-CEARÁ focused on two main areas: the analysis of the public budgets and the capacity building of civil society to use the budget as a political tool through lobbying and advocacy. They also brought out the *Child Budget Report* based on the outcome of this exercise.[60] In this report a critical analysis was made of the proposals presented by the Executive for children and adolescents. This report was made available to all organisations that fought for the rights of children and adolescents to enable them to use it as a pressure tool to intervene in the formulation of budget proposals. In the following years, many other coalitions and networks emerged that used the budget as a monitoring tool and to change policy at the city, state and federal levels.[61]

Over the years, child budget analysis has been experimented with in several countries across the world, with most efforts on a sector (education, health) or a group of children (disabled) etc; these have not been sustained efforts. In Vietnam

[55] Children's Budget Unit, *Child Budget Analysis: Training Manual* (Cape Town, IDASA, 2002).

[56] L Kgamphe in L Mahony (ed), *Using Government Budgets as a Monitoring Tool* (Minneapolis, New Tactics Project of the Center for Victims of Torture, 2004).

[57] CEDECA-CEARÁ is a non-governmental organisation that was founded in 1994. It came about as a result of networking among civil society organisations, social movements and institutions aimed at protecting children and young people. Its aim is to create a society that practices infant-juvenile human rights, by linking judicial intervention, social mobilisation and communication: www.cedececeara.org.br.

[58] MM Marques, N De Morais Bezerra and RR de Oliviera (eds), *Children And Young People In Action Participating In Budget Work* (Save the Children Sweden, 2005): resourcecentre.savethechildren.se/content/library/documents/children-and-young-people-action-participating-budget-work.

[59] Ibid.

[60] MM Marques, 'Monitoring of the Public Budget with the Participation of Adolescents: The Experience of CEDECA-CEARÁ' in E Ganguly Thukral (ed), *Every Right for Every Child: Governance and Accountability* (London, Routledge, 2011) ch 9, 258.

[61] Ibid.

in 2000,[62] a study was done focusing on education and on health services for children in China in 2006,[63] and in Suriname, a Child Friendly Budget Analysis, was made of the Education Budgets for 2004–07 in 2007.[64] In the Philippines, as part of the Social Watch Initiative, the social sector budget is analysed regularly; this also covers some children's issues such as basic health, nutrition, maternal health, immunisation and basic education.[65] In Bosnia and Herzegovina, Save the Children—the UK Bosnia and Herzegovina programme—has worked with UNICEF and the Government to estimate the impact of that state's electricity privatisation on child poverty and how to mitigate the negative consequences.[66] The assessment involved analysing existing quantitative data, plus new quantitative and qualitative information from stakeholders. This work highlights the links between increasing prices and/or limited access to schooling, school performance, health and development.[67] Although BfC analysis was initiated in Palestine in 2000, the work had to be halted in 2001 due to the intifada, and the study's recommendation could not be discussed or implemented.[68]

VII. Involving Children Themselves

As highlighted above, the UN CRC stresses both the need for children to participate in decisions that concern them and their right to be heard. However, as the Committee on the Rights of the Child has observed, 'appearing to "listen" to children is relatively unchallenging; giving due weight to their views requires real change'.[69] Hence that body has cautioned that listening to children should not be seen as an end in itself, but rather as a means for states to make their actions on behalf of children ever more sensitive to the implementation of children's rights.[70] In the field of budget analysis, efforts have been made to ensure

[62] Save the Children, *Child-Focused Budget Study: Assessing the Rights to Education of Children with Disabilities in Vietnam* (Hanoi, Save the Children, 2000).

[63] M Hong and W Xiaolin, *China's Budget System and the Financing of Education and Health Services for Children* (Beijing, United Nations Children's Fund and Office of the National Working Committee on Children and Women under the State Council, 2006).

[64] R Klein, *The Education Budget in Suriname 2004–2007 Child Friendly Budget Analysis: A Tool to Measure Results for Children and Enhance Transparency* (Suriname, UNICEF, 2007).

[65] Social Watch Philippines and Alternative Budget Initiative, Attaining the MDGs and Sustainable Growth with Equity (2008): http://www.internationalbudget.org/resources/library/Alternative_Budget2008.pdf.

[66] UNICEF, 'Child Rights Impact Assessment of Potential Electricity Price Rises in Bosnia and Herzegovina' (Florence, UNICEF Innocenti Research Centre, 2007).

[67] Submission made by SEE Programme, Save the Children UK on the General Day of Discussion, 'Budget Analysis as a Tool for Enabling Realisation of Children's Rights in South-East Europe': www.crin.org/docs/Children%20's%20Law%20Centre[1].pdf.

[68] Secretariat for the National Plan of Action for Palestinian Children, *Dollars and Sense for a Better Childhood: A Palestinian Child-Focused Budget Study* (Stockholm, Save the Children, 2000).

[69] ComRC General Comment No 5, para 12.

[70] Ibid.

children are represented and heard. This has included training and engaging children in both budget analysis and advocacy.

In 2003, CEDECA began a project to involve children and young people in the process of budget analysis and advocacy based on the understanding that the struggle for the human rights of children and young people must be premised on discussion of public policies that affect them and the knowledge and the ability to exercise social control on the allocation and spending of public resources.[71] Some important results were achieved, including an increase in social awareness of the need for understanding, monitoring and participating in the budget process, and how that contributes to the strengthening of the civil society—through the participation of children themselves. It was understood that:

> [W]hen we seek the participation of children, we seek that children and adolescents be recognised and included as subjects of rights, which can only be effective if we create real spaces of participation It also means that we do not speak on their behalf any longer but we speak along with them. Clearly, to include children and adolescents in the process of monitoring the public budget in such adverse cultural, social and political conditions, means the breaking of a way of functioning of the public administration.[72]

This was one of the first ever initiatives to engage children in budget processes.

A similar effort was instigated by the CBU in South Africa in 2004 as part of its project on *Budget Monitoring within a Rights-Based Framework: Children Participating in Governance (CPG)*.[73] In this project the CBU worked with children in four partner organisations to build their capacity to participate in governance by monitoring budgets for the realisation of their rights. These efforts were based in urban and rural contexts on a local government level. The project's objectives were to create opportunities for children in South Africa to enable them to monitor government budgets and to improve children's participation in, and monitoring of, budgets for the realisation of rights in a way that ultimately informed policy and contributed to the alignment of government budgeting with rights realisation. This required negotiating through societal and administrative pressures, without jeopardising the other rights of children, while also ensuring their physical security and comfort as well as the protection of their dignity and emotional well-being.[74]

The CBU's experience showed that advocating for children's active citizenship and their participation requires more than opening spaces for children in the decision-making process; it requires both a change in the processes of participation and increasing the knowledge and abilities of children. Most importantly, there is a need to change adult spaces of decision-making so that they enable citizenship participation and create public political spaces for children, persons with

[71] See Marques et al (eds), above n 58.

[72] Marques, above n 60.

[73] S Casseim, D Ewing and M Kgwete, 'Everywhere We Go, Our Presence is Felt: Reflections on a Governance and Budget-monitoring Project in South Africa' in E Ganguly Thukral (ed), *Every Right for Every Child: Governance and Accountability* (London, Routledge, 2011) 218.

[74] Ibid 227.

disabilities, women, illiterate persons, excluded people, people living in poverty and people living on the outside of cities. As noted by the Committee on the Rights of the Child, meaningful children's participation requires consistent and sustained support.[75] In the case of South Africa, the CPG project ended as IDASA moved its Children's Budget Unit out of Cape Town and the project managers left.[76] Elucidating on the lessons learnt from the project, Christina Nomdo concluded:

> For South African children ... the success of the project should not only be measured in terms of their ability to affect budget allocations. Children's participation in governance is still relatively new, as is the participation of citizens in general ... Most policy-making processes ignore the voices of children, and most governments fail to recognise the power of children's participation. Instead, as our interaction has witnessed, children have been used as tokens and political pawns.[77]

VIII. Some Impacts of BfC Work

The experiences of using budget analysis have been varied. These include increases in resources as well as policy changes. According to the Right to Education Project:

> Because they generally do not have access to information about the budget when it is being formulated, most CSOs [civil society organisations] have tended to focus their attention on the budget approval, budget implementation and budget auditing stages of the budget cycle, as this is where they can have the most impact ... CSOs focus their attention on budget implementation—ie on verifying whether or not government funds are being spent as intended. Some initiatives have involved monitoring from a national perspective, using data or quarterly reports from government ministries to check that expenditures are being made according to budget plans. Other initiatives have examined the expenditure of state or district level institutions responsible for the delivery of education.[78]

For example, combining CBU-IDASA's solid information and the mobilising power of Alliance for Children's Entitlement to Social Security (ACESS) has resulted in their main requests being put into practice by the Government in the 2003–04 budget. Total resources were increased in real terms, and the age until which a child could benefit from the Child Support Grant was extended to 14.[79] However, this was possible because South Africa had a government committed to

[75] ComRC General Comment No 12, paras 11, 15 and 132–135.

[76] Nomdo above n 49.

[77] Ibid.

[78] Information taken from: www.right-to-education.org/node/609.

[79] H Hofbauer, 'Sustained work and dedicated capacity. IDASA's Experience in Applied Budget Work in South Africa. Case study prepared for the research project "Lessons from Civil Society Budget Analysis and Advocacy Initiatives"'. May 2006: http://internationalbudget.org/wp-content/uploads/SouthAfricaFullReportEnglish.pdf.

reducing poverty, as well as strong advocacy organisations, which made it easier to implement the tactic. Also, South Africa's efficient treasury and rights conscious Constitution made it easier to access data.[80]

There are several examples of national successes in using budget analysis to impact on the education sector. The Right to Education Project, an international initiative which aims to promote social mobilisation and legal accountability,[81] has documented several examples of how budget analysis has been used by NGOs/ CSOs in furthering the right to education in different countries.[82]

In Ghana, community scorecards were used by national civil society organisations to track education budgets. The aim was to strengthen accountability and transparency in service delivery. For this, budget information relating to allocations and expenditure on textbooks and other learning materials were used to monitor school budgets. These findings provided parents and children with an opportunity to raise their concerns regarding service delivery in their communities. This also enabled them to assess the performance of education officials, teachers and school management committees.[83]

In Kenya, budget work was undertaken to ensure that the Government's policy of free primary education also provided for adequate financial and human resources to facilitate children's access to quality primary education. The budget analysis also assessed whether there was sufficient devolution of funds to the local level enabling speedy service delivery and increased community participation. This was achieved by training communities to monitor education policy and budget implementation, and by working to establish good governance structures in schools. Active lobbying led to a change in the Education Act.[84]

In Malawi, the Civil Society Coalition for Quality Basic Education (CSCQBE) monitors the Government's promise to provide free primary education. The coalition used budget analysis to hold the Government accountable to its commitment to free primary education by analysing whether the resources allocated to primary education were sufficient and spent as planned. The results of the education budget monitoring study showed a decrease in the percentage of the national

[80] HAQ and Save the Children, *Budget for Children Analysis*: www.haqcrc.org/sites/default/files/ Toolkit_1.pdf (2010) 11.

[81] The Right to Education Project aims to promote social mobilisation and legal accountability, looking to focus on the legal challenges to the right to education Housed by ActionAid International, and in partnership with the Global Campaign for Education and Amnesty International, the Right to Education Project is supported by the Open Society Institute and others: www.right-to-education.org.

[82] Information taken from: www.right-to-education.org/.

[83] Ghana, 'Assessing Education Delivery: The Community Scorecard Project'. Information taken from: www.right-to-education.org/node/612.

[84] Kenya, 'Improving School Governance to Support Free Primary Education'. Information taken from: www.right-to-education.org/node/613.

budget allocated to education. The results of the study were used for advocating for an increase in the share of education sector in the national budget.[85]

In Uganda, the child-led budget monitoring and anti-corruption initiatives concentrated on whether expenditure in the education sector went according to plan, and whether there was misappropriation of funds. Hence, child budget monitors in schools uncovered cases of corruption by school officials. These were reported to the district education office resulting in the dismissal of the guilty officials.[86]

In Bangladesh, national civil society organisations have developed the capacity of community audit groups to monitor both allocation of resources for education at the district level and with regard to the delivery of services in the schools. These efforts by the community audit groups have been linked to national level advocacy by Bangladesh's first parliamentary caucus on education resource which has lobbied the Government for education to be recognised as a right, as well as for increased resource allocations to the education sector.[87]

These are just some examples of rights-based budget work and its impact.[88] Clearly, systematic analysis of budgets and using the results for advocacy can bring about policy change as well as change in allocation expenditure. A systematic documentation of these efforts helps in replication of efforts.

IX. The HAQ Experience

The child budget work in India began in 2000 with a decadal analysis of the Union Budget.[89] This is because the decade of the 1990s marked many changes for India and its children. While India made some significant commitments towards ensuring children their basic rights, it also launched the 'era of globalisation'.[90] Both of these had an impact on children's lives. In the wake of its global and regional commitments, India had ratified the CRC in 1992.[91] Children's human rights protection in India was thus faced with the clash between India's commitment to its children and the process of globalisation. It was felt by HAQ: Centre for Child Rights that

[85] Malawi, 'Annual District Education Budget and Services Monitoring'. Information taken from: www.right-to-education.org/node/610.

[86] Uganda, 'Budget Monitoring to Fight Corruption in the Education Sector'. Information taken from: www.right-to-education.org/node/614.

[87] Bangladesh, 'The Power of People and Parliaments to Increase Resources for Education'. Information taken from: www.right-to-education.org/node/611.

[88] For more examples, see Save the Children, *Where's the Money Going? Monitoring Government and Donor Budgets* (London, STC, 2004).

[89] HAQ: Centre for Child Rights, 'Budget for Children': www.haqcrc.org/publications/haqs-budget-children.

[90] Ibid.

[91] UN Convention on the Rights of the Child, Art 4.

a decadal analysis would produce a comprehensive picture of the Government's commitment to children in terms of actual financial commitments.

On 19 March 1997, India submitted its first report to the UN Committee on the Rights of the Child.[92] The Committee's Concluding Observations had stressed the need for the State Party to take all necessary measures, including ensuring the allocation of required resources (ie, human and financial) and the appropriate distribution of resources at the central, state and local levels.[93] Monitoring the implementation of this recommendation was also an added reason for undertaking BfC work.[94]

Released on 11 September 2001, HAQ's Report, *India's Children and the Union Budget* was the first endeavour of its kind in India. This report established the need for such analysis and set the initial direction for developing a methodology to perform such effectively. Since then, HAQ has undertaken BfC analysis every year. This marked the start of the first phase of HAQ's work.

Most laws and programmes in India are implemented at state level. Therefore, recognising that any understanding of children and budgets would remain incomplete without undertaking child budget work focusing on the state level, 2002 saw HAQ decide to undertake BfC work in three sample states.[95] This was extended to six states in the next phase. With initial training inputs from HAQ and the Indian Council for Child Welfare, in 2000, the State of Tamil Nadu also began a state level analysis of the budget for children. Their report, entitled *Children of Tamil Nadu and the State Budget, An Analysis: 1998–2003* was published in 2003.[96]

Having analysed the extent of allocation and expenditure on children, HAQ realised that it was not enough to analyse the budgets for children at national and state level. Questions remained with regard to how the money allocated and/or spent impacted upon the child in terms of outcomes or results or services received. This was the question that the organisation set itself to answer in the second phase of its BfC work.

India, with the Seventy-Third Amendment to the Constitution 1992,[97] moved into a decentralised mode of governance through a model of Local Self Governance, known as the Panchayati Raj Institutions.[98] The funds allocated for any sector, scheme, or programme by the state budget can be traced right down

[92] Department of Women and Child Development, Ministry of Human Resource Development, Government of India, *Convention On The Rights Of The Child Country Report India* (February 1997): wcd.nic.in/CRCFEBmr.htm.

[93] ComRC 'Concluding Observations: India', UN Doc CRC/C/15/Add.115 (2000) paras 13 and 21.

[94] HAQ: Centre for Child Rights, *India's Children and the Union Budget: Budget for Children 1990–2000* above n 31, 9.

[95] See HAQ: Centre for Child Rights, 'Budget for Children in Indian States': www.haqcrc.org/budget-children-indian-states.

[96] K Rajeswaran, *Children of Tamil Nadu and the State Budget, An Analysis: 1998–2003* (Indian Council for Child Welfare, Tamil Nadu, 2003).

[97] The Constitution (Seventy-Third Amendment) Act 1992.

[98] See Second Administrative Reforms Commission, *Local Governance: An Inspiring Journey into the Future* (2007): arc.gov.in/6-1.pdf.

to the district, block and village levels, as each has its own budget; but how much of the budgeted allocations for a scheme or programme actually reaches the end user? What are the blockages in the flow of funds? (After all, efficient flow of resources and their optimum utilisation will determine efficacy of the budget.)

It was to get an answer to these questions that HAQ, together with its partner NGOs in different states, chose to undertake the tracking of the flagship national education programme, the Sarva Shiksha Abhiyaan (Education for All), from the centre/national level to the end user. This was carried out by reviewing outreach at the community level; the role of the institutions of local self-governance and the district administration. Similar efforts have also been made by other organisations.[99]

Two key questions that underpin HAQ's analysis are: do the allocations made genuinely reflect the needs of the country's children? And does the actual expenditure at the end of each year do justice to the financial planning?

The focus of analysis was identification of gaps at the following multiple levels: between the needs of the children to fulfil their rights and the national and international commitments made by India; between the commitments made by India and their translation into programmes/schemes under the various ministries and departments; between the objectives of the programmes/schemes and the financial allocations made towards them; between the allocations and actual expenditures; and between the outlays and the outcomes.[100]

Article 4 of the CRC states that State Parties must ensure that maximum resources are made available and that States Parties can draw upon international cooperation where needed. HAQ felt that this was an area for caution given the huge influence that international donors, aid agencies and international financial institutions (both bilateral and unilateral) have in determining India's fiscal situation and, at times, even the financial priorities of the Government. It was therefore critical to analyse the extent of dependence on external aid for the resourcing the rights of children. HAQ has expressed concerns about reliance on international aid in the context of realising children's rights.[101]

[99] See eg, A Mukherjee, S Bandyopadhyay and S Vyas, *Do Schools Get their Money?* (New Delhi, PAISA, 2009).

[100] The Government of India has presented the outcome budget in addition to outlays since 2005–06.

[101] 'It has been found ... that the induction of international assistance sometimes results in several problems in implementation: 1. As there is some flexibility in the operation of the foreign assisted programmes, these are more popular. 2. The foreign funding agencies insist that the projects assisted by them should be operated by separate agencies headed by separate co-ordinators at central and state level, and this creates a diarchy right in the middle of any programme of this country. 3. Highly paid consultants, high wages, access to perquisites like cars, computers, foreign tours etc. for individuals working in foreign funded projects lead to bad blood among colleagues and affect the working environment and output negatively. 4. At the district level, education department officials get sidelined in the discussions while the collectors and officials of foreign funded programmes take an active role': HAQ: Centre for Child Rights, 'Submission to the Committee on the Rights of the Child' for the Day of Discussion on "Resources for the Rights of the Child-Responsibility of the States"' (2007): www.crin.org/docs/BfC[1].%20India.pdf. Based on the Report of the National Committee of State Education

HAQ's work has shown that the state and the activist groups involved in advocacy for child rights can use budgetary data and analysis to understand budgetary trade-offs and governmental constraints, as well as to monitor national and state governments' functioning. It has also shown that the findings can be used not only by civil society groups for purposes of advocacy, but also by policymakers, implementers and legislators.

The first sign of the Government's acceptance of the BfC concept and the methodology was when the Government of India initiated child budgeting and included chapters related to it in the Annual Reports of 2002–03, 2004–05 and 2005–06 of the Department of Women and Child Development, Ministry of Human Resource and Development (now the Ministry of Women and Child Development).[102]

A further important sign of the institutionalisation of child budgeting was in 2005, when the minister in charge of Women and Child Development called a meeting of all the state representatives and announced that the Government would introduce child budgeting at the national level and asked the states to do the same.[103]

The ultimate recognition of child budgeting, however, came only when the Finance Minister, Mr P Chidambaram announced a separate statement on children when he presented the Finance Bill for Budget 2008–09 in Parliament in 2008. He said in his speech:

> We will score another 'first' this year. A statement on child related schemes is included in the budget documents and Honourable Members will be happy to note that the total expenditure on these schemes is of the order of Rs 33,434 crore.[104]

It was included in the Expenditure Budget Statement:

> Recognising that children under 18 constitute a significant percentage of the Indian population, the Government is committed to their welfare and development. This statement reflects budget provisions of schemes that are meant substantially for the welfare of children. These provisions indicate educational outlays, provisions for the girl child, health, provisions for Child protection, etc.[105]

Ministers under the Chairmanship of the Minister of Human Resource Development, *To Develop the Structure and Outlines of Implementing Universal Elementary Education in a Mission Mode* (New Delhi, Government of India, July 1999). More recently, these concerns have been echoed by Stephen Peterson when he said dependence on foreign aid is a red herring in many ways. He argues that it is imprudent to finance long-term recurrent liabilities such as teacher and health worker salaries with short-term volatile financing such as foreign aid. Foreign aid must be used for the right reasons and that cannot be for the social sector: S Peterson, 'Rethinking the Millennium Development Goals for Africa' (Fourth International Policy Conference on the African Child, Budgeting for Children, organised by the African Child Policy Forum, (Addis Ababa, 7–8 December 2010).

[102] Ministry of Women and Child Development, *Annual Report 2003–04*, Chapter 3 'Programmes for Children': wcd.nic.in/ar0304/chapter3.pdf.

[103] Ministry of Women and Child, *Annual Report 2007–08*, Chapter 7 'Child Budgeting': wcd.nic.in/ar0708/English/Chapter-7.pdf.

[104] Finance Minister, 'Budget Speech 2008–09': indiabudget.nic.in/ub2008-09/bs/speecha.htm.

[105] Expenditure Budget, Volume I, Budget 2008–09: exim.indiamart.com/budget-2008-09/expenditure-budget-08-09-vol1.html.

Today child budgeting is an integral part of the Government of India's National Plan of Action for Children 2005, which specifically includes a section on budgeting for children. The same is true of the Eleventh Five-Year Plan document of the Government of India.[106]

Yet another example of the successful utility of using BfC is the Government's acknowledgment of consistent low allocation of resources for the protection sector, and the resultant very poor indicators for the protection of children. This has led to the formulation of a comprehensive programme on child protection known as the Integrated Child Protection Scheme (ICPS),[107] and its announcement as part of the Eleventh Five-Year Plan mentioned above.

X. Budget for Children: Lessons and Challenges

The first challenge with regard to BfC work is the methodology itself and acceptance thereof. Experience shows that although one can learn from practice in other jurisdictions, each country needs to develop its own system or methodology. At the same time, while it is by now well accepted that BfC is based on disaggregating budget heads meant for children, the basis for selection of the budget heads needs to be developed and clearly articulated. In other words, it must be expressly stated in the methodology why certain programmes have been deemed relevant as part of the BfC analysis. Hence, while there is bound to be some level of subjectivity in the selection of programmes that are directed at children from the plethora of existing state budgetary interventions, effort must be made to keep this subjectivity to the minimum and to justify the choice made.

The selection of sectors is the second challenge. While in the first instance it would seem logical to divide budget heads along the different foci of the CRC (for example, the right to leisure, the right to an adequate standard of living), this is not the way in which budgets are formulated within governments. That is why HAQ decided to club programmes and schemes into three sectors—Development, Education, Health and Protection.[108] Any budget analysis can be of any one sector or issue or of the whole budget. However, while it may be more practical, and indeed easier to concentrate on a sector or an issue, HAQ's experience has shown that it is vital to calculate the share for children in the whole budget, along with carrying out a sectoral analysis. It is also important to include budgets for children's civil and political rights, especially since most governments believe

[106] The economy of India is based in part on planning through its five-year plans, which are developed, executed and monitored by the Planning Commission. See: planningcommission.nic.in/plans/planrel/fiveyr/11th/11_v2/11th_vol2.pdf.

[107] wcd.nic.in/schemes/icps.pdf.

[108] See HAQ: Centre for Child Rights, *India's Children and the Union Budget: Budget for Children 1990–2000* above n 31, chapter 1.

that if they have invested in education or—at best—health, they have done well by children.

Third, while most budget analyses have concentrated on analysing percentages that go to sectors, or examined them in proportion to Gross Domestic Product (GDP), HAQ has found that this sometimes hides anomalies and discrepancies. For example, the proportion of the budget allocated to health as a whole may have gone up, making advocates rejoice. However, what may go unnoticed is that the investment in an easily preventable disease like diarrhoea, which takes many lives in countries such as India, has actually reduced. Similarly with education—simply looking at increases in the context of GDP may hide the lack of allocation for special categories of children such as disabled or tribal children.

The devil is in the detail. Therefore, digging deeper and deeper, peeling away the layers—sector to major heads to minor heads etc—is often necessary in order to carry out BfC work effectively. For example, it was only in doing so that HAQ was able to point out how there had been a fall in the allocations for street children in a budget bill relative to the previous financial year, and the fact that the increase in midday meals given to school children was at the cost of a failure to provide any increase in resources for other initiatives needed to ensure elementary education. This forced the Government to take corrective action. The Government of India revised the allocations for street children mid-year in its revised budget. It also made sure that the rise in allocations for midday meals was separate from that for elementary education the next year. Furthermore, as already mentioned, an analysis of budgets highlighting the consistently low allocations for protecting children led to the Government finally developing a new programme for integrated child protection.[109]

Fourth, to be effective, budget analysis needs to be a sustained endeavour showing longitudinal results, rather than being only a one-time project. That way, governments also know that they are being consistently and systematically monitored, forcing them to be more transparent and accountable.

Fifth, it is important to track the entire budget cycle—the first allocation, the revised allocations that happen mid-year in most countries and the final expenditure. Most often, when governments report on budgets or investments in children, they only report on allocations; this often gives a false picture as actual expenditure may be less than what was allocated. Tracking budgets through the three stages of the cycle throws light on the planning process and the gaps therein.

Finally, as mentioned earlier, it is important to analyse the extent of dependency on foreign grants and aid as this is an important indicator of the government's commitment of its national resources to children.

Patience is the key to any budget analysis for human rights work. It took seven years for the Government of India to acknowledge and accept Budget for Children

[109] The Ministry of Women and Child Development of the Government of India launched the Integrated Child Protection Scheme (ICPS) in November 2009. The scheme concretises the government/state responsibility for creating a system to protect children in country: wcd.nic.in/schemes/icps.pdf.

and give it a status similar to the Gender Budget in India. The Ministry of Women and Child Development had adopted HAQ's methodology and included a chapter on budgeting for children in its annual report as far back as 2003,[110] and also in its National Plan of Action in 2005.[111] But it was only when the Finance Minister announced it in his Budget 2007–08 speech in 2007,[112] and included a separate statement for children in the Expenditure Budget document,[113] and when child budget was included in the Eleventh Five-Year Plan,[114] that we could be assured that it truly was a part of the Government's agenda.

There is yet another important issue with regard to specialised human rights budgets. While recognising the need to put the spotlight on a group of people, how do we ensure that they do not fall out of the larger planning process? Hence, even though undertaking BfC analysis and advocating for a separate budget statement for children in government budgets is an important strategy, how do we ensure that every ministry or department also takes ownership of children, recognises them as citizens and includes them in their plans and interventions? After all, children are part of broader society too.

A very good example of this is the National Programme of Action for Children in South Africa (NPA) which was envisaged as an instrument for ensuring that poor children are 'put first' in policy, government budgets and service delivery. In putting children first in government's budgets, the NPA called upon every department to give priority to children's needs in every decision about how to spend public funds, thereby ensuring the mainstreaming of children's needs into all budget decisions:[115]

> The concept of mainstreaming means that each government department incorporates children's issues into their respective portfolios. It calls upon each department to reflect its commitment to children, with corresponding budgetary allocation. With this approach, there is no single 'children's budget', rather, children's issues … [are supposed to] … inform every department's budget.[116]

This would mean that child rights need to be an important development indicator and every ministry or department should mainstream child rights indicators into

[110] See Ministry of Women and Child Development, *Annual Report 2003-04*: wcd.nic.in/ar0304/contents.htm.

[111] The Department of Women and Child Development's National Plan of Action for Children, 2005 commits itself to ensure all rights to all children up to the age of 18 years and it is the duty of the government to enable suitable environment for survival, growth, development and protection of all children: www.wcd.nic.in/NAPAug16A.pdf.

[112] Minister of Finance, 'Budget Speech 2007–08', paras 17 and 26: indiabudget.nic.in/ub2007-08/bs/speecha.htm.

[113] Ministry of Women and Child Development, 'Notes on Demands for Grants 2007-08': indiabudget.nic.in/ub2007-08/eb/sbe103.pdf.

[114] Planning Commission, *Eleventh Five-Year Plan 2007-2012*: planningcommission.nic.in/plans/planrel/fiveyr/11th/11_v1/11th_vol1.pdf.

[115] S Casseim, H Perry, M Sadan and J Streak, *Are Poor Children Being Put First? Child Poverty and the Budget* (Pretoria, IDASA 2000) vii.

[116] President's Office, Office on the Status of the Child 1999, *National Programme of Action 2000 and Beyond: An Assessment of the NPA and the Way Forward*, (Pretoria, Government of South Africa) cited in Casseim et al, ibid xiii.

its work. Similarly, all government policies and actions must be examined through a child rights lens. However, very few governments have emulated South Africa's approach to policy formulation in this area.

XI. Conclusion

It has taken ten years for groups and governments to accept BfC as a tool for monitoring state performance and accountability. As highlighted above, it has had some impact in a range of countries. In India, BfC work by HAQ has led to small increases in the budget of the Union Government in certain child-specific sectors. However, it may be a little premature to be able to realistically assess the impact of BfC analysis in terms of change on the ground. What is possible is to begin to assess whether there have been any changes in real terms in the budgeting process—not just in words—and how these translate into the lives of children in terms of outcomes.

This cannot be done by any one organisation. It is an exercise that calls for sharing BfC work with local communities and community leaders and building their capacities to act as the real watchdogs. This is what HAQ is now embarking upon.

In addition, HAQ's experience with budget monitoring has been that, although it is a significant tool, if it is to prove effective in terms of advocacy and lobbying, it is important to combine it with other monitoring methodologies. Examples of such activity include HAQ's status reports on children in India, and the monitoring of the judiciary and the legislature through the analysis of parliamentary questions and answers.

HAQ's experience—like that of other BfC practitioners—shows that budget monitoring cannot be one-sided. The objective cannot and must not be merely to monitor and criticise government performance; it must also involve a realistic assessment of governmental capacity, as well as engagement with the state when it seeks support. At the same time, it is extremely important to keep an eye on the information being provided and to ensure that it is correct and full-proof. Furthermore, although a very important tool, BfC can be effective only where the government is relatively transparent, rights-conscious and willing to engage with civil society. Thus, BfC faces huge challenges in states which lack transparency and commitment to rights-associated expenditure.

The ultimate indicator of success of HAQ's Children and Governance initiative would, of course, be the mainstreaming of child rights as an indicator in all planning initiatives and actions of the government. However, HAQ realises that this is a long term-goal and unlikely to happen in India in the near future.

8

Equality Proofing the Budget: Lessons from the Experiences of Gender Budgeting?

SHEILA QUINN

I. Introduction

Traditionally the budget has been viewed as a technical instrument of public finance management, one that is free from value, and which benefits all members of the public equally without distinction. Governments may acknowledge principles of equality and human rights as important goals, but when it comes to the processes of public expenditure management, such principles are barely taken into account.[1]

This chapter demonstrates the legitimacy of working with budget processes to better progress equality outcomes. Elaborating on the advancement of gender responsive budgeting as a strategy to expedite the implementation of gender mainstreaming, the chapter argues that the methodologies and approaches of gender responsive budgeting can be adapted to the broader equality agenda. This adaptability is illustrated with reference to the example of statutory obligations in Northern Ireland, where the execution of the budget, until recently, took place within a performance-based budgeting framework introduced in the United Kingdom by HM Treasury.

The chapter is based on a longer piece of work commissioned by the Equality Commission for Northern Ireland (the Commission),[2] which sought to propose a conceptual framework for how gender responsive budgeting could be adapted and extended to the broader equality agenda. That research considered in particular how the associated tools and methodologies for gender responsive budgeting can be used within budgetary processes to further assist public authorities in the promotion of equality of opportunity and good relations in compliance with

[1] A Norton and D Elson, *What's Behind the Budget?* (London, Overseas Development Institute, 2002) 23.

[2] The Equality Commission's website is at: www.equalityni.org.

statutory obligations under section 75 of the Northern Ireland Act 1998. These obligations require designated public authorities to have due regard to the need to promote equality of opportunity in carrying out their functions.

The chapter begins by providing the overall context in which the case for equality responsive budgeting is argued. This is done through preliminary overviews of the following four topics: the budget as an instrument of public policy; gender responsive budgeting; the Northern Ireland Act section 75 duties and the budget process in Northern Ireland; and the global trend toward measuring budget performance.

The discussion then turns to a more in-depth examination of gender responsive budgeting, by examining the origins of gender responsive budgeting, its uptake and the growing institutional support for the strategy, including at governmental and intergovernmental level. In presenting the tools, approaches and methodologies associated with gender responsive budgeting, the aim is to make the link to processes developed for the implementation of section 75 duties in Northern Ireland, thus facilitating an exploration of the adaptability of such processes to the broader equality agenda. The chapter concludes with some suggestions on how an equality responsive budgeting process might be initiated and promoted in Northern Ireland.

II. Overall Context

A. The Budget as an Instrument of Public Policy

Traditionally the budget has been viewed as a technical instrument of public finance management, one that is free from value and which benefits all members of the public equally without distinction. From the perspective of civil service technocrats, the budget is an instrument of control and management which, in order to obtain optimum results, is guided by concerns of economy and value for money. Within an environment of competing priorities, the primary goal is to work to ensure that available resources are allocated to ensure maximum public good.

From a policy perspective, the budget is the financial mirror of government policy. It is arguably the most important policy of government. More than any other policy document, it reflects the government's values and priorities, in that it is an articulation of support (or lack of support) for specific measures and activities through the distribution of public finances. Essentially, among all the policy positions adopted by government and its ministries, those which are matched with an allocation in the budget can be regarded as priorities.

While a full discussion of the multidimensional nature of budget formulation and execution and the relevance to the delivery of social outcomes is outside the scope of this chapter, it is important to note that budget-making is both a technical process and a political one. In advocating for an equality–perspective approach, both domains come into play. There is also, of course, the interplay between both aspects. The political dimension of budget-making is not restricted to how and why decisions of elected representatives (whether within government or Parliament) come into play in the formulation of the budget. The politics of the budget process is also about how budget decisions are made, about the assumptions informing budgets; it is about who makes decisions, who influences decisions and who is denied influence.[3]

Increasingly, in response to demands for more accountability and transparency, mechanisms such as budget submissions and consultation exercises have been introduced to allow for more public input and scrutiny.[4] In addition, there has been a shift in some of the underlying guiding principles of budget-making, away from a focus on inputs and outputs towards a focus on performance, effectiveness and the realisation of outcomes. While these are important and welcome improvements that have the potential to contribute to better social outcomes, the primary orientation in the budgetary process is a long way from that of pro-equality in any real sense.[5]

B. Gender Responsive Budgeting

Of the numerous budget initiatives in recent years that have sought to advance social goals, gender responsive budgeting has gained considerable momentum, and has provided important learning in terms of what approaches work best in making the budget more gender equitable. A 2005 report by the Commonwealth Secretariat estimated that approximately 50 countries have engaged with gender responsive budgeting to some degree.[6] Within the European Union, all Member States have undertaken a pilot project in gender responsive budgeting.[7] As evidence of the breadth of activity across Europe, it is worth noting that there are currently just over 100 members of the European Gender Budget Network, representing 25 countries.[8]

Gender responsive budgeting is a people-centred approach to the formulation and execution of the national budget. As such, it is a strategy that is complementary to other budget reform and improvement processes being undertaken

[3] Norton and Elson above n 1.

[4] Ibid section 4.

[5] Norton and Elson above n 1.

[6] See D Budlender, D Elson, G Hewitt and T Mukhopadhyay, *Gender Budgets Make Cents: Understanding Gender Responsive Budgets* (London, Commonwealth Secretariat, 2002).

[7] See Group of Specialists (EG-S-GB), *Gender Budgeting: Conceptual Framework, Methodology and Presentation of Good Practices* (Strasbourg, Council of Europe, 2005).

[8] www.infopolis.es/web/GenderBudgets/members.html.

by many governments across Europe and beyond.[9] When public services fail to deliver or fall short of the projected outcomes, medium and long-term review mechanisms—such as the spending reviews in place throughout the UK—will call for adjustments. These encompass not only adjustments in the distribution of resources across sectors, but also in the strategic targeting underpinning the delivery of funded programmes.

Measuring the impact of public spending in relation to objectives is a key element of gender responsive budgeting. In this respect, gender responsive budgeting can function as a management control by helping to facilitate the measurement of performance.[10] In Austria, for example, gender responsive budgeting has been introduced as part of a broader budgetary reform process.[11] New legislation and a constitutional amendment in 2007 paved the way for a comprehensive reform of the budgetary process with the move to performance-oriented budgeting by 2013. The entire management process and budget cycle, including the medium term strategy as well as the annual budget, the formulation, execution and control of the budget, are affected. Among the four strategic outcomes specified in the amended Constitution is that of gender equality; the others are transparency, efficiency and a true and fair view of the financial position of the federal government of Austria. The Austrian Administration views the constitutionally defined objective of gender quality as corresponding to the internationally established concept of gender budgeting or gender equitable budgeting. Gender responsive budgeting thus constitutes the financial policy instrument for the implementation of Austria's gender mainstreaming strategy.[12]

C. Gender Responsive Budgeting Defined

The Council of Europe (COE) has defined gender responsive budgeting thus:

> Gender budgeting is an application of gender mainstreaming in the budgetary process. It means a gender-based assessment of budgets, incorporating a gender perspective at all levels of the budgetary process and restructuring revenues and expenditures in order to promote gender equality.[13]

[9] R Sharp, *Budgeting for Equity: Gender Budget Initiatives within a Framework of Performance Oriented Budgeting* (New York, United Nations Development Fund for Women UNIFEM, 2003).

[10] G Steger, *Putting Tax Money to Effective Use for Citizens: Gender Budgeting the Austrian Experience*, Third Meeting of OECD-MENA, Senior Budget Officials Network (Dubai, 31 October–1 November 2010).

[11] See Bundesfinanz Akademie, Federal Budget Reform e-learning, March 2011: ratgeber.bmf.gv.at/budgetreform-elearning/haashaltsrecht.eng/index.html.for details on the Austrian experience.

[12] Steger, *Putting Tax Money to Effective Use for Citizens* above n 10, and confirmed with the author via email.

[13] See above n 7, 10.

Given the link between gender responsive budgeting and gender mainstreaming, it is important to recall the COE definition of gender mainstreaming:

> Gender mainstreaming is the (re)organisation, improvement, development and evaluation of policy processes, so that a gender equality perspective is incorporated in all policies at all levels and at all stages, by the actors normally involved in policy-making.[14]

Thus the primary and long-term goal of gender responsive budgeting is to work towards incorporating (or mainstreaming) gender as a category of analysis in the budgetary process so as to ensure better gender equality outcomes.

In relation to the more general aspect of transparency in the use of public budgets, gender responsive budgeting is part of a broader response to increasing political and public demands. Similarly, in the context of budgetary management and control, gender responsive budgeting is a tool to enhance the effectiveness of policies by taking account of the socio-economic needs of men and women.

Some budget reform experts have described gender responsive budgeting as simply 'good budgeting' and point to the positive externalities that can derive from such an approach.[15] Others acknowledge that it is the 'budget where policy objectives are reconciled and implemented in concrete terms, thus giving effect to countries' economic and political priorities'.[16]

D. Gender Responsive Budgeting—Linking Policy Making with Budget Making

The gap between stated policies and their satisfactory translation into funded measures has long been recognised as a feature of the disconnect between policymaking and resource allocation. It is common to all policy domains, not only that of gender equality. With its explicit focus on the budget, gender responsive budgeting has the capacity to bring together the policymaking process with the budget making process. Further, gender responsive budgeting brings together two sets of information that traditionally have been kept separate: information on gender equality and information on public finance.[17] Gender responsive budgeting, with its framing of gender issues in the terms of economic discourse, has the effect of 'liberating' gender from the arena of 'soft' social issues 'to the

[14] Group of Specialists, (EG-S-GM), *Gender Mainstreaming: Conceptual Framework, Methodology and Presentation of Good Practices* (Strasbourg, Council of Europe, 2004) 15.

[15] See eg, J Stotsky, 'Gender Budgeting' (2006) IMF Working Paper No 23/2006, 3.

[16] T Hutton, Director, Public Management Directorate, 'Opening Address', OECD Conference on Strengthening Economic and Financial Governance (Brussels, OECD, October 2001).

[17] D Elson, 'Gender Responsive Budget Initiatives: Some Key Dimensions and Practical Examples', paper presented at the conference on 'Gender Budgets, Financial Markets, Financing for Development' (Berlin, Heinrich-Boell Foundation, 19–20 February 2002).

level of macroeconomics, which is often thought of as technical, value-free and gender-neutral'.[18]

E. Section 75 Duties—An Introduction

Introduced in 1998 as part of the legislation to establish a power-sharing Executive in Northern Ireland, the positive duties encapsulated in section 75 of the Northern Ireland Act 1998 were widely viewed as innovative, near revolutionary and the envy of the world.[19] Since then, other jurisdictions have introduced similar legislation.[20] At a very basic level, 'positive duties' are seen as going beyond prevention and remediation of discrimination to a proactive promotion of equality.[21]

Under the legislation, in carrying out their functions relating to Northern Ireland, public authorities are required to have due regard to the need to promote equality of opportunity between nine equality categories and to have regard to the desirability of promoting good relations between persons of different religious beliefs, political opinions or racial groups.[22]

Section 75 is a mainstreaming approach to the promotion of equal opportunities and good relations. As such, the intention is to transform the policymaking process by making the goal of equality and good relations a central concern and a guiding principle for all policy processes and service delivery.[23]

The Equality Commission for Northern Ireland has developed a range of supports to assist public authorities. The Revised Guidance, issued in 2010 and based on an extensive review of the effectiveness of section 75, provided an opportunity to refocus the approach to section 75 compliance, with a shift in emphasis away from the internal work of developing processes and procedures to a more concentrated external focus on delivering equality outcomes in the lives of the people affected by the duties.[24]

A central dimension to the duties is the assessment of policies for their potential impact on the promotion of equality with a parallel objective of bringing forward policy that can best promote the goal of equality. Screening is the first step in the assessment process and, if warranted, some policies will also be subjected to a full Equality Impact Assessment (EQIA).[25] The EQIA is intended to be a thorough

[18] N Holvoet, *Gender Budgeting: Its Usefulness in Programme-Based Approaches to Aid* (Brussels, EC Gender Help Desk, 2006) 4.

[19] For an early analysis of s 75, see C McCrudden, 'Mainstreaming Equality in the Governance of Northern Ireland' (1998) 22(4) *Fordham International Law Journal* 1694, 1696.

[20] See the statutory equality duties now consolidated in the UK's Equality Act 2010, pt 11.

[21] For more on positive duties generally see S Fredman, *Human Rights Transformed: Positive Rights and Positive Duties* (Oxford, Oxford University Press, 2008).

[22] Northern Ireland Act 1998, s 75.

[23] Equality Commission for Northern Ireland, *Section 75 of the Northern Ireland Act 1998: A Guide for Public Authorities* (Belfast, Equality Commission, 2010).

[24] Ibid.

[25] Ibid.

and systematic analysis, with the primary function of determining the extent of any differential impact[26] of the policy under analysis.[27]

In guidance from the Commission, the screening process effectively involves a policy-rating scheme, with each policy categorised relative to its relevance to equality; relevance can be 'none', 'minor' or 'major'. The Commission recommends that public authorities use assessment of impact—which includes both screening and EQIA—as part of the policy development process, rather than an exercise added on when the policy is in place.[28]

F. Overview of the Northern Ireland Budget Process

The budget process in Northern Ireland relates primarily to the allocation of public expenditure. The Northern Ireland Executive has limited revenue raising powers, in that there are a limited number of fiscal policy instruments available to it.[29] There are four main sources of funding for public expenditure in Northern Ireland.[30] These are:

1. A share of UK Public Expenditure allocations. The Barnett formula determines the population-based share of UK public expenditure that goes to the devolved administrations of Scotland, Wales and Northern Ireland.
2. Regional Rates—revenue received from taxation on business and domestic property in Northern Ireland.
3. Borrowing under the Reinvestment and Reform Initiative. With a limit of £200 million per annum, this borrowing is intended for major capital infrastructure projects.
4. EU Funding.[31]

The framework for the control of public expenditure is comprised of the Departmental Expenditure Limit (DEL) and Annually Managed Expenditure (AME). DEL funds are allocated at the discretion of the Executive to address local needs and priorities. AME, on the other hand, because it is largely comprised of demand-led programmes such as social security benefits, is controlled annually.[32] The main focus then of the budget in Northern Ireland is on DEL funding, which is delineated into Current Expenditure and Capital Investment. The Programme for Government (PfG) provides the strategic framework for the budget process.

[26] The focus on differential impact, rather than on adverse, is important and is discussed in more detail later in this chapter.

[27] Equality Commission, *Section 75 of the Northern Ireland Act 1998* above n 23.

[28] Ibid.

[29] Northern Ireland Executive, *Budget 2008–2011* (Bangor, Department of Finance and Personnel, 2008).

[30] Ibid.

[31] Northern Ireland Executive, *Budget 2011–2015* (Bangor, Department of Finance and Personnel, 2011).

[32] Northern Ireland Executive, *Budget 2008–2011* above n 29, Annex A.

Modelled on the Public Service Agreement (PSA) mechanism introduced by HM Treasury, the PfG for the period 2008–11 comprised 23 PSAs.[33]

Of the many public sector reforms in relation to budgeting in the last decade, the move toward performance-based budgeting is thought to have the most impact.[34] The development of performance information has been a long-term, widespread and evolving trend. Currently most Organisation for Economic Co-operation and Development (OECD) countries present performance objectives to Parliament and the public in either government-wide performance plans or ministerial or agency plans.[35] Performance-based budgeting is a way of allocating resources to achieve specific objectives based on programme goals and measured results. According to some experts, the key to understanding performance budgeting lies with the word 'result'.[36]

The Northern Ireland Executive modelled the organisation of Budget 2008–11 on the framework that had been put in place by the UK Treasury in the late 1990s.[37] Described by the OECD as a highly advanced total-system approach to performance budgeting,[38] the framework for PSAs, and their associated Service Delivery Agreements, was the central planning control mechanism.[39] As designed by the Treasury following the 1998 Comprehensive Spending Review, PSAs represented the Government's priorities and strategic objectives with measurable targets and outcomes.[40]

The Northern Ireland section 75 duties apply to the budget process, notwithstanding the challenges of assessing impact of aggregate level budget decisions. The Commission has always stressed the universal applicability of the duty to all stages of the policy process and to all policies and has, since 2002, been meeting with the Department for Finance and Personnel (DFP), the Economic Policy Unit and the Office of the First Minister and Deputy First Minister (OFMDFM) to discuss the need to mainstream equality consideration into the budgetary process.[41]

A positive duty in relation to gender equality has been in place in Britain since 2007. In August 2010, the Fawcett Society sought a judicial review of the

[33] Ibid para 6.8.

[34] A Aristovnik and J Seljak, 'Performance Budgeting: Selected International Experiences and Some Lessons from Slovenia' (2009) Munich, University Of Munich, MPRA Paper.

[35] Organisation for Economic Co-operation and Development (OECD), Public Governance Committee, *Modernising Government: The Way Forward* (Paris, OECD Publishing, 2005).

[36] R Young, *Performance-Based Budget Systems—Public Policy & Practice* (Columbia SC, USC Institute for Public Service and Policy Research, 2002).

[37] The Programme for Government (PfG) for Northern Ireland, which provides the strategic framework for the Budget, contained 23 PSAs for the 2008–11 budget cycle.

[38] T Curristine (ed), *Performance Based Budgeting in OECD Countries*, Part 2, *Country Case Studies, Chapter 12 UK* (Paris, OECD Publishing, 2007).

[39] C Madri, *Performance Budgeting and Accrual Budgeting: A Comparison of the United Kingdom, New Zealand and Australia* (Siena, 6th Transatlantic Dialogue (TAD) on 'Rethinking Financial Management in the Public Sector', June 2010).

[40] HM Treasury, *Devolving Decision Making: Delivering Better Public Services: Refining Targets and Performance Management* (London, HMSO, 2004).

[41] AW Trotman Associates, 'Assessing the Role of the OFMDFM and the NIO in Contributing to the Effectiveness of Section 75 of the Northern Ireland Act 1998' (2007) 70: www.equalityni.org.

Government's failure to pay due regard to gender equality laws in its preparation of the emergency budget brought in earlier that year. While leave for review was denied by the High Court, the presiding judge did acknowledge that policies set to have such a dramatically different impact on women and men merit further scrutiny. The judge also pointed to the need for improved data collection and analysis in order to adequately assess the impact of budget measures on equality between men and women.[42]

Having discussed these important preliminaries, it is now time to focus more specifically on gender responsive budgeting.

III. Gender Responsive Budgeting—Origins, Approaches, Methodologies and Tools

A. Evolution of Gender Responsive Budgeting

Australia was the first country to introduce gender responsive budgeting in 1984. During the 1980s and 1990s, the exercise expanded to include all budgets at federal, state and territorial levels. The results of the analyses were published as Women's Budget Statements and became part of the official budget documentation that was presented to Parliament for debate. While the formal process of gender budget analysis has been discontinued, a form of the women's budget statement is still published by all levels of government in Australia.

The ending of apartheid and consequent establishment of new democratic structures of governance in South Africa provided the opportunity for the adoption of a range of equality focused policies, including gender responsive budgeting. The methodologies used in these two countries were adapted as a framework, which subsequently became the basis for much of the training on gender responsive budgeting around the world.

The Commonwealth Secretariat was the first international agency to actively promote gender responsive budgeting in its Member States. Beginning in 1995, it pioneered the production of tools, methodologies and capacity-building materials, engaging prominent experts in the field, including leading economists. It continues to support numerous initiatives at country level.

Several of the UN agencies, led by United Nations Agency for Women (UNIFEM) (now UNWOMEN) and including United Nations Development Programme (UNDP), the International Labour Organisation (ILO), United Nations Economic Council for Europe (UNECE) and the United Nations Entity

[42] For more details on the litigation, see: www.fawcettsociety.org.uk/fawcetts-bid-for-a-judicial-review-of-the-2010-budget/.

for Gender Equality and the Empowerment of Women (UN INSTRAW), are responsible for an extensive and ambitious portfolio of work in much of the global south and in central and eastern Europe.[43]

The Council of Europe, whose group of specialists devised the working definition and framework for gender mainstreaming that has become the international standard, did the same for gender responsive budgeting.[44] Following from that, in 2009, the Council commissioned the drafting of a manual on the practical implementation of gender responsive budgeting,[45] which has gained significant currency in many Member States.

The European Union's first formal recognition and promotion of gender responsive budgeting was in 2001 during Belgium's presidency. In conjunction with UNIFEM, the Nordic Council of Ministers and the OECD, the EU convened a High Level Conference on 'Strengthening Economic and Financial Governance through Gender Responsive Budgeting'.[46] The conference, significant for bringing into focus the need to mainstream gender in budgetary activities in order to achieve the targets of the Beijing Platform for Action, concluded by setting 2015 as a target for the adoption of gender responsive budgeting in all EU Member States.[47] A 2003 opinion of the European Union Advisory Committee on Equal Opportunities for Women and Men noted that the call for gender budgeting is rooted in the Treaty of Amsterdam.[48] The Committee called for specific actions by the Commission to ensure gender responsive budgeting within the EC budget process and to encourage and resource initiatives at national level.[49]

Since the late 1990s, a substantial body of learning has emerged from a wide range of gender budget initiatives.[50] For some countries, the project to develop gender sensitive budgets has been put on a legislative basis. In others, where gender

[43] See the Gender Responsive Budgeting website, launched in 2001 by the United Nations Development Fund for Women (UNIFEM), now UN Women, in collaboration with the Commonwealth Secretariat and Canada's International Development Research Centre (IDRC): www.gender-budgets.org/.

[44] Group of Specialists (EG-S-GB), *Gender Budgeting: Conceptual Framework, Methodology and Presentation of Good Practices* (Strasbourg, Council of Europe, 2005) 10.

[45] S Quinn, *Gender Responsive Budgeting: Practical Implementation Handbook* (Council of Europe, Strasbourg 2009).

[46] N Holvoet, 'Strengthening Economic and Financial Governance Through Gender Responsive Budgeting Report' conference report, UNIFEM-OECD-Nordic Council of Ministers-Belgium Government High Level Conference (16–17 October 2001): www.gender-budgets.org/index.php?option=com_joomdoc&view=documents&path=resources/by-type/meeting-reports-and-presentation/strengthening-economic-and-financial-governance-through-gender-responsive-budgeting-report&Itemid=154.

[47] Ibid 5.

[48] The Advisory Committee's opinion is available at: ec.europa.eu/justice/gender-equality/other-institutions/advisory-comittee/index_en.htm.

[49] European Union Advisory Committee on Equal Opportunities for Women and Men, *Opinion on Gender Budgeting, 2003*: www.lex.unict.it/eurolabor/documentazione/.../opinion_may03.pdf.

[50] A large number of publications dealing with the learning from gender responsive budgeting can be accessed at two websites: (i) BRIDGE is a research and information programme located within the Institute for Development Studies Knowledge Services: www.bridge.ids.ac.uk; and (ii) the Gender Responsive Budgeting website, launched in 2001 by the United Nations Development Fund for Women (UNIFEM), now UN Women, in collaboration with the Commonwealth Secretariat and Canada's International Development Research Centre (IDRC): www.gender-budgets.org/.

mainstreaming has been embedded in government activities, systems, procedures, tools, expertise and experience gained in a number policy domains are being applied to budgetary processes. In other places, gender budget initiatives, generally in the form of pilot projects, are in progress as a way of testing the waters.[51]

B. Adapting Gender Responsive Budgeting and Applying Equality Responsive Budgeting in Northern Ireland

Gender responsive budgeting is largely a single equality ground approach to the budget.[52] Clearly there are challenges associated with extending the approach to encompass all nine grounds of section 75. It is not within the scope of this chapter to explore the challenges involved in such an extended application. It seems reasonable to suggest, nevertheless, that they are likely to be similar to those that have already been experienced and documented in applying the section 75 duties. The perceived complexity of the task should not be a factor of discouragement or dismissal. While the legislative duty applies to all grounds, an incremental approach—that is to say, where one or a small number of grounds become the focus of a pilot project on equality budgeting—would fall within the scope of the Commission's guidance.

The next section of this chapter will look in some detail at stages, approaches and tools employed in gender responsive budgeting and will suggest how these might be applied to section 75. It is important to point out that we are talking about a mainstreaming approach to all the budgetary processes and that this includes the allocation of resources. Work with the strategic policy framework (for example, the PfG) that informs budget formulation and execution is limited unless it is clearing linked to the financial control framework.

C. The Three Stages of Gender Responsive Budgeting

Based on a review of a large number of gender responsive budget initiatives across the 27 EU states, Quinn (the author of this chapter) identified three stages of gender responsive budgeting.[53] The following outlines these stages and explains their possible relevance to the section 75 statutory duty.

i. Stage 1: Gender Sensitive Analysis of All Budgetary Activities

Gender sensitive analysis of the budget is a potent starting place in satisfying the statutory requirement in relation to the promotion of gender equality. By adding gender sensitive analysis to the tools of analysis currently employed by

[51] Quinn above n 45, 52.

[52] In some instances race, ethnicity and age have been combined with gender as the focus of analysis.

[53] These stages are based on Quinn above n 45.

government ministries, budget officials and policymakers are better equipped to make decisions that will result in better gender equality outcomes, and thus contribute to the fulfilment of their statutory duties.

The analysis usually begins with a sex-disaggregated benefit incidence analysis. A benefit incidence analysis is a method of computing the distribution of public expenditure across different demographic groups, such as women and men.[54] The procedure involves calculating the unit cost for public services—for example, the cost to put one child through primary school, the cost of a hospital bed per night or the cost per person of a labour market activation scheme. With sex-disaggregated benefit incidence analysis, the calculation is extended to determine how much has been spent on men and how much on women.

The analysis relies on the collection of data on users of public services. If the data are available, it is possible to determine the distribution across a range of demographic groups with the beneficiary group. Theoretically, it should then be possible to determine the number of each of the nine section 75 groupings that are availing of public services in Northern Ireland. In reality, data capture and management is complex and challenging; the issues are discussed in the Commission's section 75 guidance.[55]

Probing deeper from a gender perspective, the analysis can go on to demonstrate the extent to which budgetary policies, and the attendant services, have done what they were designed to do. This includes the degree to which needs of the users of public services have been satisfied and how their gendered needs and roles contribute to their level of satisfaction. In addition, the analysis should reveal the challenges and barriers faced by those in the target group who have not accessed services. The analysis should also point to how budgetary policies need to take account of women's unpaid labour, in the home and in the community and how women bear the larger burden of care work. What is often very quickly revealed through this kind of analysis is the disconnect between government gender equality policies and budgetary decisions.

Elson draws attention to a vital guiding question: for the budgetary item under analysis, what is the impact on gender inequality? Has it reduced, exacerbated or made no impact on gender inequality?[56]

Applying this level of analysis to the broader equality agenda, in the context of section 75, for example, will mean reformulating Elson's question. For example, how does this budgetary item impact on equality for people with disabilities, people with different religious beliefs and people from different racial groups? The analysis will necessarily involve drawing on a range of qualitative and quantitative data. It will also involve intra and interdepartmental consultation as well as consultation with users and/or user representatives.

[54] OECD, 'Glossary of Statistical Terms': stats.oecd.org/glossary/detail.asp?ID=6811.

[55] Equality Commission, *Section 75 of the Northern Ireland Act 1998* above n 23.

[56] D Elson, 'Gender Mainstreaming and Gender Budgeting', paper presented at the conference on 'Gender Equality and Europe's Future' (Brussels, 4 March 2003).

Just as gender responsive budget analysis enables policymakers to unpick assumptions of gender neutrality and examine potential 'gender blindness' when developing policy and evaluating policy outcomes, this level of budget analysis will enable Northern Ireland policymakers to build up a true picture of the nature and extent of the differential impact on the section 75 groupings. This is the primary purpose of the EQIA and it is a fundamental step for policymakers to gain an understanding of the nature and extent of inequality as experienced by those affected. Employing this level of analysis—even if doing so reveals no disproportionate impact on any of the groupings—can contribute to the larger project of becoming conversant with the actual needs and expectations of the full range of public service users.

ii. Stage 2: Reformulation of Spending Lines so as to Produce Better Gender Equality Outcomes

When gender sensitive analysis informs budget decisions and results in the restructuring of budgetary lines, the Government's gender equality strategy stands a better chance of being resourced and implemented. At the same time, any unintentional gender biases can be revealed and mitigated. Where analysis reveals that budget resources have not been distributed in a gender equitable way, a response from the budget is required to redress the inequity. Where the distribution of budget resources does not match the Government's gender equality policies, realignment is required. In some instances, restructuring may mean a positive action measure—a temporary additional spending line specifically targeted at an identified problem.

However, temporary or one-off solutions do not address the fundamental finding of a gender sensitive analysis, which is that budgets are not gender neutral. Accepting the gender impact of budgets requires changing the mainstream funding line so as to more permanently correct the inequity and better target the need for which the spending line was designed.

This second stage is akin to the requirement under section 75 to adjust policy so as to mitigate adverse impact or to devise an alternative policy to better promote equality. The key difference, as is the case with all three stages, is that the focus is on the budget line attached to the policy rather than limiting the impact assessment to the policy in isolation from the budget. In bridging the gap between policy design and resource allocation, it is potentially possible to respond to any revealed deficiency or needed change in design of policy by a change in the level and distribution of budgetary allocation.

iii. Stage 3: Working Systematically to Incorporate a Gender Equality Perspective within All Budgetary Processes

Gender budgeting is not just about the content of budgets.[57] Essentially, public expenditure management is a political process and not simply a technocratic

[57] See Norton and Elson above n 1.

one.[58] So that while understanding the technicalities of budget formulation and execution is important, understanding the political influences on the system is also important.[59] In many gender budget initiatives, the role of civil society to hold government accountable has played a significant part in bringing political influence to bear.

Mainstreaming gender as a category of analysis in the budgetary process is a long-term exercise of analysis, monitoring and restructuring. It is a process of refinement based on continuous analysis of budgetary performance which should result in better targeted objectives and thus spending of public money that is more effective in producing equality outcomes. Mainstreaming gender budgeting requires an ongoing commitment to understanding gender, which includes analysis and consultation, and ongoing budget readjustments to take account of the changing needs of women and men.

Stage three involves making the practice of responding to the differing needs of service users central to the budget decision-making processes. Just as section 75 was intended to ensure that principles of equality and good relations are at the heart of policymaking, keeping the focus on the budget will expedite that agenda.

Mainstreaming involves changing work practices, working systematically to embed new approaches into the everyday operational processes, changing the work culture so that considerations of equality become reflex.[60] The three stages outlined above are iterative, with the practice of analysis and reformulation becoming continuous, building capacity and developing systems to bring about a changed work culture where equality considerations become embedded.

These three stages provide the medium to long-term framework for the work of mainstreaming equality considerations in the budget. The next section of the chapter discusses ways in which the work can be initiated and progressed. Following that, a number of tools are detailed.

D. Two Approaches to Gender Responsive Budgeting

Broadly speaking there are two approaches for the introduction of gender responsive budgeting:

- Approach 1: The establishment of one or more gender equality objective(s) and the design of appropriate activities and identification of budget allocation(s) to achieve the objective(s).
- Approach 2: The systematic examination of all budgetary items with the objective of making any necessary changes to produce more gender equitable outcomes.

[58] Norton and Elson above n 1; see also the chapter by Rory O'Connell in this volume.
[59] Norton and Elson above n 1.
[60] For more on mainstreaming, see Rooney and Harvey's chapter in this volume.

The strategic difference between the two approaches is that with the former (establishing gender equality objectives) the focus is on the status of gender equality in the sector and the identification of areas for improvement. For example: what are the gender imbalances in education? Are more girls than boys progressing to third level? Are boys doing better at science? In relation to sport, the participation rates of males and females could be a focus. This sectoral analysis will lead to an understanding of how gender inequality is manifest and in turn to the identification of measures and resources to improve the situation.

With the second approach, the focus is on the existing activities/programmes and their associated budget lines. For each budgetary activity the purpose of the analysis is to discover the differential impact on men and on women; to determine if there is an adverse impact on one gender or another and to redesign the activity so as to redress the imbalance and so promote gender equality.

i. Approach 1: Establish Gender Equality Budget Objectives

This is the approach adopted by the Austrian Government as part of its introduction of gender responsive budgeting.[61] The 2007 legislation in Austria mandates that for each of the three levels of budget (chapter, global and detail) all government departments are required to set at least one gender equality objective each year.[62]

The format of the documentation used in the Austrian framework requires four questions to be considered. What is the outcome objective? Why this objective? What is planned to achieve this objective? What would success look like?[63]

A closer look at the language used in the Austrian format is useful to understanding the level of analysis that is required. Notice that the objective is described as an outcome objective. In the traditional budget formulation process the terms 'input' and 'output' are used. The input is the amount of spending allocated to an activity or measure and the output is what is produced or 'bought'. For example, within the area of spending on health care a line item of spending dedicated to doctors' salaries is considered the input and the output is the number of doctors employed. The term 'outcome' refers to something beyond the output; for example a reduction in the incidence of prostate cancer. This specific outcome would involve the input of the salaries of oncologists, as well as other inputs, such as, for example, upgrading medical equipment, improving regional access to cancer preventive services, etc. As demonstrated, the outcome of a reduction in the incidence of prostate cancer might not be achieved simply by making sure that there is enough in the budget to pay doctors.

[61] See Steger, 'Putting Tax Money to Effective Use for Citizens' above n 10; and G Steger, 'Putting Tax Money to Effective Use for Citizens: Gender Budgeting the Austrian Federal Experience', presentation made in Dar es Salaam, 21 June 2011: unpan1.un.org/intradoc/groups/public/documents/un-dpadm/unpan046609.pdf for details of the Austrian experience.

[62] Steger, ibid 6.

[63] Ibid 8.

In the context of gender responsive budgeting, specifying a gender equality outcome objective means being able to identify areas within a department's responsibility where there is room for improvement in terms of gender equality. For each sector—education, health, labour market and social security, rural and regional development, enterprise, etc—knowing where and how gender inequality exists and what the priority issues are will enable policymakers to set concrete and evidence-based objectives.

In considering how this approach could be adapted to the broader equality agenda, it is useful to recall the recommended shift in focus in the application of the section 75 duty away from the processes of implementation towards the realisation of outcomes.[64] To assist this refocus the Commission's new guidance recommends that public authorities produce an action plan in which they detail specific activities designed to promote equality.[65] This recommendation is a response to a finding of the Effectiveness Review that policymakers lacked awareness of the reality of inequality. A similar critique was levelled at gender mainstreaming when it was characterised as a strategy without an objective; Verloo argues that unless and until policymakers have quantified gender inequality as it is experienced by their local population, it is not possible to set realistic and meaningful objectives.[66] Broad, national-level gender equality objectives, such as reducing the gender pay gap, ending gender based violence or increasing women's economic independence, need to be translated into sector and location-specific objectives. Likewise, in order to set realistic and meaningful objectives for the realisation of equality of opportunity for all, assessment must become more than identifying potential adverse impact. Measuring for differential impact is of a different order of assessment than that of identifying potential adverse impact. Measuring for differential impact will allow policymakers to unpick assumptions about the homogeneity of the end users of public services and thus learn about the needs and expectations of a diverse population.

A useful starting place is an audit of inequalities. As recommended in the Commission's Guidance, an audit of inequalities will provide public authorities with a profile of the populations within their remit.[67] The nature and scale of inequality among the different groupings revealed through the audit will form the basis of equality objectives that are pertinent. In addition, the audit is an important tool towards the development of baseline data, recommended by the Effectiveness Review to enable the setting of targets and the measurement of outcomes.[68] Within a framework of equality responsive budgeting, the setting of equality objectives is undertaken in conjunction with budgetary allocation. The

[64] Equality Commission for Northern Ireland, *Keeping it Effective—Reviewing the Effectiveness of Section 75 of the Northern Ireland Act 1998—Final Report* (Belfast, Equality Commission, 2009) 8.

[65] Equality Commission, *Section 75 of the Northern Ireland Act 1998* above n 23, 47.

[66] M Verloo, 'Displacement and Empowerment: Reflections on the Concept and Practice of the Council of Europe Approach to Gender Mainstreaming and Gender Equality' (2005) 12 *Social Politics* 344.

[67] Equality Commission, *Section 75 of the Northern Ireland Act 1998* above n 23, 47.

[68] Equality Commission, *Keeping it Effective* above n 64, 28.

PSA Framework in place for the Northern Ireland Budget 2008–11 and discussed earlier in the chapter is well suited to the alignment of budgetary decisions and strategic policy decisions.

ii. Approach 2: Applying Gender Responsive Budgeting to All Budgetary Activities

The second approach is to assess each budgetary activity for its capacity to deliver gender equality outcomes. This is the approach adopted by the Belgian Government as mandated by 2007 legislation on Gender Mainstreaming.[69]

The logic of this approach is:

- Men and women (and boys and girls) are the end users of public policies and services.
- Gender mainstreaming is premised on the fact that public policies can impact men and women differently.
- The budget is an instrument of public policy and its budgeted activities can impact men and women differently.
- All budgetary activities have the potential of affecting equality between men and women.

In Belgium, this approach comes out of legislation designed to deepen the implementation of gender mainstreaming. It is a mainstreaming approach, in the sense that the intention of the legislation is for gender to ultimately be integrated as a category of analysis and control in all budget decisions. The procedures prescribed in the legislation, and communicated through standard budget circulars directed towards line ministries and other spending units, means that gender equality issues are no longer peripheral or add-ons to the budget.

This approach can also be viewed from the perspective of improving the efficiency and effectiveness of the management of public finances. In general, such improvements can be achieved by continuously updating the profile of the target group of end users in terms of size of population, geographical location and a range of demographic and socio-economic characteristics. A gender budgeting approach encompasses the needs of men and women based on their gendered roles and status. As with determinants such as age, ethnicity, disability etc, the differing social and cultural roles of men and women in the family and in society have a bearing on their needs and on their expectations of public services.

Obligations under the Section 75 duty are similar to those in the Belgian legislation, in that both mandate a mainstreaming strategy. The essential difference is that the Belgian law specifically identifies the budget as a policy domain covered

[69] See Institute for the Equality of Women and Men, *Manual for the Application of Gender Responsive Budgeting within the Belgian Federal Administration* (Brussels, Institute for the Equality of Women and Men, 2011) for details of the process in Belgium.

by the obligation to mainstream for gender.[70] As discussed earlier, it is accepted that the Northern Ireland budget is subject to the section 75 duty, though there have been difficulties in applying section 75 to high level policies like the budget.[71] Equality responsive budgeting, by adapting the tools of gender responsive budgeting, could prove useful to public authorities in Northern Ireland in addressing these challenges. The process demands that policymakers, and those responsible for the budget, work together to ensure coherence between the two domains.

E. Prioritising According to Relevance

For both approaches described above, the task of prioritising policies according to their relevance to gender is a necessary first step. Mainstreaming, necessarily, is an incremental exercise. The focus is on transforming how policy is designed and implemented, to change the culture within public administration such that gender considerations are integral to policy making, thus revealing and addressing any inherent unintentional gender bias in the system.[72] In this respect, it is an organisational change process carried out within a long-term framework[73] and, as such, how and where to begin needs to be part of the strategic planning. Some policies are more relevant than others to the promotion of equality and have, therefore, more potential to produce equality outcomes. Public authorities in Northern Ireland are minded to apply the section 75 duty to promote equality of opportunity in a way that is proportionate to a particular function.[74] It becomes necessary, therefore, to select those programmes that are most likely to have the optimum impact in response to evidence of inequality. Setting priorities is a task that will involve an exercise between those responsible for the delivery of activities, as well as those responsible for the budget. The audit of inequalities will play a key guiding role.

It is useful to look at two examples of how programmes have been prioritised in the context of gender responsive budgeting. The first is in Belgium where, as part of the statutory duty on gender equality, all spending units are required to assign each budgeted programme to one of three categories.[75] The first category applies to budget items which concern internal functioning or which do not contain a gender perspective. Category 2 is made up of those budget activities specifically

[70] Arts 2 and 5 of the 2007 Belgian law on gender mainstreaming, contained in *Manual for the Application of Gender Responsive Budgeting* for the application of gender responsive budgeting within the Belgian federal administration, ibid.

[71] The Effectiveness Review noted problems with the application of s 75 to 'high level' policies: Equality Commission, *Keeping it Effective* above n 64, 17.

[72] See eg, T Rees, *Mainstreaming Equality in the European Union* (London, Routledge, 1998).

[73] Swedish Government, *A Book of Practical Methods from the Swedish Gender Mainstreaming Support Committee* (Stockholm 2007).

[74] Equality Commission, *Section 75 of the Northern Ireland Act 1998* above n 23.

[75] See Institute for the Equality of Women and Men, above n 69, for details of the process in Belgium.

targeted to achieving gender equality. This includes any 'positive action' measures aimed at redressing past discrimination or current particular disadvantage. They are likely to be part of a gender equality strategy and are, therefore, easily identifiable. Finally, category 3 activities are those which are deemed to have a clearly and immediately identifiable gender dimension. Category 3 activities are viewed as having the most potential to affect the balance of gender equality. This process of categorisation is the first step in the application of a gender responsive approach to the budget. It is similar to the screening process associated with section 75, by which policies are designated as having 'none', 'minor' or 'major' impact on equality.[76]

In Belgium, the legislation detailing the procedure for the categorisation process has been translated into a Budget Circular issued by the Federal Public Service Budget and Management Control, which has responsibility in Belgium for all functions of the national budget. The Circular states that category 2 items are to be accompanied by a 'gender note' and category 3 items by a 'gender comment'.[77] The gender note is comprised of a series of five column entries in a table, which is the standard format for all budgetary items. The gender comment, on the other hand, is more detailed and is based on the results of a gender impact assessment. The guidance to spending units is that if there is a doubt as to which category applies then the item should be assigned to category 3 and be subjected to a gender impact assessment. There is an expectation that as capacity for gender analysis deepens, some budgetary activities will over time be re-categorised from 1 to 3.[78]

In terms of using the budget to promote equality, what is key in the Belgium situation—and, indeed, with other gender responsive budget initiatives—is that the quantitative and qualitative information contained in the gender notes and gender comments becomes part of the official budget documentation. Thus Parliament and the general public can discover how and to what extent public expenditure has been used to promote equality; the budget becomes a focus of scrutiny for equality as well as a basis for advocacy; and issues of accountability and transparency are better served.

A similar methodology of categorisation is in operation in Andalusia in Spain. A 2003 law on Fiscal and Administrative Measures provides the basis for gender responsive budgeting.[79] A key provision of the law is that the budget presented to Parliament should contain a Gender Impact Report. Referred to as the G+ project, four criteria are used to select programmes that are most relevant to advancing gender equality. They are programmes that have a transformative capacity, have the

[76] Equality Commission, *Section 75 of the Northern Ireland Act 1998* above n 23, 53.

[77] Institute for the Equality of Women and Men, above n 69, 29.

[78] Ibid.

[79] Ministry of Finance and Public Administration, Regional Government of Andalusia, *The G+ Project, A methodology for using public budgeting to improve gender equality* (Andalusia, 2010).

capacity to impact on a large scale, have the capacity to reduce gender inequality and relate to employment in the administration of the region.

There are four ratings for the G+ Scale: g0 signifies a programme with no identifiable relevance to gender equality; the scale then ranges from g1, to G and lastly G+ for programmes with maximum potential to affect gender equality. While each department is responsible for rating its programmes on the G+ Scale, the Gender Impact Commission of the Andalusian budget is required to review all programmes and recommend re-designation if necessary.[80] In the context of Northern Ireland's section 75 duty, the selection of criteria as the basis of a prioritisation mechanism could be based on the experience public bodies have of working with the inequalities.

F. Methodologies and Tools

We next examine some of the most commonly used tools in gender responsive budgeting. As will be demonstrated below, some are tools of oversight and accountability, as with the Women's Budget Statement; others are analytic tools and others are tools of management. As with most mainstreaming processes, the literature on gender responsive budgeting is very clear about the lack of a standard methodology or set of tools. Gender budgeting has the advantage over gender mainstreaming in that it is conceptually much more delineated. Nevertheless, there is no clear-cut blueprint for its implementation.[81]

The following tools are presented with a discussion as to their applicability to the section 75 equality duty, and thus to the broader equality agenda. It is clear that much more work is needed in this area not only in relation to the Northern Ireland policy regime, but also more broadly where budgetary processes are examined for their capacity to deliver a range of equality outcomes. Testing the adaptability of these tools will be an important step in terms of developing a methodology that best suits the processes already in place for the section 75 duty.

The sets of tools that will be discussed are the Women's Budget Statement, the Commonwealth Secretariat Tools and the Budget Circular.

i. The Women's Budget Statement

The Women's Budget Statement is the instrument pioneered in Australia. It is the end product of a series of analytic exercises measuring the impact of budgetary activities.[82] At its core, this is an accountability tool in that each ministry is required to account for its spending on gender equality. In Australia the

[80] Ibid.

[81] N Holvoet, 'Gender Budgeting in Belgium: Findings from a Pilot Project' (2007) 9 *European Societies* 275.

[82] See the discussion on the Commonwealth Secretariat Tools below as examples of how to analyse the budget from a gender perspective.

Office on the Status of Women, which produces an aggregate account compiled from all ministries, is situated within the Department of the Prime Minister and Cabinet. This allows for high-level access to and potential influence on top-level decisions about programmes and budgets. The production of the Statement requires a high degree of cooperation and commitment throughout the machinery of government.

When first used in the Australian administration, the analysis of government expenditure was based on the following distinction between three specific types of expenditure: expenditure on programmes designed to redress identified gender imbalances;[83] expenditure on promoting equal opportunities for government employees; and general or mainstream expenditure by all government departments.

The Women's Budget Statement, which has been modelled and adapted in many other jurisdictions,[84] and is most commonly now called a Gender Budget Statement, is instrumental in a number of key ways. It 'reveals' the level of committed resources targeted at gender equality, at both the aggregate and sector level. It allows for an assessment of the adequacy, or otherwise, of funds to address gender inequality and facilitates the identification of priority areas. The approach allows for targets and associated indicators to be revised year-on-year, thus allowing for a constant improvement of gender equality outcomes. The requirement that civil servants carry out the analysis builds their capacity in relation to awareness of gender issues and the ability to conduct gender sensitive analysis. The exercise often reveals the data deficits and thus the production of the Statement acts as a lever for the production of gender specific data. Finally, it has proven to be a useful resource for women in government, and for parliamentarians in general, to participate in debate about specific budgetary policies.[85]

In the Northern Ireland context, where a broader equality legislative mandate pertains, this tool could be adapted by the DFP to provide an accounting at the aggregate level of how the budget addresses the promotion of equality of opportunity. Its compilation will be reliant on returns from all departments. Presentation of information in this way to the Northern Ireland Executive would represent the totality of work done at all levels of the budget formulation and execution process. Within a managed structure led by the DFP in conjunction with OFMDFM and with the oversight and support of an advisory and/or coordination group, the Equality Budget Statement could act as a focus and goal for the work with a framework of transparency and accountability.

[83] These might include health programmes targeted specifically at men and women, special initiatives for girls; labour market initiatives for women, reintegration programmes for male soldiers, initiatives to address violence against women, micro credit programmes for women, and educational scholarships for women.

[84] These jurisdictions include Sweden, Norway, France, Iceland and South Korea.

[85] R Sharp and R Broornhill, 'Women and Government Budgets' (1990) 25(1) *Australian Journal of Social Issues* 1.

ii. Commonwealth Secretariat Tools

The Commonwealth Secretariat commissioned Diane Elson to develop this set of seven tools.[86] Some are modelled on conventional economic analytic tools, and most deal with the expenditure side of the budget. They were first published in 1999 and remain a mainstay of the repertoire of available tools.

a. Gender-Disaggregated Beneficiary Assessment of Public Service Delivery and Budget Priorities

The assessment is developed on the basis of qualitative information obtained via opinion polls, focus groups, attitude surveys, etc, asking actual or potential beneficiaries about the extent to which government policies and programmes reflect their priorities and meet their needs. This kind of tool—without the disaggregation by gender—is used by mainstream researchers to investigate people's perceptions of public expenditure. This is an analytic tool used to provide data on a key dimension of the effectiveness of public services.

Within the context of the section 75 duties, beneficiary assessments could be used in the performance of an EQIA, as a means of determining the degree to which public services meet the needs and expectations of service users. The tool could be adapted to further beneficiaries of public services by religious belief, political opinion, racial group, age, marital status or sexual orientation, persons with a disability and persons without and persons with dependants and persons without, in accordance with the section 75 duty. The findings of the EQIA could contribute to a section 75 Audit of Inequalities.

By the same token, an existing Audit of Inequalities could point to the need for such an assessment so as to ascertain the specificity of how public services may fail to meet the needs of one or more sections of the population.

b. Gender-Disaggregated Public Expenditure Incidence Analysis

This is a quantitative tool that measures the unit cost of public services and how public expenditure is distributed between women and men on the basis of their respective take-up of services. It involves calculating the unit cost of a service and determining how many men and how many women benefit from that service. At an aggregate level, data from household surveys, such as those carried out by the Northern Ireland Research and Statistics Agency (NISRA), can be used. To obtain a more accurate picture, the analysis is best done at programme level.

This is most commonly used as a starting point in a gender analysis of budgetary programmes. This is because it is a simple way of determining the gender balance of the population benefiting from any one public service or programme. The findings are best understood alongside a gender breakdown of the broader

[86] D Elson, 'Annex: Gender Responsive Budget Analytical Tools' in D Budlender, D Elson, G Hewitt and T Mukhopadhyay, *Gender Budgets Make Cents: Understanding Gender Responsive Budgets* (London, Commonwealth Secretariat, 2002).

target group for whom the policy/service was designed. Ideally, the gender balance of both groups should be similar. Use of this tool in the context of section 75 categories could prove challenging in terms of the data available. Lack of data, either because of inadequate systems for capturing the data or because of sensitivity in obtaining data from some of the groupings, will limit the effectiveness of this tool. Nevertheless, consideration should be given to an incremental approach by using the tool initially in relation to one or a small number of the groupings, rather than all nine.

c. Gender-Aware Policy Appraisal

This is used to evaluate the policies that underlie budget appropriations so as to identify their likely impact on women and men. It questions the assumption that budgetary policies are 'gender neutral' in their effects and asks instead: 'In what ways are the policies and their associated resource allocations likely to reduce or increase gender inequality?'[87]

In effect, this tool comprises a number of elements that are generally associated with impact assessment. It draws on a range of data sources, both qualitative and quantitative, on the demographic make-up of the target group of service users, including performance information. The appraisal necessarily involves an assessment of the articulated policy in tandem with the spending allocation.

d. Gender-Aware Budget Statement

This is used to demonstrate how public expenditure as a whole, and by sectoral ministries, is expected to address issues of gender inequality. It involves the disaggregation of projected expenditure into gender-relevant categories. Conventionally, public expenditure is organised by ministry and functional division, by recurrent and capital expenses and by line-items, for instance, personnel, equipment, etc. Examples of gender relevant categories are: the share of expenditure targeted explicitly to women and men to redress inequality; the share of expenditure targeted to income transfers of highest priority in reducing women's income inequality; the share of expenditure targeted for business support; and the share of expenditure targeted to the national gender machinery, etc.

e. Gender-Disaggregated Analysis of the Budget on Time Use

This tool is one way of identifying the relationship between the national budget and unpaid labour, often referred to as the care economy. The objective is to find a way to quantify unpaid labour, show the distribution between women and men and develop budgetary policies that take account of the contribution of unpaid labour to the economy. Women share a greater proportion of the burden of

[87] Elson above n 17.

unpaid labour and are therefore restricted in the time available to them to pursue other activities, including labour market opportunities.

f. Gender-Aware Medium-Term Economic Policy Framework

Current medium term macroeconomic policy frameworks are formulated using a variety of economy-wide models, none of which take account of gender. Building in gender could be accomplished by either disaggregating variables, where possible, or by constructing new models that are gender sensitive.

g. Gender-Disaggregated Public Revenue Incidence Analysis

This examines both direct and indirect forms of taxation in order to calculate how much taxation is paid by different categories of individuals or households.

Elson suggests that this range of tools can be used to integrate a gender dimension at the three levels of decision-making identified by the World Bank Public Expenditure Management (PEM) Handbook in relation to formulating the national budget. These are concerned with how the budget affects macroeconomic performance, allocation of resources, and the efficiency and effectiveness of resource use in service provision.[88] Elson further suggests, and indeed the experience with the tools would verify, that they are most readily implementable at two of the three levels: decisions on the allocation of resources and efficient and effective service provision.[89]

iii. Budget Circulars

Budget circular is the term given in some countries to the means used in all jurisdictions by the ministry or agency with overall responsibility for the budget to communicate instructions to the line ministries and other spending units. One of the main circulars is issued annually at the beginning of the budget drafting process. Generally it sets out the macroeconomic framework, including projections, the broad policy position of the Government, spending ceilings and any other instructions relevant on how spending units should prepare their budget submissions.

A number of jurisdictions have used the budget circular as a way of encouraging spending units to pay attention to gender equality consideration in the preparation of their budget bids.[90] In Northern Ireland, the guidance from the DFP reminds government departments that that the focus on the duty to promote equality of opportunity should be applied throughout the budget process. In addition to this general guidance, departments are reminded that spending

[88] The World Bank, *Public Expenditure Management Handbook* (Washington DC, The World Bank, 1998).

[89] D Elson, *Gender Budget Initiative Background Papers* (London, Commonwealth Secretariat, 1998).

[90] Eg, Korea, Austria, the autonomous region of Andalusia, Berlin. Also for more information on the use of the Budget Circular, see D Budlender, *Gender Responsive Budgeting Manual for Trainers* (UNDP, Bratislava, 2005).

proposals which are deemed to have a positive impact on equality, good relations, poverty, social inclusion or sustainable development will fare better in the assessment process and have a better chance of being recommended to ministers.[91]

In the context of an equality responsive budgeting approach, these guidance documents could serve to ensure that all spending departments are following the same approach and that there is clarity regarding what the central budget office requires in order to present aggregate level evidence of adequate assessment and adjustment in order to realise equality outcomes.

The Belgian approach to budget circulars is potentially instructive for the Northern Ireland context. The Federal Public Service in Belgium issues two circulars that deal with gender responsive budgeting: the circular on the drafting of the budget and the circular on gender budgeting.

a. The Circular on the Drafting of the Budget

This circular contains the full range of instructions to ministries on issues such as the budget, formulation processes, fiscal and management rules, the format in which bids are to be presented and any and all other information relevant to the current budget under preparation.

This circular first contained a mention of gender budgeting in 2009 when it stipulated that all ministries were to identify the programmes chosen for the application of a gender responsive budgeting approach.[92] Since then the information in this circular has been expanded each year and in 2011 it contained an explanation of the legal basis for gender responsive budgeting.[93] It also drew attention to the new circular dealing specifically with gender responsive budgeting.

b. The Circular on Gender Budgeting

This circular was first issued by the Federal Public Service in 2010 as part of the guidance for the preparation of the 2011 budget.[94] It covers an extensive range of issues in relation to both the legal and policy foundation for gender responsive budgeting, as well as the processes to be undertaken by each ministry. The following issues are included:

— An explanation of the legislation of 2007, the focus of which is gender mainstreaming as a way of achieving equality between men and women in all aspects of society.

[91] Department of Finance and Personnel (DFP), *Priorities and Budget 2007: Guidance for Departments* available at: archive.niassembly.gov.uk/public/2007mandate/reports/2009/report_22_09_10r.htm and *Priorities and Budget 2010: Guidance for Departments* (DFP Public Spending Directorate, June 2010).

[92] Information obtained via email and telephone conversations with Jeroen Decuyper of the Belgian Institute for the Equality of Women and Men, the agency with responsibility for advising on the implementation of gender responsive budgeting in the Belgian administration.

[93] Institute for the Equality of Women and Men above n 69.

[94] Ibid.

— Specific provisions of the law, including the mandate to integrate a gender perspective in all budgetary processes and to produce a 'gender note' for each budget line identified as having the capacity to achieve gender equality.
— Definitions of gender mainstreaming, gender budgeting, gender perspective and analysis from a gender perspective.
— The rationale and method for categorisation of budgetary items.
— Details of the four-step procedure to be applied by all the relevant actors in the implementation of gender budgeting.

In the context of an equality responsive budgeting approach, the guidance documents issued by the DFP could serve to ensure that all spending departments are following the same approach and that there is clarity regarding what the central budget office requires in order to present aggregate level evidence of adequate assessment and adjustment in order to realise equality outcomes.

G. The Role of Civil Society[95]

Civil society has been engaged in advocating for adequately resourced social policies long before gender budgeting became an available strategy. Disappointed with the inadequate implementation of gender mainstreaming, many advocates and practitioners believe that gender budgeting has the potential to reinvigorate the mainstreaming of equality.

The early literature on gender budgeting discusses the mix of players involved in gender budget initiatives worldwide.[96] Where gender budgeting has had the most impact, this has been due in part to the coexistence of civil society working 'outside' government and an 'inside' set of government players. In many situations there has been close cooperation between the two sets of players, with exchange of expertise and experience; in other instances the outside civil society group has encouraged the work inside the administration while maintaining its independence as a monitor and critic.

Academics have a significant role to play, both as members of civil society groups and as individual experts. They contribute to the development of tools and methodologies, to the elaboration and deepening of the conceptual framework and to research in the relevant fields. Civil society performs a number of functions in relation to the promotion of gender responsive budgeting. In the first instance, there is the traditional role of exercising political pressure in terms of demanding transparency and accountability in the management of public finances and lobbying for changes needed in budgetary policy. Alongside this is

[95] Adapted and updated from Quinn above n 45.

[96] See eg, Budlender, Elson, Hewitt and Mukhopadhyay above n 6; F Sarraf, 'Gender-responsive Government Budgeting' International Monetary Fund Working Paper WP/03/83 (IMF, Fiscal Affairs Department, Washington DC, 2003); and UNIFEM, *Gender Budget Initiatives: Strategies, Concepts and Experiences* (UNIFEM, New York, 2002).

the articulation of the rationale for gender budgeting, including how budgetary policy needs to address the role of women's unpaid labour and the contribution of that labour to the economy. Civil society groups are relied on to demonstrate the analytic tools required for gender budgeting and also to provide training and consultative services to public administrators. In some cases, civil society oganisations have commissioned costing exercises in relation to, for example, the cost of addressing domestic violence or providing for adequate childcare. In terms of monitoring government policy, civil society groups prepare shadow reports to present an alternative perspective to how governments report on their progress on advancing equality and human rights. Shadow reports have played an important function at the meetings of the Commission on the Status of Women at the UN in New York, where there has been an increased focus in recent years on gender responsive budgeting.[97]

Working with parliamentarians is a key element of work of civil society groups. The nature of budgetary processes—where one government department and one government minister is in charge and where decisions are made by a few—means that parliamentarians have limited input. They are often very open therefore to learning of ways of effectively intervening to challenge decisions, to present new analysis, to ensure transparency and to seek to promote the interests of the public.

Civil society in Northern Ireland has played a key role in advocating for and contributing to the implementation of section 75, albeit not to any significant degree with regard to budgetary processes. Consultation with civil society is a requirement under the legislation.[98] Lessons learned through the Effectiveness Review include ways to ensure that consultation mechanisms are targeted and efficient. The objective in this respect is not simply to lessen the risk of consultation fatigue, but also to ensure that policymakers make best use of the expertise and experience available to them.

IV. Where Next for Section 75 and Equality Responsive Budgeting?

The primary goal of equality responsive budgeting is to advance equality of opportunity and outcome. In the context of the use of public finances it is about services that take account of people's differing needs and expectations as they are determined by a whole range of demographic characteristics. It is about a constant assessment of the needs of the end users of public services, which entails measuring the differential impact on different populations. In short, equality responsive budgeting

[97] For more details, see: www.un.org/womenwatch/daw/csw/index.html#about.

[98] Equality Commission, *Section 75 of the Northern Ireland Act 1998* above n 23, 14.

- is a targeted approach—resulting in better outcomes;
- relies on assessment—resulting in better targeting;
- links equality policy with public finance management—resulting in compliance with equality duties while achieving more efficient allocation of resources.

The shift to a focus on producing measurable outcomes in relation to the implementation of section 75 duties necessarily involves considerably more attention to the gathering and management of data than currently occurs in Northern Ireland. The compiling of an audit of inequalities and action plan for measures to advance equality represent the level of information and analysis that is required. Procedures for the implementation of section 75, whether stipulated in the legislation or coming out of the recommendations of the Commission, involve

- a targeted approach to addressing inequality—resulting in better outcomes;
- an assessment of differential needs—resulting in better targeting;
- linking section 75 duties with resource allocation allowing for better targeting—resulting in better equality outcomes.

Whether moving towards reform of the budgetary processes (as in Austria) or not, government administrations are constantly seeking to improve performance in terms of management and control of public finance. This is more so in times of economic crisis when a dominant concern is stretching resources across all priorities, along with the need to spend more efficiently. Budgetary decisions that are informed by evidence of performance are likely to be better decisions.

Gender responsive budgeting, as has been demonstrated, has contributed to establishing the legitimacy of applying impact assessment processes to the budget, in compliance with government policy to mainstream gender equality in all policy domains. Developing equality responsive budgeting is a worthwhile enterprise, both in terms of the recognised demand for a deeper application of the section 75 duty to the budget process, but also in terms of the wealth of methodologies associated with gender responsive budgeting which are adaptable to the Northern Ireland context.

In order to progress towards an adequate application of section 75 processes to the Northern Ireland Executive's budget, the issue of where the responsibility lies needs to be resolved. The OFMDFM appears to believe that the responsibility lies with the individual spending departments and that it is at that level where inequality relating to programmes can best be known.[99] The Commission believes that key inequalities should be addressed through actions associated with the draft budget and the Programme for Government. The DFP has expressed support for a whole budget focus, while at the same time providing support for measures to address specific issues identified by the voluntary and community sector.[100]

[99] Trotman Associates above n 41, 73.
[100] Ibid 75.

Gender responsive budgeting posits that making decisions about spending that promote better equality outcomes can happen at all levels along the spending line. The application of an equality approach applies to both the formulation and also the execution of the budget. A number of countries in the EU (Spain, France, Belgium, Sweden and Iceland, for example) present aggregate level information on how the budget addresses gender equality. At the same time, further decisions made at departmental level and at programme level by subordinate units and agencies contribute to the budget's overall impact on equality outcomes.

In Northern Ireland, it is vital that all levels of government adopt an equality responsive approach to budgeting as a means of fulfilling section 75 duties. An important step in this is a wholehearted acknowledgement by the Executive that it is the budgeting process where equality proofing and monitoring 'is most likely to take sustainable effect'.[101]

Let us tentatively sketch the possible next steps in developing equality responsive budgeting in the Northern Ireland context. An extensive consultation process involving a number of different stakeholder groups is a necessary prerequisite for moving towards a deeper application of the section 75 positive duties in Northern Ireland's budgetary processes. This chapter could usefully provide the basis of that process to explore and flesh out how an equality responsive budgeting approach 'fits' with compliance with section 75 duties. The Equality Commission, in conjunction with the OFMDFM and the DFP, should consider convening a high-level seminar to further explore the potential for the application of budget work to the promotion of positive duties. Consideration should be given to inviting the input of senior budget officials from Austria, Belgium and Andalusia.

Much of the work on gender responsive budgeting has been initiated in the form of pilot projects. There is ample scope, within the Northern Ireland context, to identify a number of pilot projects to test the applicability of the tools. Given the range of populations covered by the equality duty, consideration should be given to creative and innovative ways of designing projects capable of yielding learning and results that will lead to sustainable application of tested methodologies. In preparation for these pilot projects, policymakers, ordinarily involved in ensuring compliance with section 75 duties, should be given the opportunity to work with the concepts and proposal set out in this chapter. This might be best achieved in a workshop type session during which exploration and debate can be facilitated. As with any new policy approach, appropriate training is an integral element of the roll out. The development of a training programme would allow for a greater number of civil servants, elected representatives and civil society groups to come to grips with the principles, values and processes relevant to equality responsive budgeting. Finally, it is important that the community and voluntary sectors are supported so as to enhance their capacity to engage with and contribute to the development of equality responsive budgeting in relation to section 75.

[101] Trotman Associates above n 41, 67.

V. Conclusion

This chapter seeks to demonstrate that the uptake of gender responsive budgeting in many jurisdictions across the world provides legitimacy to the broader project of using the budget to advance equality and social justice. It does so by giving an overview of the development of gender responsive budgeting as a strategy for the realisation of gender equality by expediting the mainstreaming of a gender perspective in all government policies. Gender responsive budgeting is a strategy which bridges the gap between policy development and implementation on the one hand, and budgetary planning and execution on the other; both are integral to the execution of government policy. It is premised on the assumption that unless gender mainstreaming is extended to include the budget, progress on gender equality will be impeded.

As highlighted in this chapter, gender responsive budgeting has gained considerable attention in many jurisdictions; in some places legislation is in place to provide for its implementation. In a number of countries where budget reform is underway with the adoption of a medium-term expenditure framework and some form of programme or performance-based budgeting, gender responsive budgeting has been incorporated, to varying degrees, as part of the reform process.

This chapter has suggested a gender responsive budgeting framework for application to the broader equality agenda under Northern Ireland's section 75 duties. The author makes the link between gender responsive budgeting as a mainstreaming strategy and the scope of section 75 as a mainstreaming strategy. Parallels are drawn between some of the tools used in gender responsive budgeting and the processes employed in the implementation of section 75. The Equality Commission for Northern Ireland has worked with the relevant parties, especially the DFP and the OFMDFM to make section 75 duties more integral to the budget process. Exploring the methodologies, tools and approaches associated with gender responsive budgeting in the context of section 75 could provide a useful way of further advancing this goal.

IV

Analysis in Action

9

The Right to Adequate Housing: A Case Study of the Social Housing Budget in Northern Ireland

EOIN ROONEY AND MIRA DUTSCHKE

I. Introduction

Previous chapters discussed the global trends in human rights-based budget analysis as well as the budget related obligations arising out of the International Covenant on Economic, Social and Cultural Rights (ICESCR). This chapter demonstrates how these obligations can be applied in practice. The first section outlines a human rights framework based on the right to adequate housing under ICESCR. The second section uses this framework to assess a number of elements of the social housing budget in Northern Ireland.[1] Despite the specific features of this case study, it has broad resonance, as the ideas that have shaped housing policy and finance in Northern Ireland are influential in many parts of the world.[2] Northern Ireland has witnessed a shift from the public provision of housing towards greater reliance on homeownership, public/private partnerships and the Private Rented Sector (PRS). Implicit and often explicit in this shift is the assumption that the market is inherently a more efficient and effective vehicle than the state for delivering housing. This chapter will demonstrate that this assumption is by no means safe in Northern Ireland.

[1] Northern Ireland is a region of the UK. The UK, having signed and ratified ICESCR, is obliged to comply with the Covenant under international law. The UK has not, however, incorporated the ICESCR provisions into its domestic law.

[2] See R Rolnik, 'Report of the Special Rapporteur on the Right to Adequate Housing as a Component of the Right to an Adequate Standard of Living, and the Right to Non-discrimination in this Context: Promotion and Protection of all Human Rights, Civil, Political, Economic, Social and Cultural Rights, including the Right to Development' (UN Doc A/HRC/10/7 2009). In this report, the Rapporteur identifies many of these developments as global trends.

II. Human Rights Framework

This section outlines a framework with which to assess housing budgets. The framework is based on the right to adequate housing—part of the right to an adequate standard of living enshrined in Article 11 ICESCR. We also set out some of the state's obligations in implementing this right. In defining the implementation obligations, the focus is on the budgetary obligations arising from Article 2(1) ICESCR. The section also draws on various General Comments issued by the Committee on Economic, Social and Cultural Rights (the Committee) (the Committee) which set out the implications of ICESCR provisions in more detail. General Comment No 3 elaborates on the meaning of Article 2(1). General Comment No 4 explains the right to adequate housing and indicates that the 'adequacy' of housing has various components, including legal security of tenure, affordability and accessibility for disadvantaged groups.[3] General Comment No 7 relates to the prohibition of evictions.

III. Progressive Realisation and Maximum Available Resources

Article 2(1) ICESCR requires states to 'take steps ... to the maximum of its available resources, with a view to achieving progressively the full realisation of the rights recognised in the present covenant'. The concept of progressive realisation implies continuous improvement in each of the elements of the right to adequate housing. It requires an expansion of access as well as an improvement of the implementation of the Covenant rights.[4] This means there is a duty to ensure that a larger *number* of people as well as a wider *range* of people progressively enjoy improving housing standards as more resources become available.[5] In light of the duty of progressive achievement, any deliberately retrogressive measures, which reduce the enjoyment of economic and social rights (ESR), have to be justified 'by reference to the totality of rights provided for in the Covenant and in the context of the full use of the maximum available resources'.[6]

As the citation from Article 2(2) indicates, the duty to realise progressively is related to the maximum of available resources (MAR). 'Resources' in this context refers to *all* resources available, including informational, technical, organisational,

[3] ComESCR General Comment No 4 on the right to adequate housing, UN Doc E/1992/23, Annex III, 114 (1991), para 8.

[4] S Liebenberg, 'The Right to Social Assistance: The Implications of *Grootboom* for Policy Reform in South Africa' (2001) 17 *South African Journal of Human Rights* 232, 241.

[5] Ibid 241.

[6] ComESCR, General Comment No 3 on the nature of States parties' obligations (art 2 (1)), UN Doc E/1991/23 (1990), para 9.

human, natural and administrative resources.[7] The duty of MAR requires that the available resources are used to maximise the enjoyment of ESR.[8] The obligation of MAR also requires that all the resources that can be used towards realising ESR, without sacrificing other essential services, are employed for this purpose.[9] Resources allocated towards the realisation of ESR must be fully expended for that purpose and must not be diverted to other non-ESR areas, if this reallocation results in a reduced enjoyment of ESR.[10]

States should keep under review the extent to which their use of resources is delivering the fastest progression of ESR, including the right to adequate housing. The most appropriate use of resources will vary from one State Party to another[11] and states should adopt whatever forms of public and private provision are suitable to the local context.[12] The most suitable approach is that which realises the Covenant obligations as expeditiously and effectively as possible.[13]

IV. Immediate Obligations

Certain aspects of the right to adequate housing are not subject to progressive realisation and have to be implemented immediately.[14] It has been argued that these immediate aspects of the Covenant obligations must be prioritised in the allocation of resources.[15] When states fail to realise certain immediate obligations claiming a lack of available resources, they must demonstrate that every effort has been made to use all the resources that are at its disposal in an effort to satisfy these duties.[16]

These immediate obligations include the duty of non-discrimination.[17] Article 2(2) guarantees non-discrimination in the enjoyment of ESR on a number of

[7] G van Bueren, 'Alleviating Poverty through the Constitutional Court' (1999) 15 *South African Journal of Human Rights* 52, 61.

[8] A Eide, 'Economic and Social Rights' in J Symondies (ed), *Human Rights: Concepts and Standards* (Farnham, Ashgate, 2000) 126.

[9] P Alston and G Quinn, 'The Nature and Scope of the State Parties' Obligations under the International Covenant on Economic, Social and Cultural Rights' (1987) 9 *Human Rights Quarterly* 156, 178.

[10] Ibid; The Maastricht Guidelines on Violations of Economic, Social and Cultural Rights' (1998) 20 *Human Rights Quarterly* 691, 697.

[11] ComESCR General Comment No 4, para 12.

[12] ComESCR General Comment No 3, para 14.

[13] V Dankwa, C Flinteman and S Leckie, 'Commentary on the Maastricht Guidelines on Violations of Economic, Social and Cultural Rights' (1998) 20 *Human Rights Quarterly* 705, 716. See also Queen's University Belfast Budget Analysis Project, *Budgeting for Economic and Social Rights: A Human Rights Framework* (Belfast, QUB, 2010) 18. Note that the state bears the burden of proving that it has been progressing towards the fulfilment of ESR using the maximum resources available.

[14] ComESCR General Comment No 3, para 1.

[15] Liebenberg above n 4, 367.

[16] ComESCR General Comment No 3, para 10 (talking about minimum core obligations). See also ComESCR General Comment No 20 on Non-discrimination in economic, social and cultural rights, UN Doc E/C.12/GC/20 (2009), para 13 with regard to the duty to ensure non-discrimination.

[17] ComESCR General Comment No 20, para 7.

grounds including race, religion and sex or other status.[18] General Comment No 20 on the right to equality states:

> [E]liminating discrimination in practice requires paying sufficient attention to groups of individuals, which suffer historical or persistent prejudice instead of merely comparing the formal treatment of individuals in similar situations. States Parties must therefore immediately adopt the necessary measures to prevent, diminish and eliminate the conditions and attitudes which cause or perpetuate substantive or de facto discrimination.[19]

In other words, the state must take immediate action to realise equal enjoyment of rights, even if achieving that goal can take time. This may require affirmative action and preferential treatment in favour of disadvantaged groups.[20] In terms of the allocation of budgets, eliminating substantive discrimination will often require additional resources towards realising the rights of traditionally neglected groups.[21] The Committee recognises that due to the interdependency of ESR, inequality in the enjoyment of one right can contribute to inequality in another right:

> [L]iving in poverty or being homeless may result in pervasive discrimination, stigmatisation and negative stereotyping which can lead to the refusal of or unequal access to the same quality of education and health care as others, as well as the denial of or unequal access to public places.[22]

It appears that efforts designed to eliminate discrimination have to be met within the existing resources, rather than with those that become progressively available. If states fail to give effect to the immediate duty not to discriminate, the higher burden of proof alluded to in previous paragraphs applies, namely that states must show that every effort has been made to address the discrimination as a matter of priority.

Like the right to equality, the duty to provide for a minimum essential level of enjoyment—also referred to as the 'minimum core'—is not subject to progressive realisation. States must immediately ensure the satisfaction of a minimum level of enjoyment of the rights. In other words, the minimum core provides a baseline from which progressive improvement must take place.[23] While the Committee does not use the term 'minimum core' in either General Comments Nos 4 or 7, it does note that the state is prima facie violating its obligations if a significant number of individuals are deprived of 'basic shelter'.[24] One can safely assume that 'basic shelter' constitutes the minimum core of the right to adequate housing. A situation in which a significant number of people lack basic shelter is thus a priority for policy and resource allocation.

[18] Ibid.
[19] Ibid para 8(b).
[20] Ibid para 9.
[21] Ibid para 39.
[22] Ibid para 35.
[23] Queen's University Belfast Budget Analysis Project above n 13, 50.
[24] ComESCR General Comment No 3, para 10.

Since the rights in the Covenant are to be realised 'progressively, States must refrain from taking deliberate retrogressive measures'.[25] Logically this duty is also immediate in nature.[26] A retrogressive measure is described as a 'general decline of living and housing conditions, *directly attributable* to policy and legislative decisions by State Parties'.[27] In terms of the right to housing, evictions and repossessions can constitute retrogressive measures if they are caused by deliberate actions or inactions of the state and are not accompanied by measures that enable people to find adequate alternative accommodation.

A number of procedural requirements, necessary for a principled rights-based approach to policymaking, are also independent of the availability of resources. State Parties are under an immediate obligation to monitor the extent to which rights are enjoyed, devise policies for their progressive realisation and ascertain the impact of those policies.[28] With respect to the right to adequate housing, states must therefore collect disaggregated data that allows the adequacy of housing for different social groups to be ascertained.[29] States must adopt a national housing strategy that 'identifies the resources available to meet goals and the most cost-effective way of using them'.[30] This strategy should be developed with the participation of those affected, including the homeless. State bodies responsible for policies that are relevant to the different aspects of the right to adequate housing have to coordinate their efforts in order to ensure their effectiveness.[31] With these obligations in mind we now examine Northern Ireland's budget for social housing.

V. Northern Ireland's Social Housing Budget

This section sets out the historical development of housing policy in Northern Ireland. The subsequent sections assess the success of that policy using a number of human rights indicators and consider in more detail some specific aspects of the social housing budget.

The roots of contemporary social housing in Northern Ireland can be traced to the establishment of the Northern Ireland Housing Executive (NIHE) in 1971. The creation of the NIHE as a single housing authority for the region was prompted by the civil rights campaign, which highlighted sectarian discrimination

[25] Ibid para 9.

[26] Ibid.

[27] ComESCR General Comment No 4, para 59 [own emphasis added]. It can be argued that the retrogressive measures can also be the result of a lack of policy and legislation, specifically during times of economic crisis and recessions.

[28] Ibid para 13.

[29] Ibid.

[30] ComESCR General Comment No.7 on the right to adequate housing: forced evictions (art 11 (1)), UN Doc E/1998/22, Annex IV (1997), para 12.

[31] ComESCR General Comment No 4, para 12.

in social housing build and allocation.[32] The stock and functions of various local providers were transferred to the NIHE, which embarked on a large-scale building programme, constructing 57,223 new homes (an average of 6358 per year) by 1979.[33]

The election of the Conservative Party in 1979 ushered in a radical transformation in social and economic policy. Under the leadership of Margaret Thatcher, the Conservatives broke from the social democratic consensus which accorded a significant role to social housing. The neoliberal ideology that underpinned the Government's agenda advocated the extension of markets and an expanded role for the private sector in the provision of public services. In housing, this thinking entailed a shift in support from social housing to homeownership. The House Sales Scheme, which subsidised social housing tenants to purchase their homes, helped to engineer this shift. Between 1979 and 2003 more than 100,000 properties in Northern Ireland were sold under this initiative.[34] In addition, investment in new social housing declined. Between 1983–84 and 1988–89 expenditure on new build in Northern Ireland halved in real terms.[35] With sales exceeding new builds, the social housing stock fell by 17.3 per cent between 1987 and 1998 while home ownership increased by 34.5 per cent.[36]

The NIHE became concerned with the adequacy of government funding for social housing,[37] and began to explore alternative sources of finance. This required creative thinking, as Treasury rules prohibited the NIHE from borrowing.[38] Housing associations (non-state not-for-profit social housing providers) which hitherto complemented the large-scale programmes of the NIHE with small-scale specialised developments,[39] appeared to offer a solution. Having previously been restricted to borrowing from government, the 1992 Housing (NI) Order permitted housing associations to obtain loans from private sources. As non-state bodies, the borrowing of housing associations was not categorised as part of public sector debt and was therefore not subject to the Treasury's borrowing rules. In effect, housing associations provided a means of circumventing these restrictions and of supplementing government funding for social housing

[32] Lord Cameron, *Disturbances in Northern Ireland: Report of the Commission Appointed by the Governor of Northern Ireland* (Belfast, Stationary Office, 1969).

[33] Personal Communication with Department for Social Development (DSD) unpublished on file with authors (10 June 2009).

[34] NIHE, *The House Sales Scheme and the Housing Market* (Belfast, NIHE, 2004) 8.

[35] Department of Finance and Personnel, *Northern Ireland Commentary on Public Expenditure Plans 1989–90 to 1991–92* (Belfast, Department of Finance and Personnel, 1989).

[36] Department for Social Development, *Northern Ireland Housing Statistics 1999–2000* (Belfast, Department for Social Development, 2000).

[37] See F Gaffikin and M Morrissey, *Northern Ireland: The Thatcher Years* (London, Zed Books, 1990) 160.

[38] House of Commons Northern Ireland Affairs Select Committee, 'Social Housing Provision in Northern Ireland: Sixth Report of Session 2002–04' (2004) Memorandum submitted by Chartered Institute of Housing (CIH).

[39] These developments were typically geared towards servicing specific local areas or particular client groups (such as elderly or disabled tenants).

with what was categorised as 'private' borrowing. On this basis, responsibility for building and managing new social housing was transferred from the NIHE to housing associations in 1998. The NIHE remains the landlord for social housing built before this date.

This new direction in the delivery of social housing coincided with broader political change as part of the 'peace process'. The Belfast (or Good Friday) Agreement 1998 established new arrangements for the governance of Northern Ireland, which had been subject to 'direct rule' by the UK Government since 1972. The Northern Ireland Act 1998 devolved a range of functions to a new Northern Ireland Assembly, an Executive and eleven government departments. The Assembly receives the vast majority of its budget in the form of a 'block' grant from the UK Government, the size of which is determined by changes in spending in England via the 'Barnett Formula'. Housing policy is a devolved matter, meaning that it is the responsibility of a department within the Northern Ireland Executive—namely the Department for Social Development (DSD), which sponsors and oversees the NIHE. However, other policy areas are reserved to the UK Government. For example, most taxation powers reside with the UK Government and social security, though officially devolved,[40] is provided on the basis of parity with the rest of the UK. In any case, amid continued political instability, devolution operated intermittently and was suspended over the entire period from October 2002 to May 2007. Consequently, between 1998 and 2007, devolution had little effect on housing policy in Northern Ireland.[41] Certainly the social housing stock continued to decline—between 2001–02 and 2010–11, the number of social housing units fell from 132,300 to 117,400 and from 21.0 per cent to 16.6 per cent of all occupied stock.[42]

The Assembly reassumed its functions on the cusp of a global economic crisis, to which housing finance was central. Deregulation of the financial sector permitted lenders to provide mortgages with a high risk of default (known as the 'sub-prime' market), to disperse these debts throughout the global financial system via complex financial products[43] and to use these dubious assets as leverage for further borrowing. When a rise in interest rates in 2006 caused many households in the United States to default on their mortgage payments, property values collapsed. Facing substantial losses, uncertain of the value of their assets and short on reserves, banks reined in their lending. As credit and confidence dried up, the UK economy went into recession. Under the New Labour Government the UK assumed substantial

[40] See s 87 Northern Ireland Act 1998; B Fitzpatrick and N Burrows, *An Examination of Parity Principles in Welfare and Wider Social Policy* (Belfast, NICCY, 2012).

[41] C Paris, 'Changing Housing System in Northern Ireland 1998–2007' (2008) 7 *Ethnopolitics* 119, 120.

[42] Department for Social Development, *Northern Ireland Housing Statistics 2010–2011* (Belfast, Department for Social Development, 2012).

[43] Specifically Collateralised Debt Instruments, Credit Default Swaps and Structured Investment Vehicles.

debt[44] in an attempt to recapitalise financial institutions, kick-start lending and stimulate aggregate demand. The Conservative–Liberal Democrat coalition Government, which came to power in 2010, undertook to reduce the deficit, primarily through cuts in public spending. Consequently, in real terms the Northern Ireland Assembly's current budget for 2014–15 will be 8.0 per cent less than it was in 2010–11 while its capital spending will be 40.1 per cent less.[45]

VI. Progressive Realisation of the Right to Adequate Housing?

The changes in housing policy in Northern Ireland since 1979 are characteristic of the shift from social democracy to neoliberalism. The private sector (particularly homeownership) has been promoted and social housing has assumed a more residual role. Responsibility for providing new social housing has been transferred from the state to the voluntary sector (ie, housing associations), with government providing financial support and oversight.

The Committee's General Comment No 3 makes clear that various economic systems can be compatible with the principles of the Covenant as long as they are democratic and respect the full range of human rights.[46] Transferring resources from the public to the private and voluntary sectors can be commendable as an 'enabling'[47] strategy if it forms part of an overall scheme towards the full realisation of everyone's right to housing.[48] The Committee accepts that the realisation of the right to adequate housing may involve a mixture of public and private initiatives appropriate to the country's specific context. The key point is that the chosen initiative realises the right to adequate housing for everybody in the shortest possible time.[49]

Social housing waiting lists and homelessness are two of the measures used by the Committee to assess the extent to which the right to adequate housing is realised.[50] Figure 1 shows the number of households on the waiting list for social housing in Northern Ireland between 2002–03 and 2010–11. It also displays the number of households in 'housing stress' (those assessed by the NIHE as being in severe need of accommodation). Over this eight-year period the waiting list

[44] Net public sector debt increased from 36% of GDP in 2006–07 to 52% in 2009–10. HM Treasury Public Finances Databank (August 2012) Table A5.

[45] Northern Ireland Executive, *Budget 2011–15* (Belfast, Northern Ireland Executive, 2011) Table 3.1. Forecasts for inflation in the UK have since been revised upwards suggesting that these estimates are conservative.

[46] ComESCR General Comment No 3, para 8.

[47] ComESCR General Comment No 4, para 14.

[48] Ibid.

[49] Ibid.

[50] See Committee on Economic, Social and Cultural Rights. 'The Guidelines on Treaty-Specific Documents to be Submitted by State Parties under Articles 16 and 17 of the International Covenant on Economic, Social and Cultural Rights' (UN Doc HRI/MC/2008/3) 29.

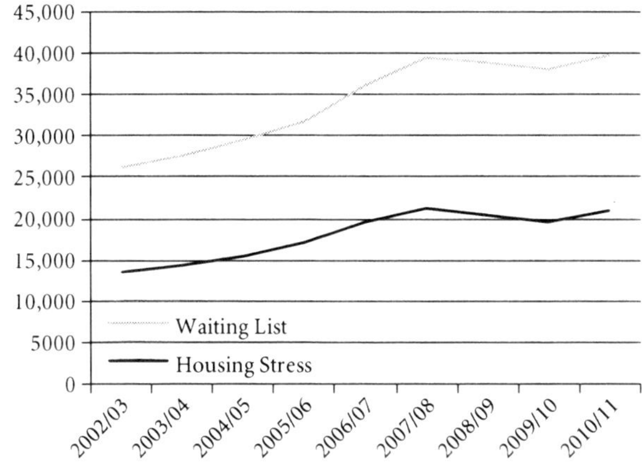

Figure 1: Social Housing Waiting List and Housing Stress 2002–03 to 2010–11

Source: DSD (2011) NI Housing Statistics 2010–11

for social housing in Northern Ireland increased by 52.0 per cent (from 26,248 to 39,891 households) and housing stress increased by 56.4 per cent (from 13,402 to 20,967 households). Both the waiting list and housing stress increased each year between 2002–03 and 2007–08. They then declined in 2008–09 and 2009–10 before increasing again in 2010–11. This indicates that the right to adequate housing has not been progressively realised.

Figure 2 (p 204) shows that the number of households presenting to the NIHE as homeless between 2002–03 and 2010–11 increased by 22.7 per cent from 16,426 to 20,158. As with the waiting list and housing stress, homelessness grew each year from 2002–03 to 2007–08, declined in 2008–09 and 2009–10 and increased in 2010–11. Again, the rise in homelessness indicates that progressive realisation of the right to adequate housing is not taking place. Indeed, it could constitute retrogression, which the state should be avoiding as a matter of priority. The Committee itself, in its 2009 Concluding Observations, expressed concern with the extent of homelessness in the UK as a whole,[51] and with the chronic shortage of social housing in Northern Ireland specifically.[52]

Other data also brings into question the capacity of the private sector to compensate for the decrease in social housing. Affordability is a key component of the right to adequate housing. The Committee is clear that housing costs should be commensurate with income levels and should not threaten the satisfaction of other basic needs.[53] However, a review commissioned by DSD calculated that

[51] Committee on Economic, Social and Cultural Rights, 'Concluding Observations: United Kingdom', UN Doc E/C.12/GBR/CO/5 2009, para 29.

[52] Ibid.

[53] ComESCR General Comment No 4, para 8c.

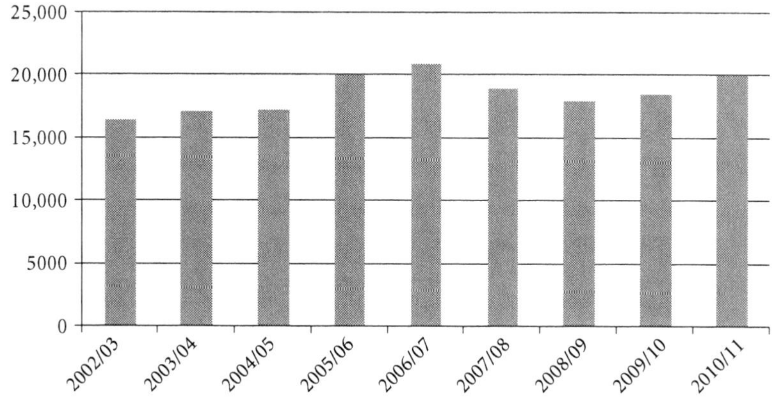

Figure 2: Households Presenting as Homeless 2002–03 to 2010–11

Source: DSD (2006) NI Housing Statistics 2005–06 and (2011) 2010–11

in 18 of the 26 district council areas, fewer than 10 per cent of owner-occupied homes were affordable for a household on a median income (Table 1).[54]

Table 1: Affordability by Northern Ireland District Council 2006

District Council	% Affordable	District Council	% Affordable
Antrim	9	Down	0
Ards	62	Dungannon	1
Armagh	2	Fermanagh	1
Ballymena	9	Larne	13
Ballymoney	0	Limavady	0
Banbridge	20	Lisburn	3
Belfast	1	Magherafelt	0
Carrickfergus	40	Moyle	0
Castlereagh	26	Newry and Mourne	1
Coleraine	0	Newtownabbey	26
Cookstown	3	North Down	11
Craigavon	1	Omagh	14
Derry	1	Strabane	4

Source: Review into Affordable Housing: Final Report

[54] This report defined mortgage repayments as unaffordable if they exceeded 35% of household income. Mortgage repayments were estimated on the basis of a 25 year mortgage with an interest rate of 6.75%, and a loan to value ratio of 0.95. J Semple, *Review into Affordable Housing: Final Report* (Belfast, Department for Social Development, 2007) 56.

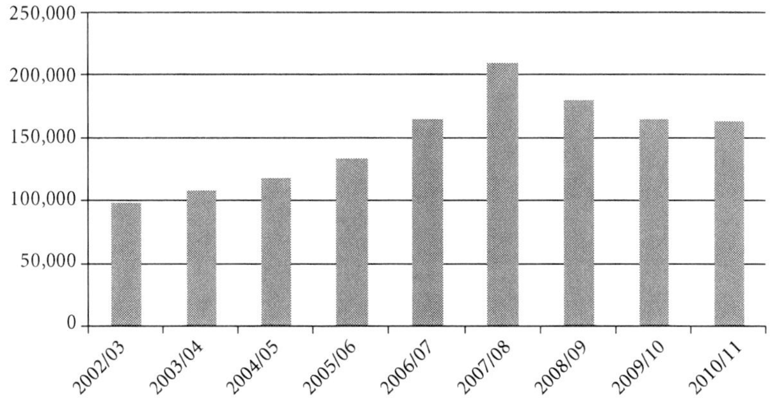

Figure 3: Average Price of New Houses in Northern Ireland 2002–03 to 2010–11

Source: DSD (2011) NI Housing Statistics 2010–11

This lack of affordability largely arose from the exorbitant increase in house prices. As Figure 3 shows, the average price of a new house more than doubled between 2002–03 and 2007–08 from £97,900 to £210,700. The drop in house prices that accompanied the 2007 economic crisis might have been expected to improve the affordability of homeownership. However, as banks were reluctant to lend, particularly for property, accessing mortgages became more difficult.[55] Indeed despite the fall in prices, the number of house sales declined from 6136 in 2006–07 to 2141 in 2008–09.[56]

Furthermore, as recession took hold many households struggled to meet their mortgage repayments. As Figure 4 shows, actions for repossession increased from 2401 to 3894 between 2007–08 and 2008–09 (by 62.2 per cent).[57]

The difficulties in accessing social housing and homeownership placed a greater onus on the PRS, which between 2001–02 and 2010–11 increased from 6.6 per cent to 14.9 per cent of occupied stock. Of particular interest to this chapter, which is focused on social housing, is the fact that the PRS increasingly accommodated low-income households that were traditionally associated with social housing.[58] The state subsidises the rent of many of these households via Housing Benefit (a social welfare payment). A total of 66,475 PRS tenants received housing

[55] Council of Mortgage Lenders, *Northern Ireland Factsheet: Housing and Mortgage Market Update* (Belfast, Council of Mortgage Lenders, 2009) 2.

[56] Department for Social Development, *Northern Ireland Housing Statistics 2008–2009* (Belfast, Department for Social Development, 2009) 69.

[57] Ibid 68.

[58] Of households with incomes of less than £5000, 21% lived in the PRS compared with 12% of all households. U McAnulty and P Gray, *Private Rented Sector in Northern Ireland: Report Three* (Belfast, Northern Ireland Executive, 2009) 9.

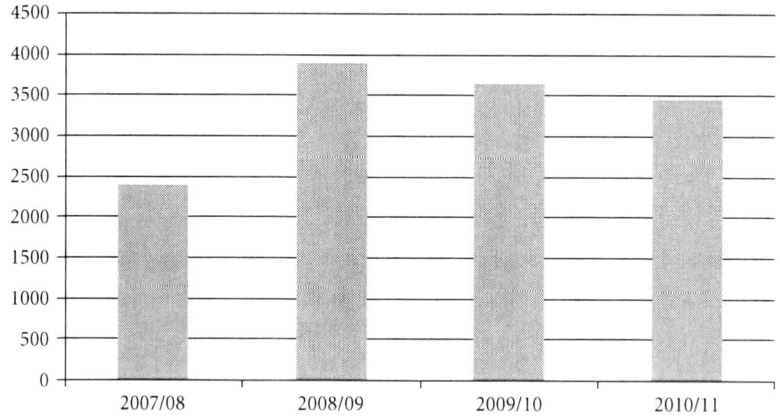

Figure 4: Actions for Mortgage Repossession 2007–08 to 2010–11

Source: DSD (2011) NI Housing Statistics 2010–11

benefit in 2010–11.[59] Although the NIHE does not record the monetary value of this expenditure it is likely to be in the region of £270.3 million.[60]

The increased use of the PRS to accommodate low-income households avoids the capital costs associated with new social build but also misses out on the social and economic benefits associated with housing development, including employment.[61] In addition, while surpluses accrued by a housing association will be reinvested in social housing, there is no guarantee that surpluses accumulated by private landlords will be reinvested to advance the right to adequate housing. Therefore payments to private rather than social landlords arguably constitute a diversion of resources away from the right to adequate housing.

The affordability of the PRS is also a concern. Tenants have reported difficulties in paying the shortfall between housing benefit and rent, which on average amounted to £28.00 per week in 2006,[62] and this has contributed to the rise in homelessness in Northern Ireland.[63] The gap between rent and housing benefit is likely to widen as the UK Government's programme for welfare reform will

[59] www.nihe.gov.uk/housing_benefit/.

[60] Ibid. PRS and housing association housing benefit totalled £361.4 million. The PRS represented 75% of claimants. Seventy-five per cent of £361.4 million is £270.3 million.

[61] '[F]or every 10 jobs created by expanding the social housing programme at least a further 7 jobs will be sustained elsewhere in the economy'. M Smyth and M Bailey, *Addressing the Economic Downturn: The Case for Increased Investment in Social Housing* (Belfast, Department for Social Development, 2009).

[62] Northern Ireland Executive, *The Private Rented Sector in Northern Ireland* (Belfast, Northern Ireland Executive, 2007) 6 and 36.

[63] Ibid 36.

reduce government support for housing costs at the same time as PRS rents are increasing (see Table 2 below).[64]

Table 2: Increase in Average Private Sector Rent (Belfast) between 2010 and 2011 (First Quarter)

Bedroom	Increase %
1 bed	10.1
2 bed	4.7
3 bed	6.9
4 bed	1.1

Source: Citylets (2011) Trends in Belfast Private Rented Sector

The above trends suggest that in a number of respects, the shift from social housing to homeownership and private renting has not resulted in progressive realisation of the right to adequate housing. The waiting lists for social housing, housing stress and homelessness have each increased substantially between 2001–02 and 2010–11. While there was some improvement in 2008–09 and 2009–10 this did not compensate for the previous decline and any progress has been largely reversed in 2010–11. The decrease in the affordability of home ownership and the PRS further indicate that the emphasis on the private sector has not progressively improved the right to adequate housing.

The next section assesses the potential links between this failure to progressively improve the right to adequate housing and the use of available resources. The analysis examines four aspects of the financing of social housing: the use of private borrowing to deliver new build; levels of investment in new social housing; the reliance of the new build budget on capital receipts gained from house and land sales; and finally the expenditure on land for housing developments.

VII. The Model for Financing New Social Housing

Housing associations finance new build from three main sources: a grant from the DSD known as Housing Association Grant (HAG); reserves (including surpluses from rent and house sales) and borrowing.[65] HAG constitutes approximately 60 per cent of the funding for new build developments. This system represents a

[64] For a list of changes to housing benefit and an analysis of the impact of welfare reform on Northern Ireland, see Institute for Fiscal Studies, 'The Impact of Tax and Benefit Reforms to be Introduced between 2010–11 and 2014–15 in Northern Ireland': www.ifs.org.uk/bns/bn114.pdf.

[65] www.nifha.org/about-us/what-is-a-housing-association/.

Public–Private Partnership (PPP), although unlike many PPPs, the private parties in this case (ie, housing associations) operate on a not-for-profit basis.[66] At face value, by supplementing HAG with borrowing, the use of housing associations appears to maximise the resources available for social housing. As a former DSD minister, Margaret Ritchie, argues:

> Housing associations, unlike the Housing Executive, can attract private finance without it scoring as public expenditure. Therefore housing associations can deliver more social housing for a given amount of public funding. Since the introduction of private finance, housing associations have raised some £340 million in private funding, which means that they have provided the equivalent of about 5,000 new homes at no cost to the Exchequer.[67]

While it is true that the borrowing of housing associations is not officially counted as public debt, the impact on the Exchequer deserves closer examination. Housing associations are financed, and therefore repay their debts, using income directly provided by government (HAG) or forgone by government in relinquishing ownership of new build (rental income and capital receipts from house sales). Therefore all else being equal, the cost to the Exchequer in the long run is the same regardless of whether the NIHE or housing associations borrow. However, all else may not be equal. With multiple housing associations negotiating loans as opposed to a single body, additional transaction costs are likely to be incurred. In addition, it is generally the case that government bodies can borrow on more favourable terms than private parties. As the director of the Chartered Institute of Housing (CIH) noted, this is aggravated by the small size of many housing associations:

> Each of the [housing] associations is actually going with limited appeal to lenders because their stock levels are quite small. If the Housing Executive with a stock base of just less than 100,000 was actually going to the market ... I think more favourable rates would be forthcoming.[68]

In the credit-friendly environment that prevailed until recently, the disparity may not have been too significant. For example, a House of Commons committee noted that prior to the economic downturn, housing associations in England were 'recognised as a good triple A investment'[69] and were 'able to secure loans at very competitive rates'.[70] However, the capacity of housing associations to borrow on

[66] It is important to note that delegating functions to third parties does not divest the state of its responsibilities under international human rights law.

[67] Northern Ireland Assembly, (AQO 238/07) Monday 2 July 2007: archive.niassembly.gov.uk/record/reports2007/070702.htm.

[68] House of Commons, Northern Ireland Affairs Committee, 'Social Housing Provision in Northern Ireland: Sixth Report of Session 2003–04' Vol 2: Oral and Written Evidence House of Commons Papers (2003–04 493-II Q) 11.

[69] House of Commons, Communities and Local Government Committee, 'Housing and the Credit Crunch: Third Report of Session 2008–09' (2009) 27.

[70] Ibid.

such favourable terms may come under threat given the widespread reluctance to lend, particularly for property, following the economic crash of 2007–08.

The move from a single to a multi-provider system may also have involved a loss of economies of scale and consequently diminished efficiency. The NIHE anticipated that housing associations would merge in order to reclaim economies of scale,[71] but to date this has not materialised. While the DSD has organised housing associations into procurement groups in an effort to realise economies of scale, the issue of mergers remains a live issue.[72]

The obligation to use the MAR refers to all resources, including those of a human, organisational or technical nature, and not just financial resources.[73] In this context the loss of the NIHE's expertise also represents a cost. The capacity of housing associations to deliver large-scale housing developments relative to the NIHE was queried in the course of an investigation by the Northern Ireland Affairs Select Committee into social housing. In his testimony to the Committee, the Policy Advisor for the CIH stated that 'one of the difficulties with [housing] associations is that only a handful really has the capacity to undertake new development'.[74] In his contribution, Professor Paddy Gray commented that 'possibly the [housing] association movement is still relatively small and does not have the expertise of delivering a new build programme that the housing executive has'.[75] For its part, the Northern Ireland Federation of Housing Associations (NIFHA) has rejected any suggestion of a lack of expertise. When the interim report of the *Review into Affordable Housing* expressed 'doubts about the capacity of housing associations to deliver an enhanced social [housing] programme'[76] the NIFHA responded in the following terms:

> We would strongly refute this suggestion, and point to both recent and past evidence which shows that the housing associations have continued to deliver a substantial development programme despite facing a variety of planning and land acquisition difficulties which have been outside of their control. The skills and capacity necessary to deliver new social housing are already in place, but have been inhibited by other factors.[77]

[71] Northern Ireland Housing Executive, *Building for Success: Northern Ireland Housing Executive Response* (Belfast, Northern Ireland Housing Executive, 1996) 39.

[72] For example, in January 2011 the Minister for Social Development stated that he had asked housing associations 'to do more on joint procurement and to consider mergers and working together on shared services'. Northern Ireland Assembly, Monday 31 January 2011: archive.niassembly.gov.uk/record/reports2010/110131.htm.

[73] Van Bueren above n 7, 61.

[74] House of Commons, Northern Ireland Affairs Committee above n 68, Q 9.

[75] Ibid Q 318.

[76] J Semple, *Review into Affordable Housing: Interim Report* (Belfast, Department for Social Development, 2006) 29.

[77] NIHE and NIFHA, *Response to the Recommendations of the Review into Affordable Housing Interim Report* (Belfast, NIHE and NIFHA, 2007) 10.

However, in 2011, the Northern Ireland Audit Office highlighted 'significant problems with the registered housing association sector'[78] and noted that 'there are currently seven housing associations which have been suspended from building further houses'[79] by DSD.

Affordability is also a concern as housing associations, facing greater financial pressures than the NIHE, are likely to charge higher levels of rent. The NIHE raised this issue when the transfer of its responsibilities to housing associations was proposed, arguing that 'the major effect of introducing private finance will be to increase rents'.[80] In comparing NIHE and housing association rents it is important to appreciate that there are differences in house size, age, location and standard. Setting aside the issue of quality, comparative average rents nevertheless provide an indication of differences in affordability. Figure 5 shows that in 2002–03 average weekly housing association rent was £10.78 more than that of the NIHE.[81] By 2010–11 this differential had grown to £28.93 per week.

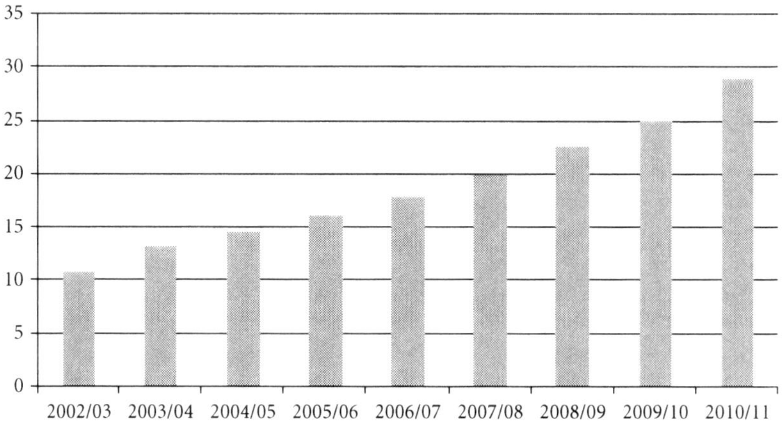

Figure 5: Difference in Average Weekly Rent Levels (£) 2002–03 to 2010–11[82]

Source: DSD (2011) NIHE Housing Statistics 2010–11

[78] NIAO, *Financial Auditing and Reporting: General Report by the Comptroller and Auditor General for Northern Ireland—2011* (Belfast, NIAO, 2011) 42–43.

[79] Ibid 43.

[80] *Building for Success* above n 71, 39.

[81] Department for Social Development, *Northern Ireland Housing Statistics 2003–2004* (Belfast, Department for Social Development, 2004).

[82] Rent levels are inclusive of rates and service charges.

VIII. Levels of Investment

Given the rising need for social housing (Figures 1 and 2), a corresponding increase in investment in new build would be expected in order to progressively realise the right to adequate housing, or at least to prevent regression.

Figure 6 shows real[83] expenditure on new social build between 2002–03 and 2011–12, together with projected spend for 2012–13 to 2014–15. In the graph:

— 'public' refers to HAG and the co-ownership scheme;[84]
— 'private' represents funding levered in by housing association borrowing and reserves;
— 'total' is the sum of public and private investment.

The graph shows that in general, total investment in new build increased from 2002–03 to 2010–11, although expenditure did not increase in every year (it dipped in 2006–07 and 2008–09). While this increase in resources was not sufficient to prevent retrogression in the waiting list for social housing, it at least indicates that increasing resources were, by and large, being allocated to the task.

The graph also shows that total investment dropped from £271 million in 2010–11 to £208 million in 2011–12 (a fall of 23.2 per cent); the budget for the next three years falls further below the 2010–11 level of spend, to £175 million, £165 million and £178 million respectively. This is primarily due to a fall in public spending, the result of budget cuts imposed by the UK coalition Government that are ostensibly aimed at reducing the UK deficit. Setting aside the debate on the economic validity of this strategy,[85] reducing the new build budget as need continues to rise could constitute a retrogressive measure in human rights terms. States are obliged to guard against a general decline in housing and living standards during times of economic contraction.[86] The Rapporteur on the Right to Adequate Housing has specifically commented that funding for social housing may need to increase at times of economic crisis in order to protect the most vulnerable.[87]

[83] Using Treasury GDP deflators.

[84] The co-ownership scheme helps people to access home ownership but the NIHE was unable to provide figures for HAG alone.

[85] This largely replicates the long-running debate between 'Hayekian' monetary policy and 'Keynesian' demand management.

[86] ComESCR General Comment No 4, para 11.

[87] Rolnik above n 2, para 83.

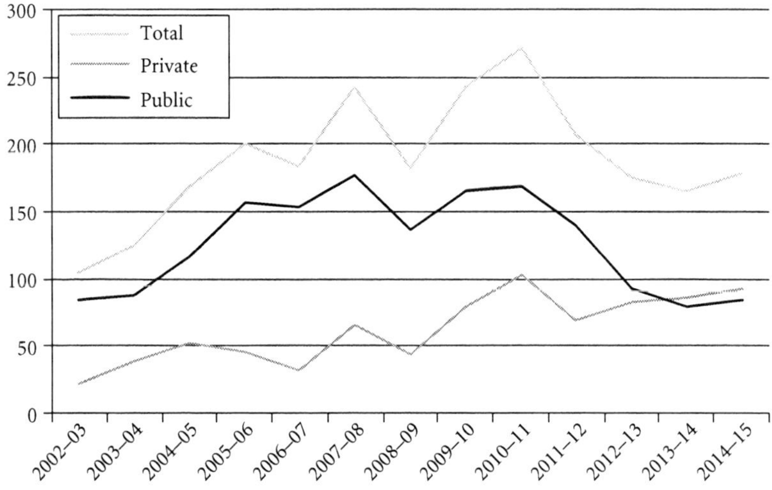

Figure 6: New Build Expenditure (£m) 2002–03 to 2014–15 (2011–12 values)

Source: DSD

If resources are not rising in line with need, the right to adequate housing may still be progressively realised if those resources are used to deliver a higher level of outputs, ie, housing units. However, the level of new builds completed has been erratic (Figure 7) and, as the NIHE acknowledges, 'has failed to keep pace with the steadily rising need for social housing'.[88]

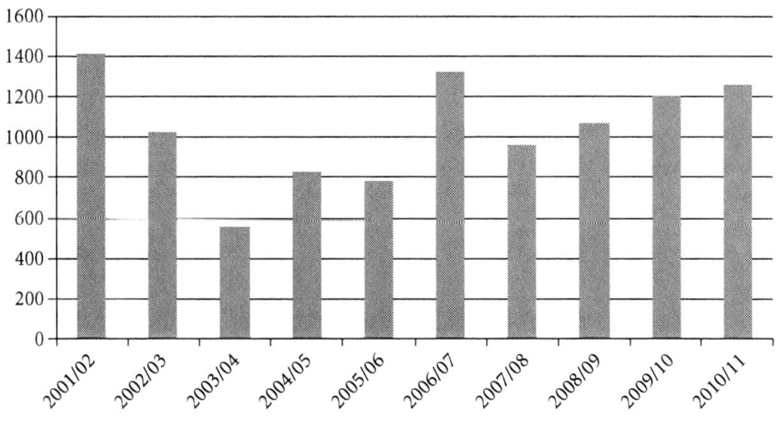

Figure 7: New Social Build Completions 2001–02 to 2010–11

Source: DSD NI Housing Statistics 2005–06 and 2010–11

[88] Northern Ireland Housing Executive, *Northern Ireland Housing Market: Review and Perspectives 2009–2012* (Belfast, Northern Ireland Housing Executive, 2009) 18.

Looking ahead, the University of Ulster Net Stock Model projects that at least 2500 new social housing units are required each year in order to prevent the waiting list from growing.[89] However, only 4600 new social homes are planned between 2012 to 2014–15 (an average of 1533 annually).[90] This is unlikely to ensure progressive realisation.

IX. Expenditure on Land

One difficulty in translating investment into housing units is the cost of land, which increased substantially in the years preceding the economic crash. Between 2000 and 2006 the market value for 'small sites' increased by 370 per cent while 'bulk land' prices increased by 310 per cent.[91] This significantly affected the new build programme because the NIHE purchases land at market value. Having typically constituted 25–30 per cent of the new build budget, land increased to approximately 50 per cent of the cost of development by 2007. As noted in the *Review into Affordable Housing*, the 'very rapid rise in land costs [was] fuelled by land banking and speculation'.[92]

The Committee states that policies and legislation should 'not be designed to benefit already advantaged social groups at the expense of others'.[93] Paying excessive prices for land and allowing land banking and speculation arguably unduly benefits an already privileged group of landowners and speculators at the expense of taxpayers and those in need of social housing. Consequently, it raises an equality issue, as those who are most in need should receive the greatest levels of protection, especially during times of economic retraction. This situation is also unlikely to be consistent with the duty of MAR since those resources that are available could be used to more effectively advance the right to adequate housing.

There are many ways of maintaining land prices at a level that is fair to all parties. The NIHE and NIFHA have proposed a range of options, including greater use of the former's vesting powers.[94] The *Review into Affordable Housing* included a recommendation that DSD 'monitor the effectiveness of the Northern Ireland Housing Executive's existing vesting powers and consider strengthening them, if necessary'.[95] It also called on the Planning Service to 'take advantage of any opportunities that arise to dezone housing land which is being held for

[89] Northern Ireland Housing Executive, *Northern Ireland Housing Market: Review and Perspectives 2011–2014* (Belfast, Northern Ireland Housing Executive, 2012) 16.

[90] Northern Ireland Executive, Programme for Government 2011–15 (Belfast, Northern Ireland Executive, 2012) 38.

[91] Semple, *Review into Affordable Housing: Interim Report* above n 76, Annex 2.

[92] Ibid 10.

[93] ComESCR General Comment No 4, para 9.

[94] NIHE and NIFHA, *Response to the Recommendations* above n 77, 5.

[95] Semple, *Review into Affordable Housing: Final Report* above n 54, 4.

speculative reasons'.[96] Another measure—a tax on derelict land—was considered in the course of a DFP review of the domestic rating system. The consultation document produced as part of the review explained the purpose of the tax in the following terms:

> The rationale behind this proposal was that it would act as a disincentive to excess land banking, whereby developers and others hold on to land with the aim of making capital gains. The intention was that this would free up further sites for development, assist with the issue of housing affordability, as well as bringing broader economic development and regeneration benefits. Initial research by the University of Ulster also suggested that the tax could generate several million pounds of additional revenue per year.[97]

However, in October 2008 the DFP Minister, Nigel Dodds, announced that the tax would not be introduced on the following basis:

> [T]he market conditions which led to the development of this proposal have reversed since the time of the rating review in 2007. The supply of land has increased and prices have dropped dramatically, with increasing pressures on the development sector and in particular the viability of house building ... It would not be right to proceed further with this proposal during the life of this current Assembly, a move which I hope will be welcomed by the development sector, which has enough to contend with at the moment, without the prospect of a new tax on land holdings.[98]

While the market conditions have certainly changed since the tax was proposed, the need for affordable land to support social housing remains and has arguably increased. In the absence of alternative measures, rejecting a policy aimed at bringing derelict land into productive use does not appear to ensure that the MAR are employed to progressively improve the right to adequate housing. Rather than giving priority to disadvantaged groups, the above rationale suggests that the interests of landowners—who benefited considerably from the bubble in land and property values during the 'boom' years at some expense to taxpayers and those in need of social housing—are also to take precedence in the midst of a property crash.

X. Use of Capital Receipts

The economic crisis has further reduced the resources available for new social housing as the new build budget is partly dependent on receipts from land and house sales. The values of these assets collapsed following the recession. Therefore, under the current financing system, fewer resources are available for new social

[96] Ibid.

[97] Department of Finance and Personnel, *Review of Domestic Rating: A Consultation Report* (Belfast, Department of Finance and Personnel, 2009) 50.

[98] Northern Ireland Executive, *Dodds Announces Decision Not to Introduce Derelict Land Tax*, 23 October 2008: www.northernireland.gov.uk/news-dfp-231008-derelict-land-tax.

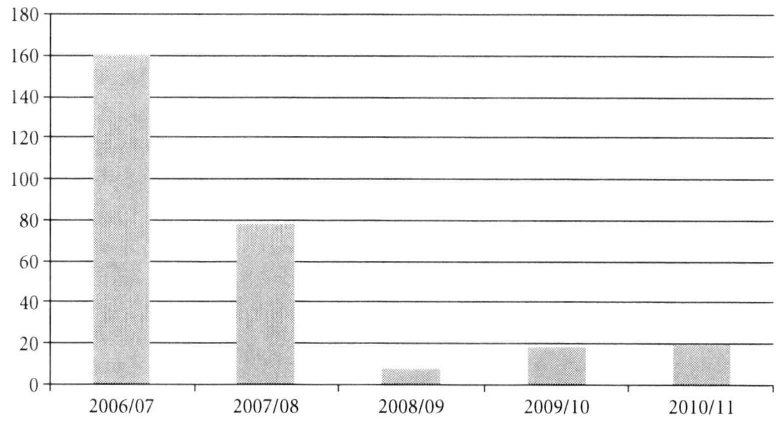

Figure 8: NIHE Receipts from House and Land Sales (£m) 2006–07 to 2010–11 (nominal)

Source: DSD (2011) NI Housing Statistics 2010–11

housing. The DSD estimated that the decline in capital receipts from land and house sales (Figure 8) created a shortfall of £85 million in the social housing programme for 2009–10. According to former DSD minister Ritchie, this was reduced to £35 million 'through in-year monitoring rounds and diversions of DSD resources from other budget lines'.[99] However, the minister added that a shortfall of £100 million was anticipated for each of the next two financial years, which 'is equivalent to the loss of 1,000 new build houses per annum'.[100] Decoupling the social housing budget from capital receipts would help to prevent retrogression, particularly during this economically difficult time in which the need for social housing is likely to increase for more vulnerable sections of society.

While it appears that the new build programme is expected to bear the cost of any shortfall in projected receipts from house and land sales, surpluses from house and land sales are not reinvested in new stock. Indeed, the budget for new social build was cut at the same time as a substantial surplus from social house sales was generated, and amid rising need. When the Minister of State in the Northern Ireland Office, John Spellar, informed the Committee that the DSD had reduced its new build target to 1300 as the Department 'only have funding for 1,300' the NI Affairs Select Committee concluded that it was

> wrong that the target has been arbitrarily reduced from 1,750 to 1,300 houses in the current year because funding has only been made available for the smaller number. This is particularly unfortunate when, despite strong evidence of escalating housing stress

[99] NI Assembly, Monday 2 February 2009: www.niassembly.gov.uk/record/reports2008/090202.pdf 164.

[100] Ibid.

> and homelessness, around £37 million annually from record levels of sales of existing Housing Executive stock is returned to the Treasury, when that could be used for the benefit of the homeless.[101]

Diverting existing resources away from the realisation of ESR, in this case, the right to adequate housing is contrary to the duty of MAR, which requires that all the resources that are available for the realisation of ESR are actually used towards that purpose. This situation arguably also raises an equality issue, as those dependent on social housing are likely to be particularly vulnerable. As social housing plays a key role in protecting the rights of vulnerable social groups it should be given priority in the allocation of resources, especially in light of the increasing need.

XI. Conclusion

This chapter has applied obligations generated by ICESCR—in particular the duty to progressively realise the right to adequate housing using the MAR—to the financing of social housing in Northern Ireland. Over the last three decades social housing has assumed an increasingly marginalised role in favour of homeownership and, to a lesser extent, private renting. Local social housing providers demonstrated considerable ingenuity in compensating for declining public expenditure and borrowing restrictions. Housing associations were used to circumvent central government borrowing constraints and to raise additional funding. However, this was essentially an exercise in creative accounting as the finance borrowed by housing associations is repaid with revenue forgone by government (ie, rent and capital receipts) or provided by government (HAG). Indeed, it came with possible drawbacks such as a loss of economies of scale in moving from a single to a multi-provider system, and a loss of the NIHE's expertise in delivering large-scale housing developments. Greater use of the PRS for low-income households also represents an inventive means of making up for the shortfall in social housing funding. However, it is questionable whether the PRS can adequately provide low-income households with an affordable alternative to social housing, particularly as government support for housing costs is set to decline amid rising rents. Despite the innovations, growing waiting lists for social housing and declining affordability of both homeownership and private renting suggest that the Government's approach has failed to progressively realise the right to adequate housing.

Although it has some specific features, the case study has wider resonance given the global impact of the 2007 financial crash. The Special Rapporteur concluded her 2009 annual report to the UN Human Rights Council by saying that the global economic crisis may result in a reduction in income for some sectors of the

[101] House of Commons, Northern Ireland Affairs Committee, 'Social Housing Provision in Northern Ireland' above n 68, 17.

population, thus making affordable housing even more necessary.[102] On this basis she called for increased investment in social housing in order to protect the rights of the most vulnerable.[103] The case for increased investment in social housing in Northern Ireland is certainly compelling. At a time of considerable economic insecurity and hardship it would provide a safety net for vulnerable households, ease demand in the private housing sector and help rebalance the Northern Ireland housing system as a whole. New house building would also provide a much needed economic stimulus. However, the UK Government's plan to cut public expenditure has increased the financial constraints faced by the Northern Ireland Executive and has further undermined the new build programme.

The case study also strikes a chord with other parts of the world given the global dominance of neoliberal ideas on housing policy. The Special Rapporteur on the Right to Adequate Housing notes that in many countries, home ownership has been prioritised[104] and that a 'reduction in public housing has resulted in long waiting lists'.[105] This, and the disastrous impact of the global economic crash, itself facilitated by the neoliberal policy of deregulating financial markets, calls for a fundamental reassessment of housing policy and the ideology that has underpinned it. As the Special Rapporteur on the Right to Adequate Housing comments, the current crisis represents an opportunity for reflection on how to improve housing systems, policies and programmes so as to ensure adequate housing for all.[106] ICESCR provides a useful framework with which to appraise the options.

[102] Rolnik above n 2, para 82.
[103] Ibid para 83.
[104] Ibid para 35.
[105] Ibid para 34.
[106] Ibid para 75.

10

Assessing the Impact of the Public Spending Cuts: Taking Human Rights and Equality Seriously

JAMES HARRISON AND MARY-ANN STEPHENSON

I. Introduction

This chapter will argue that the legal standards contained in equality and human rights legislation can be the basis for important examination of the impact of public spending decisions, particularly in the context of widespread public spending cuts. However, our scrutiny of current practice in the United Kingdom identifies the need for the development of more robust methodological frameworks of analysis and the engagement of a broader range of actors in future assessments.

The chapter begins by arguing that cuts to public spending are likely to disproportionately affect the most vulnerable and disadvantaged. The impact of these cuts are often complex and interrelated. It is therefore important to work out very carefully what the impact of multiple cuts by a range of different agencies are likely to be on the most vulnerable and disadvantaged in our communities.

We examine one policy instrument—equality and human rights impact assessments (EHRIAs)—and draw on UK and international experience to suggest that these can provide a potentially important and valuable process through which relevant actors can identify and then tackle the negative impacts of budget cuts.

The chapter explores the example of a recent equality and human rights impact assessment of the impact of the cuts on women in Coventry, which was carried out by the authors of this chapter.[1] It is argued that this EHRIA highlights a range of potential impacts on the most vulnerable and disadvantaged women in the city and provides a blueprint for how EHRIAs should be conducted in the future.

The chapter presents evidence that many existing equality (and more rarely human rights) impact assessments, which are undertaken by central and local

[1] MA Stephenson and J Harrison, *Unravelling Equality? A Human Rights and Equality Impact Assessment of the Public Spending Cuts on Women in Coventry* (Warwick, University of Warwick, 2011): www2.warwick.ac.uk.

government in the UK in order to comply with their legal obligations, are superficial processes. At their worst, they can be no more than bureaucratic tick-box exercises, which validate decisions that have already been made.

However, the legal standards contained in equality and human rights legislation should be the basis for important analysis of the impact of public spending decisions on the poorest and most disadvantaged in our communities. Therefore EHRIAs should not be rejected as policymaking tools; rather efforts should be made to enhance existing practice. This contribution therefore makes a number of suggestions for how future practice can be improved. To achieve a meaningful EHRIA process which can potentially give rise to profound re-evaluations of budget-cutting priorities, EHRIAs must be based on a genuinely participatory consultation process, significant gathering of evidence and robust analysis of the combined impact of cuts on particularly vulnerable groups. EHRIAs would also benefit greatly from explicit consideration of economic, social and cultural rights.

The primary obligation to assess the impact of the public spending cuts falls on public authorities. However, this chapter concludes by arguing that academics can also play an important role in advancing the use of equality and human rights frameworks to address the public spending cuts. This is particularly important when it comes to economic, social and cultural rights. Academic endeavour can have most influence where it is closely linked to the actual impact of the cuts on the lives of individuals and communities.

II. Budget Cuts and the Disadvantaged

There are strong grounds for thinking that cuts in public spending will generally affect the poorest and most disadvantaged people hardest, unless concerted and focused action is taken to prevent this. This is because poorer people, as well as many other disadvantaged groups, are likely to receive a higher proportion of their income from welfare benefits and are more likely to rely on public services. This can be seen in an analysis of the UK's current public spending cuts.

Research from the Institute of Fiscal Studies has demonstrated how cuts to benefits and changes to tax announced in the UK's 2010 emergency budget will hit the poorest and disadvantaged hardest.[2] The Fawcett Society and Women's Budget Group have shown how poor women in particular will be badly hit by cuts to public services and welfare benefits.[3] Disability Alliance has shown how

[2] J Browne and P Levell, *The Distributional Effect of Tax and Benefit Reforms to be Introduced Between June 2010 and April 2014: A Revised Assessment* (London, Institute of Fiscal Studies, 2010): www.ifs.org.

[3] UK Women's Budget Group, The Impact on Women of the Budget 2011 (April 2011): www.wbg.org.uk.

spending cuts announced by the Coalition Government are likely to significantly increase the number of disabled people living in poverty.[4]

Local authorities across England alone are facing collective reduction in income of over £4.7 billion in 2011.[5] Further budget cuts will mean that available funds will continue to be reduced in relation to the years to come. At the same time, ring-fencing is being lifted from many budget streams meaning that local authorities have a great deal more freedom in what they decide to fund. In a number of areas across the UK this has led to severe cuts for particularly vulnerable and disadvantaged groups. For example, 60 per cent of all UK refuge services have no funding agreed after March 2011,[6] and Birmingham City Council has recently lost a case in court for cutting care services for severely disabled people.[7]

Overall, the current budget-cutting processes in the UK involve cuts to jobs, services and benefits by a wide range of different public authorities. As a result, individuals in a particular area may be hit by cuts from national government, local government and a range of other agencies, as well as cuts to voluntary services. For example, disabled people will be affected by cuts to the payments they receive to assist them to carry out their everyday activities such as washing and buying food;[8] they will also be disproportionately affected by cuts to housing benefit where 19 per cent of those affected will be disabled.[9] Disabled people will also be affected by cuts to adult social care services, cuts to voluntary support and advocacy services and the move from Incapacity Benefit to Employment Support Allowance.[10] Disabled people are also disproportionately likely to require civil legal aid, which is being cut in England and Wales at a time when the number needing legal advice to deal with benefit problems in particular is likely to go up.[11]

Where budgets are being cut by different agencies with multiple impacts on vulnerable and disadvantaged individuals, there is a particular need to work out very carefully what the impact of cuts on the most vulnerable and disadvantaged in our communities will be. Equality and human rights impact assessment is one important tool through which impacts on the vulnerable and disadvantaged can potentially be measured and action taken as a result.

[4] Disability Alliance, 'Emergency Budget Summary' (30 November 2010): www.disabilityalliance.org.

[5] Audit Commission, 'Tough Times: Councils' Response to a Challenging Financial Climate' (November 2011) 4: www.audit-commission.gov.uk.

[6] Women's Aid, 'Women's Aid's Survey Reveals Fear that Over Half of Refuge and Outreach Services Could Face Closure' (March 2011): www.womensaid.org.uk.

[7] *R (on the application of W) v Birmingham City Council* [2011] EWHC 1147 (Admin).

[8] Disability Living Allowance is being replaced by Personal Independence Payment. The total budget available for such payments will be cut by 20%. See Disability Alliance above n 4 for more details on the changes and their impact.

[9] Department for Work and Pensions, 'Equality Impact Assessment for Changes to the Local Housing Allowance Arrangements and Housing Benefit Size Criteria for People with Non-Resident Overnight Carers' (2010) 12: www.dwp.gov.uk.

[10] See Stephenson and Harrison, 'Unravelling Equality?' above n 1, 40–41.

[11] Of those requiring legal aid in welfare benefits cases, 63% are sick and disabled: Ministry of Justice, 'Legal Aid Reform: Scope Changes, Equalities Impact Assessment' (November 2010) 63: www.justice.gov.uk.

III. Equality and Human Rights Impact Assessments

Internationally, 'human rights impact assessment' (HRIA) is a recognised term that is used to indicate a process of measuring actual or potential human rights impacts of a policy, project or other form of intervention.[12] Impact assessments can assess activities that have happened in the past (ex post) as well as planned future activities (ex ante). A common thread in defining all HRIAs by those undertaking them is the evidence-based nature of the exercise.[13] The aim of an HRIA is to 'build attention to human rights into the project [or policy] cycle'.[14] Just as policymakers consider environmental, social or economic impacts by conducting impact assessments to explore these issues, HRIAs aim to make policymakers consider the impact of their policies and practices on the protection and promotion of human rights.

HRIAs are increasingly demanded by international human rights actors including UN treaty monitoring bodies, particularly the Committee on Economic, Social and Cultural Rights (the Committee), the Committee on the Rights of the Child and the Committee on the Elimination of Discrimination Against Women.[15] Other UN human rights actors—including the UN Special Representative on Business and Human Rights, the UN Special Rapporteur on the Right to Health and the UN Special Rapporteur on the Right to Food—as well as European human rights bodies like the European Court of Human Rights and European Committee of Social Rights have also called for HRIAs to be undertaken.[16]

Partly as a result of such calls to action, human rights impact assessments have been used by a range of different organisations to measure the impact of human rights on a wide range of different policies and practices. The majority of methodologies, toolkits and individual HRIAs have been undertaken by civil society organisations. HRIAs have created a language and framework for such

[12] See the Human Rights Impact Resource Centre: www.humanrightsimpact.org/hria-guide/overview.

[13] S Bakker, M Van Den Berg, D Duzenli and M Raadstake, *Human Rights Impact Assessment in Practice: The Case of the Health Rights of Women Assessment Instrument (HeRWAI)* (2009) 1 *Journal of Human Rights Practice* 436, 442.

[14] T Landman, *Studying Human Rights* (Abingdon, Routledge, 2006) 128.

[15] G De Beco, 'Human Rights Impact Assessments' (2009) 27 *Netherlands Quarterly of Human Rights* 139, 143; J Harrison and A Goller, 'Trade and Human Rights: What Does 'Impact Assessment' Have to Offer?' (2008) 8 *Human Rights Law Review* 587, 589.

[16] See eg, P Hunt, 'Report of the Special Rapporteur on the right of everyone to the highest attainable standard of physical and mental health—Mission to Peru' (UN Doc E/CN.4/2005/51/Add. 3), para 50; O De Schutter, 'Report of the Special Rapporteur on the Right to Food on Building Resilience: A Human Rights Framework for World Food and Nutrition Security' (UN Doc A/HRC/9/23); J Ruggie, 'Report of the Special Representative of the Secretary-General on the Issue of Human Rights and Transnational Corporations: Mapping International Standards of Responsibility and Accountability for Corporate Acts' (UN Doc A/HRC/4/035), para 77. In relation to European actors, see De Beco, ibid 143.

organisations to campaign and lobby on issues where they have a long-standing interest and expertise. This practice is briefly summarised below but has been catalogued comprehensively in other work by the authors of this chapter.[17]

There is considerable experience of undertaking HRIAs in relation to the rights of specific groups—in particular women and children. In terms of child rights impact assessments, the United Nations Children's Fund (UNICEF) has catalogued methodologies developed by state and non-state actors including Finland, Ireland, New Zealand, Scotland and Sweden.[18] Leading examples of impact assessments include a study by UNICEF, in collaboration with various non-governmental organisations (NGOs) on the impact of price rises in electricity on the rights of children in Bosnia-Herzegovina, a review of legislation to protect vulnerable groups in Scotland, assessments of high density housing on children in Auckland and the impact of waste management in Makau, New Zealand.[19]

The NGO, Aim for Human Rights are the pioneers in the field of women's rights. They have developed the Health Rights of Women Assessment Instrument (HeRWAI) which has been heavily utilised by a number of NGOs globally to undertake assessments.[20] Aim for Human Rights has also developed two further tools in relation to anti-trafficking laws and policies and domestic violence.[21] These models are both being piloted, and a recent HRIA was completed by a UK based NGO on UK anti-trafficking policy.[22]

Use of HRIAs is also prominent in the international economic sphere. A wide range of methodologies has been developed for conducting human rights impact assessments of multinational corporations (MNCs).[23] A number of HRIAs of MNCs have

[17] See J Harrison and MA Stephenson, *Human Rights Impact Assessment: Review of Practice and Guidance for Future Assessments* (Scottish Human Rights Commission, 2011) 1–98: www.scottish-humanrights.com; J Harrison 'Human Rights Measurement: Reflections on the Current Practice and Future Potential of Human Rights Impact Assessment' (2011) 3 *Journal of Human Rights Practice* 162.

[18] UNICEF, 'Draft Child Rights Toolkit', on file with author.

[19] UNICEF, *Child Rights Impact Assessment of Potential Electricity Price Rises in Bosnia and Herzegovina* (Florence, UNICEF Innocenti Research Centre, 2007): www.unicef.org; Scottish Commissioner for Children and Young People, 'Vetting and Barring Arrangements in the Protection of Vulnerable Groups Bill: A Full Impact Assessment' (Edinburgh, SCCYP, 2006): sccyp.net; Office of the Children's Commissioner New Zealand, *Undertaking Child Impact Assessments in Aotearoa New Zealand Local Authorities: Evidence, Practice, Ideas* (Auckland, AUT University 2009): www.unicef.org.nz.

[20] For an overview of this work see the Health Rights of Women Assessment Instrument (HeRWAI) Resource Centre: www.humanrightsimpact.org.

[21] Aim for Human Rights, *The RighT Guide: A Tool to Assess the Human Rights Impact of Anti-Trafficking Laws and Policies* (2010): www.humanrightsimpact.org.

[22] X: Talk Project, 'Human Rights, Sex Work and the Challenge of Trafficking: Human Rights Impact Assessment of Anti-Trafficking Policy in the UK' (2010): www.xtalkproject.net.

[23] Cataloguing this experience see, J Harrison, 'Measuring Human Rights: Reflections on the Practice of Human Rights Impact Assessment and Lessons for the Future' (2010) Warwick School of Law Research Paper No 2010/26, 10: papers.ssrn.com. Rights and Democracy have also developed a model which has been utilised by NGOs to undertake assessments in the Philippines, Tibet, the Democratic Republic of Congo, Argentina and Peru. See Rights and Democracy, *Human Rights Impact Assessments for Foreign Investment Projects: Learning from Community Experiences in the Philippines, Tibet, the Democratic Republic of Congo, Argentina, and Peru* (Rights and Democracy, 2007): www.dd-rd.ca.

now been published, including HRIAs of BP's Tangguh LNG Project, Goldcorp's Marlin mine in Guatemala, Paladin Energy's Kayelekera Uranium Project in Malawi, Green Resources Tree Plantations in Tanzania and Aimec Minerals gold and silver mine in Indonesia.[24] HRIAs have also been used to assess the human rights impacts of international trade agreements. These include an HRIA of the Thailand–US Free Trade Agreement, an HRIA of the impact of the intellectual property provisions of the Central American Free Trade Agreement and a number of HRIAs which consider the impact of trade liberalisation of particular agricultural products on the right to food in Ghana, Honduras, Indonesia, Uganda and Zambia.[25] A number of further HRIAs of trade agreements are currently in progress.

There are a number of other HRIAs that have been conducted in other areas beyond those mentioned above.[26] One model which is particularly worthy of mention is that of the EU Commission. It has adopted a model of integrated impact assessment (IIA) to assess its policymaking and formulation of legislative proposals. The integrated model includes extensive mention of the need to assess the impact of policies on EU fundamental rights.[27]

It is interesting to note, in the context of the current volume, that existing HRIAs have tended to 'reflect the interdependence and inter-relatedness of human rights' and have often included analysis of economic, social and cultural rights impacts alongside civil and political rights impacts.[28] Methodologies simply focus on those rights that are of most concern.[29]

The quality of existing practice is variable, but there is considerable good practice and this allows for the identification of solid principles on which to base future HRIAs.[30] These principles were utilised by the authors in the development of their methodology for an equality and human rights impact assessment of the public spending cuts on women in Coventry and so will be elaborated upon below in that context.

In the United Kingdom, equality and human rights impact assessments (EHRIAs) have become prevalent largely because of obligations on public authorities rather than initiatives by civil society organisations.[31] Equality impact assessments were developed as a tool for public authorities to ensure compliance with their duties

[24] For references to all these studies see Harrison, 'Measuring Human Rights' above n 23, 10.

[25] Thailand National Human Rights Commission, *Report on Results of Examination of Human Rights Violations* (2006) on file with author. For access to all the agriculture studies see FIAN, 'Agricultural Trade and the Right to Food': www.fian.org/programs-and-campaigns/projects/agricultural-trade-and-the-right-to-food.

[26] For a complete review, see Harrison, 'Measuring Human Rights' above n 23.

[27] European Commission, 'Impact Assessment Guidelines' 15 January 2009 (SEC 2009) 92: ec.europa.eu.

[28] S Walker, 'Human Rights Impact Assessments: Emerging Practice and Challenges', paper presented at the Expert Meeting on Contemporary Issues in the Realisation of Economic, Social and Cultural Rights (Geneva, 10–11 February 2011).

[29] Ibid.

[30] For an elaboration on principles for undertaking future assessments see Harrison, 'Human Rights Measurement' above n 17.

[31] Harrison and Stephenson, 'Human Rights Impact Assessment' above n 17, 36.

to prevent discrimination and promote equality under equalities legislation.[32] In Great Britain, these duties have recently been amalgamated together through the Equality Act 2010.

The Equality Act, which covers England, Scotland and Wales, contains a general duty to have 'due regard' to the need to eliminate unlawful discrimination, harassment and victimisation and other conduct prohibited by the Act, to advance equality of opportunity between people who share a protected characteristic and those who do not and to foster good relations between people who share a protected characteristic and those who do not.[33] With a few minor exceptions, the Equality Act does not apply in Northern Ireland. However, section 75 of the 1998 Northern Ireland Act requires public bodies to have 'due regard' to the need to promote equality and good relations. This obligation has also given rise to significant practice of undertaking equality impact assessments.

Equality impact substantial should be seen as a form of HRIA, in that they measure discrimination through the lens of a range of equality issues, in particular race, gender, disability, age, religion or belief and sexual orientation. Alongside this, a number of public authorities have developed models for undertaking joint EHRIAs which aim to ensure that public authorities are not breaching their duties under the UK's Human Rights Act.[34]

There is now substantial practice in the UK of utilising equality impact assessments (and more rarely HRIAs) in order to measure the impact of various budget-cutting measures. Such impact assessments have the potential to identify and tackle the types of impacts on vulnerable and disadvantaged persons identified in section II above. We discuss this practice in section IV below. First, we present the experience of the current authors in undertaking their own equality and human rights impact assessment of public spending cuts.

IV. An EHRIA of the Public Spending Cuts on Women in Coventry

The EHRIA undertaken by the authors of this chapter analysed the public spending cuts that are currently underway and their potential human rights and equality impacts on women in Coventry. The EHRIA was a joint project of the Centre for Human Rights in Practice at the University of Warwick and Coventry Women's Voices (CWV), a Coventry based women's voluntary organisation. The Centre for Human Rights in Practice (CHRP) has developed significant

[32] Equality and Human Rights Commission, *Equality Impact Assessment Guidance: A Step-by-Step Guide to Integrating Equality Impact Assessment into Policymaking and Review* (EHRC, November 2009).

[33] Equality Act 2010, s 149.

[34] Harrison, and Stephenson, 'Human Rights Impact Assessment' above n 17, 25f.

international expertise over a number of years in designing methodologies for undertaking EHRIAs.[35] CHRP wanted to utilise this expertise in order to work with a local group to undertake a model EHRIA process and to create a blueprint methodology that could be more widely utilised by groups and individuals interested in analysing particular human rights and equality dimensions of the public spending cuts.[36]

The EHRIA process adopted by CHRP and CWV included eight core elements identified as vital to any EHRIA process. The authors of this chapter have provided detailed analysis of these elements elsewhere and of what is required to ensure that they are carried out robustly.[37] In this section, we limit ourselves to describing each of these elements and highlighting what each involves. This will then inform the overarching discussion in the final section of this chapter of how practice can be enhanced in the future.

The first element of the process was 'screening'. Here we decided the particular aspects of the cuts on which we would focus in the study; the range of local and national cuts being implemented by many different authorities meant it would have been impossible to cover everything. The screening stage is important to allow focused attention on the most important issues for the affected groups. Based on extensive consultation with the groups and individuals who make up CWV, we decided to focus on eight priority areas. These were: employment; housing; tax and benefit changes; education; violence against women; health, social care and other support services; legal advice; and women's voluntary organisations.

Second, we undertook 'scoping'. 'Scoping' is deciding the information that needs to be gathered and the questions that need to be asked once the decision to undertake an EHRIA has been made. Scoping essentially provides a road map for the rest of the assessment, setting out what is being assessed and how it is to be assessed. For each of the eight areas of our study, we asked a series of key questions to inform our assessment before taking any further action. These included, who did we need to consult with in Coventry? What other evidence did we require in order to inform our analysis of the issue? What were the human rights and equality issues that potentially arose from public spending cuts in each of these areas?

Our whole study was therefore framed by an equality and human rights perspective. It was not simply a case of addressing the legal obligations of equality and human rights legislation at the end of our analysis. The equality perspective meant that we were specifically focusing on ways in which the public sector spending cuts might disproportionately affect women (as well as particular

[35] For more details of this work see the website of the Centre for Human Rights in Practice at: www2.warwick.ac.uk/fac/soc/law/chrp.

[36] One such study has already been produced. See Bristol Fawcett Society, *Cutting Women Out in Bristol: A Report of the Human Rights and Equality Impact Assessment of the Public Spending Cuts on Women in Bristol* (Bristol Fawcett, October 2011): www.bristolfawcett.org.uk. Several other studies are currently being undertaken.

[37] Harrison, 'Human Rights Measurement' above n 17, 172f; Harrison and Stephenson, 'Human Rights Impact Assessment' above n 17, 40f.

groups of women—disabled women, black, Asian and minority ethnic (BAME) women etc). The human rights perspective meant that we were specifically focusing on ways in which the public sector spending cuts might have the most severe impacts on women.

The third element was consultation. We conducted semi-structured interviews with organisations and individuals in Coventry as well as relevant national organisations.[38] These were undertaken in order to better understand the impacts of the public spending cuts at the Coventry level. This consultation also ensured that the voices of those likely to be affected by the policy were heard and taken into account in the EHRIA process.

At the same time as the consultation we also gathered evidence about the impact of the cuts (element four). We collected information from a variety of different sources to inform analysis of the policy. The consultations we conducted with local groups provided vital information. This was supplemented by national level analysis of the gender impact of the public spending cuts or the impact of the cuts on particular groups (for example, by the Institute for Fiscal Studies, Fawcett Society, National Family and Parenting Institute, Women's Budget Group, Shelter, Citizen's Advice, Disability Alliance, Carers UK etc). We also collected Coventry-specific data on the numbers of women or particular groups of women (for example, carers) who would be impacted by the cuts from relevant government departments, the Office for National Statistics, Coventry City Council and so on.[39]

We then analysed the policy area in question utilising principles and standards from relevant human rights and equality legislation (element 5). We focused primarily on the human rights provisions contained in the European Convention on Human Rights that are protected in the UK by the Human Rights Act 1998, and the equality duties set out in the Equality Act 2010. The rationale for this was that these were the obligations that have most 'bite' with respect to the public authorities whose policies we were scrutinising. The assessment also included consideration of the UK's other international human rights obligations where they were particularly relevant. This included the International Covenant on Economic, Social and Cultural Rights (ICESCR), as will be discussed further below in section V.

[38] Organisations consulted included: Age Concern Coventry; Council of Disabled People (Coventry and Warwickshire); Coventry and Warwickshire Primary Care Trust; Coventry Carers; Coventry Citizen's Advice Bureau; Coventry City Council; Coventry Cyrenians; Coventry Ethnic Minority Action Partnership; Coventry Haven; Coventry Law Centre; Coventry Multi Faith Forum; Coventry Pensioners; Coventry Primary Care Trust; Coventry Rape and Sexual Abuse Centre; Coventry Refugee Centre; Coventry Somali Women's Network; Coventry University Students Union; Coventry Women' Forum; Foleshill Women's Training; Foleshill Children's Centre; Grapevine Coventry; Stoke Community Culture Project; Trades Union Congress; Unite, the Union; Valley House; and Voluntary Action Coventry.

[39] Where we could not find Coventry-specific data, we used national level data to give an indication of the scale of the problem.

Based on the preceding analysis, we then identified what the main human rights and equalities impacts were for each area of the study and made recommendations for what action was required (element six). The EHRIA also includes recommendations for further monitoring that is required in order to assess what the actual impact of the cuts will be on women in Coventry over the next few years (element seven). Finally, the EHRIA was published and widely circulated to relevant actors (element eight).

Our EHRIA identified a range of potential and actual equality and human rights impacts across all the areas examined. We found that there were equality impacts of the (potential) cuts on women in relation to cuts in employment, housing benefit, education funding, changes and cuts to the tax and benefit system, cuts in social care and other support services, cuts to legal advice services and cuts to funding for voluntary organisations. We also found potential negative impacts on women's human rights in relation to cuts to support for women who are the victims and survivors of violence, cuts to legal advice services and cuts affecting women who need care. Cuts to welfare benefits and housing benefit may also push women into poverty, impacting on their right to health or even their right to life.[40]

There is no space in this short contribution to catalogue all those impacts. Here, we concentrate on the impact on one particular group, which demonstrates the importance of an equality and human rights impact assessment. For both equality and human rights impacts, it is the combination of cuts in different areas that is particularly troubling. There are a number of areas where a combination of cuts, often by a variety of different agencies, will impact on particularly vulnerable or disadvantaged women with potentially devastating effects. Our EHRIA identifies cumulative impacts on a range of groups such as lone parents, BAME women and those giving and receiving care. Here we take one example—the effect of the cuts on victims and survivors of violence and abuse.

Women victims and survivors of violence and abuse will be affected by a range of cuts in Coventry. Such cuts are being replicated (often more severely) in many other parts of the UK.[41] Our research identified six different types of cuts that would impact on such women. First, services for women facing violence are under threat. Some agencies have already lost significant funding and funding for other services is under review, leaving organisations very uncertain about their future. Second, the police and Crown Prosecution Service (CPS) are both facing budget cuts which voluntary organisations fear may reduce the support available to victims and survivors. For example, the number of specialist domestic violence officers in Coventry has been cut from eight to two.[42] Third, the NHS is facing a

[40] See Stephenson and Harrison, 'Unravelling Equality?' above n 1. Individual chapters of the report catalogue impacts in particular areas and these impacts are then summarised in ch 10 of the report.

[41] J Towers and S Walby, *Measuring the Impact of Cuts in Public Expenditure on the Provision of Services to Prevent Violence against Women and Girls* (Trust for London and Northern Rock Foundation 2012) 3: www.trustforlondon.org.uk.

[42] Stephenson and Harrison, 'Unravelling Equality?' above n 1, 35.

budget cut which may reduce the level of support available to victims of violence and the funding for voluntary organisations. Fourth, cuts to legal aid will reduce the ability of women suffering violence to get the legal help and support they need. Fifth, cuts and other changes to welfare benefits will make it harder for women to leave violent relationships. Sixth, cuts to housing benefit will make it harder for some women to move area to get away from their attacker.[43]

In conducting interviews with a wide range of organisations for our EHRIA, it became obvious to us that individual agencies working in a particular field were often not aware of the kind of cumulative impacts identified above. Therefore there was the potential for a series of smaller individual impacts to add up to a 'perfect storm', which might seriously prejudice equality and human rights outcomes for particular women. Our EHRIA therefore recommends that public authorities should make sure that they create coherent and collective strategies for dealing with such issues. This includes ensuring that they coordinate their policies and practices where multiple agencies have an impact on a particular issue (for example, for violence against women—the City Council, health services, police, CPS and voluntary services). It also includes ensuring that each public authority has strategies in place so that policies and practices are not seen in isolation from one another in any individual agency.[44] This is often a problem in existing impact assessments undertaken by public authorities, an issue which we go on to address in the next section.

V. Poor Quality Impact Assessments

As highlighted above, there is now significant practice in the UK of public authorities employing equality impact assessments (and, to a more limited extent, human rights impact assessments) so as to assess the impact of various budget-cutting measures.[45] This practice allows public authorities to argue that they are complying with their equality and human rights obligations. Such impact assessments also have the potential to identify and tackle the types of impacts on vulnerable and disadvantaged persons identified above. This can then potentially become the basis for a reconsideration of spending priorities in order to take into account equality and human rights outcomes. But the reality of this practice is that it largely fails to live up to its transformational potential.

Our research has found that UK equality impact assessments (EQIAs) can become a 'tick-box' exercise with little use of evidence to support conclusions. In

[43] For detailed evidence in relation to all the cuts mentioned in this paragraph and their impacts, see Stephenson and Harrison, 'Unravelling Equality?' above n 1, ch 6.

[44] Stephenson and Harrison, 'Unravelling Equality?' above n 1, 58.

[45] For a number of examples see Harrison and Stephenson, 'Human Rights Impact Assessment' above n 17, 20f.

many cases, there was minimal consultation, limited understanding of key human rights and equality principles and little real impact on decision-making.[46] Similar problems affect joint equality and human rights impact assessments where they are carried out. Indeed, a great many guidance documents produced by public authorities to help their staff carry out such impact assessments specifically mention the need to avoid a tick-box approach.[47] However, despite these warnings, a great many EQIAs and EHRIAs reviewed by the authors of this chapter were of poor quality. Some of the key failings of these assessments are set out below.

First, EHRIAs can take a narrow or misguided view about the key human rights or equality principles behind the assessment. Some EHRIAs appear to fundamentally misunderstand the meaning of a human rights or equality impact. For example, assessments by Aberdeen City Council concluded that policies to reduce funding for homelessness provision, reduce provision of services to older people, and cut staff posts responsible for domestic abuse policy, would have no potential human rights impact. However, policies to increase charges for allotment holders, reduce maintenance of sports facilitates and introduce car park charges were all judged to have a possible Article 8 impact (private and family life).[48] Furthermore, the Aberdeen EHRIA tool asks if the policy will have an impact on community cohesion and good relations (to which public bodies are obliged to have 'due regard' under the Equality Act).[49] However, many of the assessments undertaken addressed this question purely in terms of potential negative media coverage for a council decision, rather than considering the impact on affected communities.[50] Such problems are by no means unique to the Aberdeen process. Many other equality impact assessments we analysed, undertaken by a range of agencies, took a very limited approach on key principles such as disproportionate impact or failed to consider those impacts at all.[51]

[46] See examples provided below as well as Harrison and Stephenson, 'Human Rights Impact Assessment' above n 17, 25f; Harrison, 'Human Rights Measurement' above n 17, 171.

[47] See eg, NHS Wiltshire, *Promoting Equality Respecting Diversity, Being FAIR (Fair, Accessible, Inclusive and Responsive) Staff Guidance and Templates for Conducting Equality Impact Assessment*: www.wiltshire.nhs.uk; Solicitors Regulation Authority, 'Equality Impact Assessments': www.sra.org.uk. Department for Work and Pensions, *Housing Benefit: Uprating Local Housing Allowance by the Consumer Price Index, Equality Impact Assessment* (2011): www.dwp.gov.uk.

[48] For further analysis see Harrison and Stephenson, 'Human Rights Impact Assessment' above n 17, 23f and 45. Aberdeen City Council EQIAs can be viewed at: www.aberdeencity.gov.uk/xeq_EHRIA_Search.asp.

[49] Equality Act 2010, s 149.

[50] Aberdeen City Council EQIA above n 47.

[51] In some cases EQIAs do not even give a breakdown of the proportion of people affected by a policy who are from different groups; instead they simply state that the policy will affect all those people affected equally. An example of this is the Treasury Equality Impact Statement for the increase in mileage allowance from 0.40p to 0. 0.45p a mile. This provides tax relief for payments to employees who use their own car or van for business use. The Treasury equality impact statement states: 'The change is a relieving provision which applies equally to all employees who use their own car or van for business mileage'. The Women's Budget Group and Fawcett have pointed out that the policy is likely to benefit more men than women since men are more likely to use a car for work. See 'Women's Budget Group and Fawcett, *The Impact on Women of the Budget* (2011): www.fawcettsociety.org.uk/.

Second, assessments are generally only related to the particular functions of an individual subdivision within a single public authority. For instance, Coventry City Council published a series of EQIAs of changes to policy as a result of their 2011–12 budget.[52] Each of these relate to the functions of particular departments. This meant that, for example, an adult social care impact assessment only considered the impact of local authority budget cuts on those receiving care and carers, rather than the potential cumulative impact of cuts on these individuals which was highlighted in section II above.

Third, assessments can appear rushed and lacking in analysis of existing data. Of the 15 EQIAs published by Coventry City Council, nine concluded that it was not yet possible to assess the equality impact of the policy examined and that the impact would be reviewed at a later date. These included cuts to the budgets of Connections (careers advice for young people), public safety and housing, adult social care, community services, as well as the voluntary redundancy programme.[53] While ongoing monitoring of actual impacts is extremely important, EQIAs should also be used to project likely impact based on existing data and consultation with affected groups. For example, the EQIA of job losses across the council did not provide a breakdown of the background of staff working for the council, which would have shown that 78 per cent of council staff are women, and accordingly job losses are likely to have a disproportionate impact on employment for women in the city.[54] More generally, the EQIAs carried out by Coventry contained little evidence that existing data had been analysed. In some cases, where potential reference was made to possible equality impact, there was no data given to show the numbers affected or the extent of the impact.[55]

Fourth, and related to this, assessments often ignore earlier assessments or other relevant data that does not suit the political context of the current analysis. For instance, in the June 2010 budget, the coalition Government announced changes to Local Housing Allowance (LHA).[56] In November 2010, the Department for Work and Pensions produced an EQIA of some of these changes.[57] Among the changes was the introduction of a cap on LHA so that the maximum amount that could be claimed was for a four-bedroom property. The EQIA does recognise that 'as some ethnic minority groups tend to have a higher proportion of large families, these measures may impact on them disproportionately' but goes on to say that '[i]t is not possible to provide the specific impact of this measure on race

[52] Coventry City Council, 'Equality Impact Assessments on Budget Setting 2011/12': www.coventry.gov.uk.

[53] Ibid.

[54] Office for National Statistics, 'Labour Market Profile for Coventry 2009–10': www.nmweb.dur.ac.uk.

[55] See eg, the Neighbourhood Services equality impact assessment in Coventry City Council, 'Equality Impact Assessments on Budget Setting 2011/12' 15: www.coventry.gov.uk.

[56] HM Treasury, 2010 Budget (June 2010) 48: www.hm-treasury.gov.uk.

[57] Department for Work and Pensions, 'Equality Impact Assessment, Housing Benefit' (November, 2010): www.dwp.gov.uk.

equality due to limitations in data'.[58] However, in 2009 the Department produced a detailed impact assessment of the introduction of the previous five-bedroom cap. This showed that although the proportion of BAME families receiving LHA was broadly in line with the ethnic composition of the general population (10 per cent), 37 per cent of families in properties that were five bedroom or larger were BAME.[59] This EQIA concluded that 'there is likely to be a disproportionate percentage of customers from minority ethnic groups entitled to six or more bedroom properties, raising concerns of indirect discrimination'.

The above is just a small sample of the very many examples of poor quality impact assessments uncovered during analysis of existing practice by public authorities in the UK. It is clear that such poor practice is not sufficiently robust or rigorous to have any transformational effect on policy so that equality and human rights impacts are seriously taken into account in budget-cutting processes. But EHRIAs, when carried out properly, can form the basis of informed policymaking which takes into account key human rights and equality impacts that are otherwise likely to go unnoticed. However, the coalition Government and the UK courts have reacted in almost polar opposite fashion to the problems of current practice.

New guidance from the coalition Government on public authorities' specific duties in England under the Equality Act stresses that there is no legal obligation to carry out EQIAs (specific duties vary between England, Scotland, Wales and Northern Ireland as discussed below).[60] This is clearly in part a reaction of the low standards of existing practice,[61] but it also has a more ideological bent. The Government has described its approach as

> minimising the risk that public bodies would feel compelled to do more than is needed, by following arduous and ineffective bureaucratic processes which go against the Government's drive to free the public sector from unnecessary process requirements and top-down targets.[62]

The Government has also made it clear in a number of different contexts that individuals and local communities should be key mechanisms for holding public authorities accountable for their performance.[63] This is equally true in the equality context where the Government has stated that: 'Challenge from the public will

[58] Ibid 13.

[59] Department for Work and Pensions, 'Equality Impact Assessment, Local Housing Allowance, Larger Properties' (2009) 7: www.dwp.gov.uk/.

[60] Government Equalities Office, 'The Equality Act 2010: Specific Duties to Support the Equality Duty, A Quick Start Guide for Public Sector Organisations' (September 2010): www.homeoffice.gov.uk/equalities.

[61] Government Equalities Office, 'The Public Sector Equality Duty: Reducing Bureaucracy' (17 March 2011) 4: www.homeoffice.gov.uk.

[62] Ibid.

[63] For instance, in the field of criminal justice, the Government has created 'street-level crime maps' with the express intention of local communities directly holding police to account for their performance. See Home Office, 'Street-Level Crime Maps': www.homeoffice.gov.uk.

be the key means of holding public bodies to account for their performance on equality'.[64]

However, our research demonstrates that in relation to the human rights and equality impacts of budgetary processes, it will be very difficult for the average citizen or local community group to undertake their own analysis of the impact of the cuts in any meaningful way. Relevant data is hard to access and robust analysis requires considerable expertise, particularly where cumulative impacts of multiple cuts are affecting the same individuals in a variety of different ways. Groups will require considerable support and guidance as well as the most valuable commodity—a great amount of their own time—to undertake such analysis.

At the same time, the UK courts are sending a very different signal to public authorities about the nature of their equalities duties. A series of cases in relation to the equalities duties under previous equalities legislation made it clear that, whatever their *specific* duties, public bodies' *general* duties to pay 'due regard' to promoting equality between different groups entails undertaking a process that looks very much like a good impact assessment process when they carry out budget-cutting measures—including consultation, evidence-gathering and analysis of impacts.[65] Similar principles have now been confirmed with regard to the new section 149 duty under the Equality Act.[66]

At the time of writing it is too early to tell what overall impact the Government guidance and court cases will have on the practice of public bodies. However, when researching the Coventry EHRIA, we observed that there was a belief among a number of public sector staff that the Government's proposals for the specific duties under the Equality Act weaken the obligations that previous equality legislation placed on them to assess and monitor policies for their equality impact. The Equality and Diversity forum has already warned that the specific duties may give 'public bodies the inaccurate impression that they do not have to do much in order to comply with the statutory equality duty'.[67] But the case law identified above suggests that these authorities may find it hard to demonstrate that they have complied with their *general* equality duties when faced with legal challenge if they do not carry out and publish some form of assessment of the impact of their policies.

It will be interesting to see how the practice of assessing impact diverges across the UK. In Wales and Scotland, the specific duties developed by the relevant governments include specific obligations to assess the equality impact of policies and

[64] Government Equalities Office, 'The Public Sector Equality Duty' above n 61, 4.

[65] See eg, *R (on the application of W) v Birmingham City Council* [2011] EWHC 1147 (Admin); *R v London Councils (ex parte Hajrula and Hamza)* [2011] EWHC 151; *R v Birmingham City Council (ex parte Rotao Rahman)* [2011] EWHC 944 (Admin).

[66] *R (on the application of Kirsty Green) v Gloucestershire County Council* [2011] EWHC 2687 (Admin). See in particular paras 118–31.

[67] Equality and Diversity Forum, 'Submission in Response to the Public Sector Equality Duty: Reducing Bureaucracy Consultation' (20 April 2011): www.edf.org.uk.

practices.[68] Section 75 of the Northern Ireland Act 1998 also explicitly requires public authorities to assess the likely impact of their policies on the promotion of equality of opportunity.[69] There are no such specific obligations in England.[70] It could be that the practice in England varies considerably from that in Scotland, Wales and Northern Ireland, and that substantive equality outcomes could differ as a result as well. The impact of these different specific duties will therefore have to be monitored carefully.

Whatever variations in practice across the UK do occur, it is vital that public authorities understand how to undertake a meaningful and robust analysis of their public spending decisions. The Coventry case study highlights what a good equality and human rights impact assessment should look like and the issues it can uncover. Therefore, in the final part of this chapter, we consider the key issues for ensuring that future EHRIAs are meaningful and potentially transformational processes.

VI. Lessons for Future Equality and Human Rights Impact Assessment by Public Bodies

EHRIAs could become a powerful tool for analysing and thereafter addressing some of the most damaging impacts of the public spending cuts on the most vulnerable and otherwise disadvantaged in our society. But in order to realise their potential, they need to avoid many of the pitfalls set out above which have blighted much of the existing practice by public authorities. Below we set out six mechanisms through which EHRIAs by public authorities can be significantly improved and enhanced. We concentrate here on assessments of public authorities because they are the bodies making the spending decisions, and because they have the legal duties under human rights and equality legislation. In the final section of this chapter we then go on to argue that EHRIAs can and should also be undertaken by other actors to monitor the impact of the spending cuts—many of the same methodological issues discussed below also apply in that context.

A. Improved Guidance and Examples of Good Practice for those Carrying out Assessments

To be widely transformative, good quality EHRIAs need to be conducted by public authorities extensively across the country. The public officials undertaking

[68] The Equality Act 2010 (Statutory Duties) (Wales) Regulations 2011/1064 reg 8; the Equality Act 2010 (Specific Duties) (Scotland) Regulations 2012/162 reg 5.
[69] Northern Ireland Act 1998, sch 9(4)(2).
[70] The Equality Act 2010 (Specific Duties) Regulations 2011/2260.

assessments are going to need considerable support and guidance in order to be able to undertake meaningful assessment processes and to avoid the kinds of problems set out in section IV above.

There are many handbooks and manuals that purport to guide users through various assessment processes,[71] but much of the existing guidance is deeply flawed. Some materials are so concise that they do little more than state the relevant human rights law (in one case, this meant simply reproducing the European Convention on Human Rights as an annex).[72] Other guidance is set out at such a high level of abstraction that it is difficult to see how it can be utilised by individual users in order to guide them in terms of the various key elements of the assessment process (for example, evidence-gathering, consultation, analysis etc).[73] Most guidance tends to focus on the process of completing the assessments and the elements of the 'form' that must be filled in. Instead they should be focusing on the human rights principles and how they should be applied; upon the evidence-gathering techniques needed in order to inform a meaningful assessment; and upon the barriers to effective consultation etc.

There is, therefore, a need to develop more dynamic, integrated and context-specific forms of guidance for those undertaking assessments. Guidance should be accessible, clearly linked to elements of the assessment process and contain as many examples of practical application as possible, so that assessors can see how human rights principles are used in practice and the type of evidence that can justifiably support any conclusion reached. Written guidance also needs to be the start rather than the end of support for assessment. Extensive and ongoing training is likely to be necessary (particularly for those with limited human rights expertise) not just in the process (the how) but in the underlying human rights issues (the why) of the assessment process.[74]

As important as the guidance itself, there is a need to put resources and time into the creation of 'good practice' pilot studies by public authorities which demonstrate what a robust, evidenced-based and methodologically-sound process looks like. These will then provide useful case studies for those undertaking future assessments and demonstrate that EHRIAs can be meaningful and worthwhile. The Coventry EHRIA provides a starting point for this endeavour. However, it was undertaken as a collaboration between academics and civil society organisations. Public authority approaches will inevitably differ to a degree in terms of the way the studies are undertaken and presented. Accordingly, good practice needs to be developed specifically by public authorities, including in relation to cumulative

[71] See Harrison and Stephenson, 'Human Rights Impact Assessment' above n 17, 92f for examples of guidance and toolkits.

[72] See eg, Sussex Partnership NHS Foundation Trust, 'Equality and Human Rights Impact Assessment': www.sussexpartnership.nhs.uk.

[73] See eg, Aberdeen City Council, 'Equality and Human Rights Impact Assessment: the Form': www.aberdeencity.gov.uk.

[74] Bakker et al above n 13, 452.

impacts, as a result of cuts affecting the same individuals from multiple agencies and departments.

B. Developing a Shared Evidence Base

There is a strong need to develop ways of sharing the evidence base for impact assessments. Currently, assessments undertaken by public authorities appear to occur largely in splendid isolation from one another. Therefore, each official trying to understand the impact of cuts to jobs, services or benefits has to identify for him or herself what the evidence base to support the assessment should be.

To compound the problem, finding much of the key data can be a complex and time-consuming process. A great deal of data is available online, but can be hard to find for people who do not know where to look. Assessors would benefit hugely from access to the types of data that others have utilised before to underpin their assessments. This data needs to be accessible in a user-friendly format so that it can be obtained and understood by a wide range of public officials. Therefore the creation of central repositories of such data, specifically for use in assessment processes, would be an important resource to improve the general quality as well as feasibility of EHRIAs.

C. Monitoring of Practice

There is a need for effective monitoring of practice by public authorities. Currently, there is a danger that poor impact assessment has no consequence other than in extreme situations, such as where EHRIAs are so poor that they are criticised in judicial review proceedings. For example, in November 2011, the High Court ordered Gloucestershire and Somerset County Councils to revisit their plans to close library services on the grounds that they had failed to meet their obligations to assess the impact of the decision on equalities.[75] However, few individuals or organisations have the resources to take judicial review proceedings against a public authority that has not carried out a proper assessment of equality impact. As a result, the focus for many public authorities is primarily on making sure that the process is completed rather than the quality of the assessment and the results to which it gives rise.

Robust monitoring by a credible independent body would greatly incentivise better practice. In England and Wales, the Equality and Human Rights Commission (EHRC) is the body primarily responsible for ensuring compliance with the

[75] *R (on the application of Kirsty Green) v Gloucestershire County Council* [2011] EWHC 2687, para 131. Judge Martin McKenna stated that: 'In order to discharge their respective duties Gloucestershire County Council (GCC) and Somerset County Council (SCC) should have undertaken a sufficiently thorough information-gathering exercise and then properly analysed that information. In this case I conclude that both GCC and SCC failed to comply with that obligation'.

Equality Act and the Human Rights Act. It has the power, for instance, to issue a compliance notice to a body that it believes has not met its obligations under the Equality Act. It has launched a review of whether the Treasury complied with the Equality Act in its 2010 spending review.[76] However, it would take a great change in strategic priorities if the EHRC were to effectively monitor practice across the whole of the public sector. In addition, the EHRC has experienced severe budget cuts and does not currently have the resources to undertake this endeavour. The EHRC should be resourced to carry out proper monitoring and this should be seen as a strategic priority, given the potential impact of robust and meaningful EHRIA practice. This monitoring should highlight good practice, which can then become part of the evidence base for future assessments. It should also highlight poor and inadequate practice. As a result, those public bodies that are conducting superficial assessments will find that their practice is scrutinised and the validity of the exercises they have undertaken is questioned. With appropriate resourcing, bodies such as the Scottish Human Rights Commission, the Equality Commission for Northern Ireland and the Northern Ireland Human Rights Commission could also play similar roles in their own domestic contexts.

D. Addressing Combined Impact

A key finding of the Coventry study was that it was the combination of a series of different cuts on the same individuals that was likely to have the most damaging effect in terms of undermining equality and human rights protection. They are also the types of impact that are most likely to go unnoticed and are not acted upon. In the example given above, women victims and survivors of violence and abuse were likely to be affected by cuts made by a range of actors including national government, local government, the Primary Care Trust, the police, the CPS and voluntary organisations.

But impact assessment processes are generally only undertaken by a specific department within a single authority in relation to their own services. While this process *may* still lead to some valuable results, it is often undertaken by junior members of staff who are relatively inexperienced in equality and human rights issues and it is too narrow to capture the problems caused by combinations of cuts on groups and individuals. An impact assessment process with a much broader scope is required—such as our case study in Coventry. Public authorities need to consider the context of cuts made by other organisations when assessing the impact of their own policies on particular groups. This may well require public bodies working together to produce an assessment of combined impact on particularly vulnerable groups.

[76] Equality and Human Rights Impact Assessment, 'Section 31 Assessment of HM Treasury': www.equalityhumanrights.com.

E. Considering Economic, Social and Cultural Rights

EHRIAs could also benefit greatly from explicit consideration of economic, social and cultural rights. Many of the most serious impacts identified through our research are most clearly and obviously seen as economic, social and cultural rights issues. Current EHRIA practice in the UK tends to focus exclusively on the rights contained in the Human Rights Act and the Equality Act. This is because public authorities are subject to relatively strong and enforceable legal obligations with respect to these legal instruments unlike, for instance, the ICESCR, which provides no direct mechanism for challenging public authority decision-making. However, both the Human Rights Act and Equality Act are circuitous and inadequate mechanisms for addressing the underlying social, economic and cultural rights issues which are raised by many public spending measures.

For example, our EHRIA in Coventry showed how the right to health of women may be affected not only by cuts to spending on the health service, but also by a series of other cuts and changes: cuts to welfare benefits may push women into poverty with consequent impacts on their health; cuts to adult social care services may have a severe impact on the physical and mental health, not only of those needing care, but on friends and family members providing unpaid care; cuts to support services for women victims and survivors of violence will make it harder for them to deal with the trauma they have experienced with a potentially serious impact on their mental health.[77]

An HRIA of this issue based on the obligations contained in the Human Rights Act will probably only engage the human rights framework if the extent of suffering reaches a level where it can be described as inhuman and degrading treatment under Article 3 of the European Convention on Human Rights. Existing case law on Article 3 demonstrates how extreme the situation needs to be before positive obligations on the state to provide care and other support services are found to exist.[78] As such, serious deteriorations in services and in health outcomes will not be picked up by a human rights approach constrained by a sole focus on the Human Rights Act.

The right to the highest attainable standard of physical and mental health as set out in Article 12 ICESCR, on the other hand, provides a more appropriate analytical framework within which to assess whether cuts, changes and reductions in services have in fact led to deteriorations in the availability, accessibility, affordability and quality of health care services. Internationally there has been considerable work to pioneer methodologies and to undertake individual human

[77] These impacts are all catalogued at various points in Stephenson and Harrison, 'Unravelling Equality?' above n 1.

[78] See eg, *R (Q and Others) v Secretary of State for the Home Department* [2004] QB 36.

rights impact assessments that focus on the right to health.[79] Such practice could form the basis for assessments in the UK.

Economic, social and cultural rights issues can also be addressed indirectly via obligations under the Equality Act 2010. But such issues are only addressed indirectly if a policy can be seen to disproportionately affect a particular equality group. Socio-economic status was planned as one of the protected characteristics when the previous Labour Government introduced the Equality Act, but these provisions have not come into force under the new Government. So, for example, the Department for Business Innovation and Skills assessment of the increase in tuition fees considers the impact across various equality categories (gender, race, disability and so on) in terms of differential impact but not in terms of the right to education.[80] This means that where there are issues that affect the right to education across all groups or in relation only to groups who are not protected by equality legislation, equality duties will not be engaged. Again this demonstrates the advantages of adopting an approach that directly focuses on economic, social and cultural rights such as the right to education.

F. Balancing Rigour with Usability

The process of human rights impact assessment can vary greatly between two extremes. At one extreme, EHRIAs can represent a very simplistic process with brief methodological frameworks, little or no use of evidence, no analysis beyond the opinions of the decision-makers and tick-box conclusions. At the other extreme, EHRIAs can be highly technical and very complex mechanisms with detailed methodologies, complex quantitative and qualitative research methods, extensive consultation, high levels of analysis and very detailed and thorough final reports.

Clearly, there are problems with the simplistic extreme. Such a process is highly unlikely to advance human rights protection and may well undermine faith in human rights approaches by coming to unsupportable conclusions, as demonstrated in the examples provided in section IV above. It is right that rigorous and scientific assessment methods are demanded so that the conclusions that are drawn are as robust and secure as possible.[81] However, there is a trade-off here. Demands for 'academic' quality research can make tools less attractive and less

[79] As mentioned above, the NGO, Aim for Human Rights, is very much the leader in this field. UN actors, such as the UN Special Rapporteur on the Right to Health, have further encouraged work in this field and produced extensive guidance. For instance, see P Hunt and G MacNaughton, 'Impact Assessments, Poverty and Human Rights: A Case Study Using the Right to the Highest Attainable Standard of Health' (2006) Health and Human Rights Working Paper No. 6 (Paris, UNESCO/WHO): www.who.int.

[80] Department for Business Innovation & Skills, 'Interim Equality Impact Assessment: Urgent Reforms to Higher Education Funding and Student Finance' (November 2010): www.bis.gov.uk.

[81] Landman above n 14, 139.

effective to potential users.[82] Generally the more rigorous and demanding EHRIA tools are, the more lightly used they are in practice. It is no accident that reviews of existing international practice discover almost as many toolkits and methodologies as actual human rights impact assessments.[83] If EHRIAs can only be utilised by a very few experts they are unlikely to have a significant or widespread impact on practice. Therefore, care needs to be taken to design models that combine usability and rigour. The development of improved guidance, pilot studies of 'good practice' and a shared evidence basis for assessments will help improve quality. But there is also a need to iteratively reflect on the process, how widely it is utilised, what it is achieving and how it can be enhanced.

VII. The Role of the Academic

It is highly unlikely that public authorities, in assessing the equality and human rights impact of public spending cuts, will unilaterally improve their practice in the ways described above. Certainly bodies like the Equality and Human Rights Commission and Government Equalities Office should be pushing public bodies hard to undertake the kind of robust analysis suggested here. But there is also a key role for academic experts in becoming involved in the type of analysis suggested in this chapter. As we have argued above (see section IV), the UK Government has made it clear that individuals and local communities should be the primary mechanisms for holding public authorities to account for their equalities and human rights performance. But our research demonstrates that in relation to public spending cuts, it will be very difficult for the average citizen or local community group to evaluate the complex impacts identified above, without considerable support and guidance. Academic expertise could and should be harnessed in order to assist in the development of robust assessment processes that are based on sound evidence and proper analysis.

Too often endeavours by academics and human rights bodies stop at the point of highlighting the general problem, designing indicators and producing toolkits.[84] Indicators and toolkits can be useful, but by themselves they will not affect change or convince people of the value of employing the framework (particularly the economic, social and cultural rights framework) where the weakest legal obligations exist. It is in the application of the rights and equality-based approach to specific instances of suffering and deprivation that their significance and importance is revealed.

[82] Humanist Committee on Human Rights, 'Human Rights Impact Assessment in Practice, Conference Report' (2007) 37–40: www.humanrightsimpact.org.

[83] Harrison, 'Human Rights Measurement' above n 17, 181.

[84] For instance, as stated above, in the field of human rights impact assessment, there are almost as many toolkits as there are individual HRIAs; see Harrison, 'Human Rights Measurement' above n 17, 181.

Organisations like the Women's Budget Group, which brings together academics, trade unionists and voluntary sector representatives, have combined equality impact assessment with lobbying of ministers, civil servants and backbench MPs. This linking of academic researchers with campaigners and activists was a key element of the Coventry project. The Centre for Human Rights in Practice worked in partnership with voluntary organisations, trade unions and others through CWV to ensure that our work reflected the needs and priorities of women who were likely to be affected by the cuts.[85] Our findings have already been used by voluntary organisations in Coventry to support their advocacy to protect funding for local services.[86] The findings of the Coventry research have also been used as the basis of a toolkit published by the TUC and CWV to support trade unions and voluntary organisations in carrying out further local assessments across the country.[87]

The public spending cuts in the UK offer an opportunity to demonstrate the importance of equality, human rights and economic, social and cultural rights in particular. This framework needs to be rigorously applied to the cuts that are affecting people and communities up and down the country. Academic analysis can have most impact where it is closely linked to the actual impact of the cuts on the lives of individuals and communities, ideally carried out in partnership with voluntary and civil society groups. In this way, the high principles and lofty ideals of the human rights and equality language are made to connect and resonate with the everyday experience of individuals and communities.

[85] See Harrison and Stephenson, 'Unravelling Equality?' above n 1, Appendix 1.

[86] Personal communications on file with authors.

[87] MA Stephenson, *The TUC Women and the Cuts Toolkit* (TUC and Coventry Women's Voices, 2011): www.tuc.org.uk.

INDEX